NORTH CAROLINA

Civil Commitment Manual

Second Edition
2011

Benjamin M. Turnage
John Rubin
Dorothy T. Whiteside

North Carolina Indigent Defense Manual Series
John Rubin, Editor

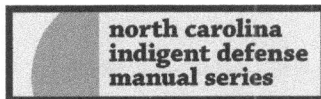

**north carolina
indigent defense
manual series**

Production of this series is made possible by funding from
the North Carolina Office of Indigent Defense Services

UNC | SCHOOL OF GOVERNMENT

The School of Government at the University of North Carolina at Chapel Hill works to improve the lives of North Carolinians by engaging in practical scholarship that helps public officials and citizens understand and improve state and local government. Established in 1931 as the Institute of Government, the School provides educational, advisory, and research services for state and local governments. The School of Government is also home to a nationally ranked graduate program in public administration and specialized centers focused on information technology, environmental finance, and civic education for youth.

As the largest university-based local government training, advisory, and research organization in the United States, the School of Government offers up to 200 courses, seminars, and specialized conferences for more than 12,000 public officials each year. In addition, faculty members annually publish approximately fifty books, book chapters, bulletins, and other reference works related to state and local government. Each day that the General Assembly is in session, the School produces the *Daily Bulletin*, which reports on the day's activities for members of the legislature and others who need to follow the course of legislation.

The Master of Public Administration Program is a full-time, two-year program that serves up to sixty students annually. It consistently ranks among the best public administration graduate programs in the country, particularly in city management. With courses ranging from public policy analysis to ethics and management, the program educates leaders for local, state, and federal governments and nonprofit organizations.

Operating support for the School of Government's programs and activities comes from many sources, including state appropriations, local government membership dues, private contributions, publication sales, course fees, and service contracts. Visit www.sog.unc.edu or call 919.966.5381 for more information on the School's courses, publications, programs, and services.

Michael R. Smith, Dean
Thomas H. Thornburg, Senior Associate Dean
Frayda S. Bluestein, Associate Dean for Faculty Development
Todd A. Nicolet, Associate Dean for Operations
Ann Cary Simpson, Associate Dean for Development and Communications
Bradley G. Volk, Associate Dean for Administration

FACULTY

Gregory S. Allison
David N. Ammons
Ann M. Anderson
A. Fleming Bell, II
Maureen M. Berner
Mark F. Botts
Michael Crowell
Shea Riggsbee Denning
James C. Drennan
Richard D. Ducker
Joseph S. Ferrell
Alyson A. Grine

Norma Houston (on leave)
Cheryl Daniels Howell
Jeffrey A. Hughes
Willow S. Jacobson
Robert P. Joyce
Kenneth L. Joyner
Diane M. Juffras
Dona G. Lewandowski
James M. Markham
Janet Mason
Christopher B. McLaughlin
Laurie L. Mesibov

Kara A. Millonzi
Jill D. Moore
Jonathan Q. Morgan
Ricardo S. Morse
C. Tyler Mulligan
David W. Owens
William C. Rivenbark
Dale J. Roenigk
John Rubin
John L. Saxon
Jessica Smith
Karl W. Smith

Carl W. Stenberg III
John B. Stephens
Charles Szypszak
Shannon H. Tufts
Vaughn Upshaw
Aimee N. Wall
Jeffrey B. Welty
Richard B. Whisnant
Gordon P. Whitaker
Eileen R. Youens

© 2011
School of Government
The University of North Carolina at Chapel Hill

Printed in the United States of America
21 20 19 18 17   3 4 5 6 7
ISBN 978-1-56011-664-6

About the North Carolina Indigent Defense Manual Series

The North Carolina Indigent Defense Manual Series is a collection of reference manuals addressing law and practice in areas in which indigent defendants and respondents are entitled to the representation of counsel at state expense. The series was created to address the need for comprehensive, up-to-date reference materials for public defenders and appointed counsel, who devote their time, skill, and effort to representing poor people. In addition to assisting indigent defenders with their responsibilities, the manuals also may be useful to others who work in the court system and who need a reference source on the law. In keeping with the School of Government's commitment to practical scholarship, the manuals are written by authors with subject-matter expertise in their respective fields, experience in developing effective educational materials, and knowledge of how things actually work in practice. The editor of the series is John Rubin, a member of the School of Government faculty who specializes in indigent defense education. For a current listing of manuals in the series, see indigentdefense.unc.edu. Production of the series is made possible by funding from the North Carolina Office of Indigent Defense Services, which is responsible for overseeing and enhancing the provision of indigent defense representation in North Carolina.

About the Authors of the North Carolina Civil Commitment Manual, Second Edition

Benjamin (Ben) M. Turnage is Special Counsel at Cherry Hospital in Goldsboro, North Carolina. Ben has practiced law in Wayne, Greene, and Lenoir Counties for sixteen years, working primarily in the area of indigent defense. He has represented indigent defendants in district and superior courts in addition to representing parents in abuse, neglect, and dependency cases, juveniles alleged to be delinquent, and respondents in guardianship proceedings. His duties include serving as a resource for appointed counsel for respondents in civil commitment cases.

John Rubin is Professor of Public Law and Government at the School of Government. He joined the faculty in 1991 and specializes in criminal law and procedure and indigent defense education. Before this appointment, he practiced law for nine years in Washington, D.C., and Los Angeles. He teaches, writes for, and consults with indigent defenders, judges, magistrates, prosecutors, and others who work in the court system.

Dorothy (Dolly) T. Whiteside is Special Counsel Supervising Attorney for the Office of Special Counsel of the North Carolina Office of Indigent Defense Services. She has practiced in the civil commitment field since 1979 and is responsible for overseeing the provision of legal representation for respondents by Special Counsel attorneys and appointed counsel in civil commitment proceedings.

Table of Contents[*]

---

[*] Each chapter contains a detailed listing of contents.

Chapter 3
Involuntary Commitment of Adults and Minors for Substance Abuse Treatment

Chapter 4
Voluntary Admission of Adults for Substance Abuse Treatment

Chapter 5
Voluntary Admission of Incompetent Adults   **103**

Chapter 6
Voluntary Admission of Minors   **111**

Chapter 7
Automatic Commitment—Not Guilty by Reason of Insanity   **125**

Appendix A
Forms

Administrative Office of the Courts (AOC) Forms

Department of Health and Human Services, Division of Mental Health, Developmental Disabilities, and Substance Abuse Services (DMH) Forms

Appendix B
Motions

Sample Motions

Appendix C
Working with Clients

Judith L. Kornegay, "Working with Clients," *from* Training in Civil Commitment Law: Representing People Facing Commitment (Feb. 21–22, 2003)

Appendix D
Involuntary Commitment and the Federal Gun Control Act

Robert Stranahan, "Involuntary Commitment and the Federal Gun Control Act," *from* Second Annual Civil Commitment Conference (Jan. 23, 2004)

Appendix E
Common Abbreviations

Common Abbreviations (source unknown)

Preface to the Second Edition

We are proud to release this second edition of the North Carolina Civil Commitment Manual. Our aim has been to create a clear, usable resource for attorneys appointed to represent respondents in civil commitment cases. We hope this edition of the manual continues to meet that goal. We also hope the manual will be a useful source of information for others who work in this challenging area.

We have the honor of writing this preface, but much of the credit for the manual belongs to others. First, the manual reflects the extraordinary work of the first edition's lead author, Lou Newman, who practiced law for many years in Wake County. She had just the right combination of qualities to get the project off the ground: experience as a respondent's attorney, expertise in the law, and a talent for synthesizing the valuable input we received from the editorial board on the first edition.

Second, thanks go to Rob Stranahan, Special Counsel, Central Regional Hospital, who read drafts of this edition, and to the members of the first edition's editorial board—Mark F. Botts, Associate Professor of Public Law and Government, UNC School of Government; Becky C. Zogry, Esq., Kernersville, NC; Judith L. Kornegay, Esq., Rocky Mount, NC; Willia G. Mills, Special Counsel, John Umstead Hospital; Rob Stranahan; and Eric J. Zogry, Juvenile Defender, Office of Indigent Defense Services. They volunteered their time to review each chapter, offer their insights into the civil commitment process, and endure long meetings to see the manual to its conclusion.

Third, we gratefully acknowledge the talents and contributions of Kathryn Burke, legal editor, who read, scrutinized, tightened, and improved every aspect of our work.

Last, this manual would not have been possible without the support of the Office of Indigent Defense Services and the UNC School of Government. Their collaboration on this and other educational projects has enhanced the resources available to indigent defense attorneys and has improved the service that indigent defenders are able to provide their clients. We also want to thank Owen Dubose, Katrina Hunt, Kevin Justice, and Angela Williams with the publications division of the School of Government for their assistance in designing, producing, and distributing the manual.

Comments and suggestions are welcome. They may be sent to John Rubin at the School of Government, CB #3330, Knapp Building, The University of North Carolina at Chapel Hill, Chapel Hill, North Carolina, 27599-3330. He also can be reached by telephone at (919) 962-2498 or by e-mail at rubin@sog.unc.edu.

Respondents' counsel who have additional questions about civil commitment cases are encouraged to contact Ben Turnage. He may be reached by telephone: (919) 731-3437;

e-mail: Ben.M.Turnage@nccourts.org; or mail: Cherry Hospital Courthouse, Stevens Mill Road, Goldsboro, NC 27530.

Ben Turnage
John Rubin
Dolly Whiteside

January 2011

Chapter 1
Overview of Manual

1.1   Purpose of Manual

This manual reviews the provisions of the North Carolina mental health and substance abuse laws as they pertain to commitments and admissions to 24-hour facilities and to outpatient commitments. Relevant statutes are found in Chapter 122C of the North Carolina General Statutes (hereinafter G.S.), entitled "Mental Health, Developmental Disabilities, and Substance Abuse Act of 1985." North Carolina appellate court and U.S. Supreme Court decisions are discussed where pertinent. Collateral consequences that may ensue as a result of commitment are explored as well as special provisions applicable to respondents committed through involvement with the criminal justice system.

The manual is designed to assist the attorney representing a respondent or minor facing a commitment, admission, or detention under an involuntary commitment custody order before admission to a 24-hour facility. The primary focus of the manual is on admissions and commitments requiring judicial review and thus on proceedings requiring the appointment of counsel. However, also discussed is pre-admission detention of respondents in involuntary commitment proceedings for which counsel may not have been appointed. This chapter presents a brief overview of the major topics presented.

1.2 Terminology Used in this Chapter

"Admission," although not defined in the statutes, denotes the entrance of a person into a 24-hour facility through the voluntary action of the affected individual or of that individual's legally responsible person. "Admission" to a 24-hour facility also occurs if approved after the second evaluation by a facility physician before the ten-day court hearing during involuntary commitment proceedings. *See infra* § 2.3K.

"Commitment," although not defined by statute, is a legal status denoting the court-ordered treatment of a person for mental illness or substance abuse either on an inpatient basis in a 24-hour facility or on an outpatient basis.

"Legally Responsible Person" means: "(i) when applied to an adult, who has been adjudicated incompetent, a guardian; (ii) when applied to a minor, a parent, guardian, a person standing in loco parentis, or a legal custodian other than a parent who has been granted specific authority by law or in a custody order to consent for medical care, including psychiatric treatment; or (iii) when applied to an adult who is incapable . . . and who has not been adjudicated incompetent, a health care agent named pursuant to a valid health care power of attorney." G.S. 122C-3(20).

"Respondent" is the person who is the subject of an involuntary commitment proceeding or who is admitted as a voluntary patient to a 24-hour facility by a legally responsible person.

"24-hour facility" is a facility providing around-the-clock treatment in a structured environment. G.S. 122C-3(14)g.

1.3 Involuntary Commitment

A. Three Types of Involuntary Commitment

There are three types of involuntary commitments for both adults and minors:

- involuntary inpatient commitment for mental health treatment;
- involuntary outpatient commitment for mental health treatment; and
- involuntary commitment for substance abuse treatment.

As these commitments by definition infringe on an individual's liberty interests involuntarily, judicial review is required. North Carolina statutes provide for representation by Special Counsel or an appointed attorney for all indigent and minor respondents, as well as non-indigent adults without counsel, on admission to a 24-hour facility. *See* G.S. 122C-270(a), (d), (e), 122C-224.1, 122C-268(d); *see also infra* §§ 2.1A and B, 2.5A, 3.4A.

B. Inpatient vs. Outpatient Commitment

Inpatient commitment requires that an individual receive therapeutic treatment from qualified professionals within the confines of a 24-hour facility. Outpatient commitment allows the individual to be treated in the community by a local treatment provider. A crucial component of outpatient commitment is that the respondent is *ordered* to attend appointments during the term of commitment. The appointment of counsel on a request for outpatient commitment is in the discretion of the court.

An examining physician or eligible psychologist may recommend inpatient or outpatient commitment at any step in the involuntary commitment process. Either type of commitment can be ordered by a court regardless of the physician's or eligible psychologist's request. After admission, the treating physician may evaluate whether the respondent continues to meet the criteria for commitment. At any time during the process, if the respondent does not meet criteria for commitment, he or she must be discharged by his or her physician unless committed as incapable of proceeding on a violent crime.

The appearance of the respondent may not be waived at a hearing initiated on the basis of an outpatient commitment request. If the court orders inpatient commitment for a respondent under outpatient commitment, the outpatient commitment is terminated. As the state continues to shift patients from an inpatient setting to outpatient treatment, there may be an increase in the number of commitments that begin solely as outpatient commitment requests.

For a further discussion of inpatient and outpatient commitment, see *infra* Chapter 2.

C. Maximum Periods of Mental Health Commitment

On the initial petition, the statute allows a respondent to be committed as an inpatient for a maximum of ninety days. At the expiration of an initial ninety-day commitment, the physician may request a first rehearing where the court may order up to 180 days of inpatient or outpatient commitment. The court may order up to 365 days of commitment on any subsequent request for inpatient treatment. On a second or subsequent request for rehearing on an outpatient commitment, the court may order a maximum of only 180 days.

The court also may order "split commitment," which is a combination of inpatient and outpatient commitment, within the statutory time limits (e.g., a 30/60 split commitment). The "split commitment" is typically ordered on an initial commitment. During a "split commitment," the treating physician may find that additional inpatient treatment is necessary. On the physician's request for rehearing, the court may order inpatient commitment or outpatient commitment for "up to" 180 days.

For further discussion of maximum periods of mental health commitment, see *infra* §§ 2.7, 2.9D.

D. Substance Abuse Commitment

A substance abuse commitment provides for treatment on either an inpatient or outpatient basis throughout the term of commitment. The use or abuse of the substance must be in a way or to a degree so as to impair the user's personal, social, or occupational functioning. The appearance of the respondent is not waivable at a substance abuse commitment hearing; however, the court's subpoena power may be necessary to compel the respondent's appearance at the hearing.

Initially the term of commitment may be up to 180 days. The respondent is committed to the treatment of an area authority or physician rather than to a 24-hour facility. The area authority or treating physician then evaluates whether the individual will be treated on an inpatient or outpatient basis. At the forty-five day review, the court may order additional inpatient services up to a maximum of ninety days. At each review, the court may order outpatient services during the remainder of the commitment period or discharge the respondent from further commitment. On a physician's request for rehearing at the expiration of the initial 180-day commitment, the court may order a maximum of an additional 365-day recommitment.

For a further discussion of substance abuse commitment, see *infra* Chapter 3.

E. Substance Abuse vs. Mental Health Commitment

Involuntary commitment for treatment of mental illness has been the traditional mode of treatment in a 24-hour facility. The person is committed for a period of inpatient treatment with the maximum term being set by statute. The treating physician may discharge the individual at any time during the commitment if the criteria for inpatient treatment are no longer met. With the increasing need for substance abuse treatment, it became clear that traditional mental health commitment did not best meet the needs of some clients. The General Assembly therefore amended the statutes to provide a discrete procedure for substance abuse commitment. There are two primary differences from a mental health commitment:

- the initial maximum term of a substance abuse commitment can be longer, up to 180 days versus 90 days for mental health treatment; and
- the responsible professional determines within that term how much of the treatment will be on an inpatient basis in a 24-hour facility and what portion will be on an outpatient basis.

Although a petition may initially request treatment for substance abuse, the final court order may be for mental health treatment, or vice versa. This is not a statutory provision, but rather a result of negotiation between the parties with approval by the court. For example, the parties may agree to convert a substance abuse commitment to a mental health commitment because loss of driving privileges may result from a substance abuse commitment. *See infra* §§ 3.6C, 12.4.

1.4 Voluntary Admission

There are three types of voluntary inpatient admissions for either mental health or substance abuse treatment. The first is the admission of a competent adult on the individual's own application. As this is the only truly voluntary admission, no attorney representation is required and there is no judicial review. Discussion of this type of admission is included in this manual so that the attorney will be aware of it as a possible alternative for an involuntary client and because a voluntary admission may be part of a client's psychiatric history.

The following two types of admissions are also called "voluntary" in the statutes, but they are not truly voluntary on the part of the patient:

- voluntary admission of an incompetent adult, in which an adjudicated incompetent adult is admitted on application of the guardian of the person or general guardian; and
- voluntary admission of a minor, in which the admission application is signed by the legally responsible person for the minor.

Because someone other than the client signs the admission application, the statute provides for judicial review of the admission and for an appointed attorney for the individual.

For a discussion of voluntary admissions, including the dispositional alternatives for voluntary admissions, see *infra* Chapters 4, 5, 6, and 10.

1.5 Commitments and Admissions through the Criminal Justice System

Special provisions apply to individuals committed or admitted for mental health or substance abuse treatment through the criminal justice system. These include those automatically committed after being found not guilty by reason of insanity ("NGRI") and those charged with a crime and found incapable of proceeding. Commitments for defendants who are incapable are subdivided into two categories depending on whether the crime charged is a violent crime. These commitments are commonly known as "Involuntary Incapable" when the underlying crime is a non-violent crime or "House Bill 95" when the underlying crime is a violent crime. Specific provisions apply as well for the commitment and admission of inmates and parolees. For a further discussion of commitment and admissions through the criminal justice system, see *infra* Chapters 7, 8, and 9.

1.6 Collateral Consequences

Serious consequences may ensue beyond the loss of freedom resulting from commitment for treatment. Counsel should advise clients of these possible consequences so that they can best make decisions throughout the judicial process. For a further discussion of collateral consequences, see *infra* Chapter 12.

1.7 Admissions Not Requiring Judicial Review

Individuals also may be admitted to a 24-hour facility through an advance instruction or a health care power of attorney. Each of these methods was created by legislation as a means to allow inpatient admission without the need for judicial process.

A. Advance Instruction

An advance instruction allows a person "of sound mind" to execute a document consenting to or refusing mental health treatment in advance of the need. The document becomes effective only if the person becomes incapable of making these decisions at a later date and is revocable as long as the person is not incapable. There is a limit of ten days of inpatient treatment pursuant to an advance instruction. For a further discussion of advance instructions, see *infra* § 11.3.

B. Health Care Power of Attorney

A health care power of attorney allows a competent individual to execute a document designating a "legally responsible person" to make decisions relating to mental health treatment in the event of incapacity. As with an advance instruction, the document is revocable as long as the person is competent, and it is effective only upon the incapacity of the individual. For a further discussion of health care powers of attorney, see *infra* § 11.4.

Although there is no judicial review, and thus no attorney representation, counsel may occasionally receive telephone calls from patients or staff with questions regarding these admissions. It is important to know that these alternative procedures exist and to be able to determine if a particular admission is in compliance with statutory requirements. However, a respondent's appointed counsel should not provide legal opinions to hospital personnel and instead should refer hospital personnel to the hospital's own attorney.

1.8 Administrative Office of the Courts Forms

The Administrative Office of the Courts provides forms that may be used in the commitment and admission process. Copies of these forms are included in Appendix A of this manual. These forms are available online at the Judicial Department website, www.nccourts.org, under "Forms." As these forms are being constantly reviewed and updated, the website should be checked for the latest version.

1.9 Division of Mental Health Forms

The Department of Health and Human Services, Division of Mental Health, Developmental Disabilities, and Substance Abuse Services, publishes forms that are used in the commitment and admission process. Copies of these forms are included in Appendix A of this manual. These forms are available online at the Department of Health and Human Services website, Manuals and Forms page, www.ncdhhs.gov/mhddsas/statspublications/manualsforms/index.htm, under "Legal Forms for Hospitals."

Appendix 1-1
Commitments and Admissions: Quick Summary

Involuntary Commitment for Mental Health Treatment

- Law applies to adults and minors
- District court hearing within 10 days of date respondent taken into custody
- Maximum term of 90 days of inpatient commitment at initial hearing
- Maximum term of 180 days of inpatient commitment at first rehearing, and maximum of one year of inpatient commitment at second and subsequent rehearings

Involuntary Commitment for Substance Abuse Treatment

- Law applies to adults and minors
- District court hearing within 10 days of date respondent taken into custody
- Commitment is to treatment of area authority or physician rather than to 24-hour facility
- Treatment may be on either inpatient or outpatient basis, as determined by area authority or physician
- Maximum term of 180 days of substance abuse commitment, with maximum of one year of substance abuse commitment at second and subsequent rehearings
- Maximum 45 consecutive days of inpatient treatment without supplemental hearing

Outpatient Commitment

- Law applies to adults and minors
- District court hearing within 10 days of date respondent taken into custody
- Appointment of counsel in discretion of court
- Treatment on outpatient basis, not in 24-hour facility
- Can be initiated either by physician or eligible psychologist or recommended by examiner or attending physician at any stage in the involuntary commitment process

Voluntary Admission

- By application of guardian of the person or general guardian of incompetent adult—judicial review required and attorney appointed
- By application of legally responsible person for minor—judicial review required and attorney appointed
- By application of competent adult—judicial review not required and no attorney appointed

Commitment and Admission through Criminal Justice System

- Automatic commitment following verdict of not guilty by reason of insanity
- After defendant found incapable of proceeding
- Special provisions for commitment and admission of inmates and parolees

Admissions Not Requiring Judicial Review

- By advance instruction
- By application of health agent appointed pursuant to health care power of attorney

Chapter 2
Involuntary Commitment of Adults and Minors for Mental Health Treatment

2.1   Overview of Involuntary Commitment Process

A. Right to Counsel

Involuntary commitment is the judicial procedure for compelling people to receive mental health treatment, either on an inpatient or outpatient basis. In the majority of proceedings for involuntary commitment, respondents are represented by appointed attorneys. Counsel is appointed because the process represents a significant infringement on a respondent's liberty interest. In addition, the process restricts a respondent's freedom of movement, making it potentially difficult for an otherwise financially capable respondent to make appropriate contacts for the purpose of hiring counsel.

In inpatient proceedings, Special Counsel or an appointed attorney represents all respondents who have not arranged for private representation. They represent respondents at private hospitals, state psychiatric hospitals, and treatment centers throughout the state. Section 122C-270(a) of the North Carolina General Statutes (hereinafter G.S.) provides that Special Counsel represents "all indigent respondents at all hearings, rehearings, and supplemental hearings" held at state facilities. *See also infra* § 2.5A.

A respondent has the right to counsel through all stages of the proceedings for involuntary inpatient commitment. On appeal from a district court involuntary commitment order, counsel is assigned by the Office of the Appellate Defender.

Generally, in involuntary inpatient proceedings, counsel is appointed after the respondent's second evaluation. It is after the second evaluation that the respondent is admitted to the facility, thereby establishing venue of the district court hearing according to the location of the inpatient facility. Appointment after the second evaluation and admission to a 24-hour facility has been the most feasible time after custody for effectuating the right to counsel established in G.S. 7A-451(b) for commitment proceedings, but delays may occur, as discussed below.

Appointment of counsel for indigent respondents in outpatient commitment proceedings is discretionary with the court. Respondents who are not indigent have the right to hire private counsel for outpatient commitment proceedings.

B. Possible Delays in Appointment of Counsel

A potential deviation from the general practice of appointment of counsel for inpatient commitment proceedings may be caused by G.S. 122C-263(d)(2). This statute allows the first evaluator to detain a respondent up to seven days after the issuance of a custody order if a 24-hour facility is not immediately available or appropriate to the respondent's medical condition. If detention is to extend beyond the seventh day, the evaluator must notify the clerk to terminate the proceedings. If deemed necessary, the evaluator can begin the commitment process with a new petition and affidavit and new allegations.

This creates a possibility of consecutive seven-day detentions, without appointment of counsel, as delays may occur in placing the respondent at a 24-hour facility. In light of this potential delay, a respondent arguably has the right to have counsel appointed upon the filing of a second petition resulting in another first evaluation rather than after a second evaluation and admission to a 24-hour facility. Appointment of counsel is determined according to rules adopted by the Office of Indigent Defense Services (IDS), but the rules currently do not address this situation. Local rules also may address the timing of appointment. For a discussion of possible responses to this situation, see *infra* § 2.3J.

C. Statutory Procedures

The statutory involuntary commitment procedures apply to both adults and minors. Chapter 122C of the North Carolina General Statutes outlines the typical commitment procedures:

- initiation of the process by petition before a magistrate or the clerk of superior court;
- custody and transport of the respondent for an initial examination by a physician or eligible psychologist;

- a second examination if inpatient commitment is initially recommended by the first examiner; and
- district court review of all involuntary commitments within ten days of the date the respondent is taken into law enforcement custody.

D. Responsibilities of Counsel

Generally, counsel is assigned upon the respondent's admission to a 24-hour facility. *See supra* § 2.1A (discussing right to counsel). Upon receiving a case, the attorney should review all court documents for compliance with the statutory requirements discussed in this chapter. A meeting with the client is most important in preparing the case, with follow-up meetings as necessary. The attorney must explain the legal procedures involved, discuss the underlying facts with the client, explore dispositional alternatives (what the client might agree to, what the attending physician recommends, and what the court might order), and determine whether the client wants to contest commitment at the district court hearing. Other responsibilities of the attorney include reviewing the client's medical/psychiatric records, consultation with treatment providers, and talking with potential witnesses and opposing counsel.

E. Outpatient Commitment

A court order requiring an individual to receive psychiatric treatment outside a residential facility is an outpatient commitment. An outpatient commitment may be initiated by request of a physician or eligible psychologist or may be recommended by an examiner at any point in the commitment process. Outpatient commitment also may be recommended after the individual has been admitted to a 24-hour facility. Because the possibility of outpatient commitment exists throughout the commitment process, references to outpatient commitment, also involuntary, recur throughout this chapter. Counsel should be alert for opportunities to resolve a case by agreement to outpatient commitment, which involves less restriction of freedom and fewer collateral consequences than an inpatient commitment.

F. District Court Hearing

A district court hearing must be calendared and held within ten days of the respondent being taken into custody pursuant to a petition for involuntary commitment. An evidentiary hearing, with findings of fact and conclusions of law, is held in every case. If the respondent is not contesting, this hearing may consist only of the court reviewing the physician's affidavit by stipulation. Upon finding that the statutory criteria are met, the court may order outpatient commitment, inpatient commitment, a combination of inpatient commitment followed by outpatient commitment, or unconditional discharge of the respondent.

2.2 Terminology Used in this Chapter

"'Area authority" is the "area mental health, developmental disabilities, and substance abuse authority." G.S. 122C-3(1). For a more detailed discussion of area authorities, see *infra* § 3.2.

"Area facility" is "a facility that is operated by or under contract with the area authority or county program." G.S. 122C-3(14)a. An area facility is part of a local program of services and cannot be a state facility.

"Custody order" is the order signed by the clerk of superior court or a magistrate authorizing a law enforcement officer or other authorized person to take a respondent into custody for examination or to provide other transportation required within the commitment process.

"Dangerous to self" means that within the relevant past:

"1.   The individual has acted in such a way as to show:

    I.   That he would be unable, without care, supervision, and the continued assistance of others not otherwise available, to exercise self-control, judgment, and discretion in the conduct of his daily responsibilities and social relations, or to satisfy his need for nourishment, personal or medical care, shelter, or self-protection and safety; and

    II.   That there is a reasonable probability of his suffering serious physical debilitation within the near future unless adequate treatment is given pursuant to this Chapter. A showing of behavior that is grossly irrational, of actions that the individual is unable to control, of behavior that is grossly inappropriate to the situation, or of other evidence of severely impaired insight and judgment shall create a prima facie inference that the individual is unable to care for himself; or

2.   The individual has attempted suicide or threatened suicide and that there is a reasonable probability of suicide unless adequate treatment is given pursuant to this Chapter; or

3.   The individual has mutilated himself or attempted to mutilate himself and that there is a reasonable probability of serious self-mutilation unless adequate treatment is given pursuant to this Chapter.

Previous episodes of dangerousness to self, when applicable, may be considered when determining reasonable probability of physical debilitation, suicide, or self-mutilation."

G.S. 122C-3(11)a.

"Dangerous to others" means that:

> "within the relevant past, the individual has inflicted or attempted to inflict or threatened to inflict serious bodily harm on another, or has acted in such a way as to create a substantial risk of serious bodily harm to another, or has engaged in extreme destruction of property; and that there is a reasonable probability that this conduct will be repeated. Previous episodes of dangerousness to others, when applicable, may be considered when determining reasonable probability of future dangerous conduct. Clear, cogent, and convincing evidence that an individual has committed a homicide in the relevant past is prima facie evidence of dangerousness to others."

G.S. 122C-3(11)b.

"Local management entity" or "LME" means an area authority, county program, or consolidated human services agency that contracts with an area facility for services. *See* G.S. 122C-3(20b).

"Qualified Physician's Examination report (QPE)" is the term commonly used to refer to the Department of Health and Human Services form completed by an examining physician when prepared for use in court. *See infra* Appendix A, DMH Form 5-72-01. It is forwarded to the clerk of court when involuntary commitment is recommended following the filing of a petition or when a rehearing on commitment is requested by the attending physician.

"Special Counsel" is the attorney assigned to represent all indigent respondents at state facilities for the mentally ill. The attorney is a state employee of the Office of Indigent Defense Services with an office at the state facility. G.S. 122C-270(a), (b); *see also infra* § 2.5A.

"State facility" is a facility under the supervision of the Secretary of the Department of Health and Human Services for the provision of "services for the care, treatment, habilitation, or rehabilitation of the mentally ill, the developmentally disabled, or substance abusers." G.S. 122C-3(14), 122C-3(14)f.

"24-hour facility" is a "facility that provides a structured living environment and services for a period of 24 consecutive hours or more." G.S. 122C-3(14)g. A "'residential facility,' which is a 24-hour facility that is not a hospital, including a group home," is included in this definition. G.S. 122C-3(14)e.

2.3   Involuntary Commitment: Prehearing Procedures

It is important for counsel to be familiar with the statutory requirements of the first and second evaluation and other prehearing procedures, even if counsel did not represent the respondent at that time, in order to identify defects in legal process that might be raised in a later motion to dismiss.

A. Affidavit and Petition Before Clerk or Magistrate

Affidavit and petition. Involuntary commitment begins with an individual appearing before either the clerk of superior court or a magistrate to file a petition seeking to have another person taken into custody for an examination to see if that person should be involuntarily committed. The petition is filed in the county in which the respondent either resides or is present. The petitioner must have knowledge that the person "is mentally ill and either (i) dangerous to self . . . or dangerous to others . . . or (ii) in need of treatment in order to prevent further disability or deterioration that would predictably result in dangerousness." G.S. 122C-261(a). An affidavit containing the underlying facts supporting the request for commitment is executed by the petitioner. *See infra* Appendix A, Form AOC-SP-300.

The statute also requires the affiant to state if there is reason to believe the respondent is also mentally retarded. G.S. 122C-261(a). This is necessary because state policy is to treat people who are mentally retarded in facilities separate from those dedicated to treating people with mental illness alone. The clerk or magistrate must therefore contact the area authority prior to issuing a custody order for a person alleged to be mentally retarded, and the area authority must designate the facility to which the person will be taken for examination. G.S. 122C-261(b).

Case law: An unsworn petition and a petition without facts supporting conclusory statements are grounds for dismissal.

In re Ingram, 74 N.C. App. 579 (1985). The North Carolina Court of Appeals held that the failure of a petition to be signed by oath or affirmation before a duly authorized certifying officer when required by statute is a jurisdictional defect and is grounds for dismissal of the petition. The statutory requirements for the signing of the petition under oath must be "followed diligently," and involuntarily committing a respondent without the required oath deprives the respondent of "liberty without legal process."

Although a motion to dismiss based on an unsworn petition should be granted, counsel should advise the respondent of the possible consequences. Because an order of dismissal on this basis is not res judicata, the original petitioner or a current treatment provider may file a sworn petition that could initiate a new involuntary commitment proceeding. Prevailing on the motion to dismiss could serve in effect as an unwanted continuance because the new petition could be filed before the respondent is released from custody and the new ten-day period for a hearing would start from the date the new petition was filed, thus extending the time the respondent would be in custody prior to a hearing on the merits.

No facts supporting conclusory statements. The petition must contain facts supporting the allegations that the respondent is mentally ill and dangerous to self or others. In *Ingram,* the petition stated:

> "Respondent has strange behavior and irrational in her thinking. Leaves home and no one knows of her whereabouts, and at times spends night away from home. Accuses husband of improprieties."

74 N.C. App. at 579.

The court held that the paragraph quoted above contained conclusory statements and statements that did not provide facts illustrating mental illness and danger to self or others. These statements did not form a sufficient basis for a determination of reasonable grounds for issuance of a commitment order. *Id.* at 581.

Filing a motion to dismiss based on the insufficiency of the allegations in the petition may be a better strategy than moving to dismiss because of an unsworn petition, as it is based more on the substance of the case. The petitioner would not be allowed to refile a petition with the same allegations, and the original petitioner might not have observed the more recent actions of the respondent. On the other hand, the attending physician at the facility might have sufficient information on which to file a new petition. This might lead to a delay in the hearing, just as with a dismissal based on the technical insufficiency of the petition. Counsel should advise the client of the possibility of the petition being refiled and discuss the pros and cons of filing a motion to dismiss with the client to enable the client to make an informed decision on how to proceed.

Case law: A petition may be based on hearsay.

In re Zollicoffer, 165 N.C. App. 462 (2004). The North Carolina Court of Appeals affirmed that it is permissible for a petition for involuntary commitment to be based on hearsay information. In *Zollicoffer,* the respondent appealed the failure of the lower court to grant his motion to dismiss the petition based on the hearsay contained therein. The court held that there was no requirement that the petition be based on first-hand knowledge and that the petition before the magistrate [or clerk of superior court], which the court characterized as a hearing, was not subject to the rules of evidence.

B. Custody Order for Examination

The clerk or magistrate must first review the petition to determine if there are "reasonable grounds to believe that the facts alleged in the affidavit are true." G.S. 122C-261(b). There must be a determination of whether the respondent is "probably mentally ill and either (i) dangerous to self . . . or dangerous to others . . . or (ii) in need of treatment in order to prevent further disability or deterioration that would predictably result in dangerousness." *Id.* If these conditions are met, the clerk or magistrate must issue an order to a law enforcement officer, or other authorized person, to take the respondent into custody for examination by a physician or eligible psychologist. *Id.*; *see infra* Appendix A, Form AOC-SP-302.

Where reasonable grounds are not found, the respondent is free from the threat of detention for involuntary commitment based on the petitioner's current allegations. This is the first of four opportunities prior to the district court hearing for the commitment process to end and for the respondent to be released from further involuntary detention. The respondent also may be released by the examining practitioner at either the first or second examinations or by the treating physician prior to the district court hearing.

On issuance of a custody order, the clerk or magistrate must provide the petitioner and respondent, if present, with specific information regarding the next steps that will occur. G.S. 122C-261(b).

Practice note: If the petitioner reports not knowing that he or she was requesting an involuntary commitment from the clerk or magistrate, counsel should inquire as to what information about the proceedings was provided to the petitioner by the clerk or magistrate when that official took the petitioner's affidavit. In a contested case, if it appears that no official notified the petitioner that he or she was requesting involuntary commitment, this violation of the requirements of G.S. 122C-261(b) should be brought to the attention of the court in support of the respondent's request for discharge.

G.S. 122C-261(b) presumes that the magistrate will issue the custody order within a reasonable time after presentation of the affidavit and petition. However, a significant delay in issuance of the custody order may subject the entire process to dismissal at the district court hearing, particularly when the length of delay indicates that the magistrate is accommodating non-statutory interests. *See infra* Appendix 2-2, Memorandum to Magistrates from Mark Botts (Nov. 15, 2009).

C. Transportation Procedures

Although the respondent's attorney is not involved in transportation arrangements for the client, counsel may be asked to answer questions concerning transportation to the hospital, between hospitals, to court, and home after discharge. Transportation considerations also may affect commitments. For example, an involuntary commitment petition might be filed by a law enforcement officer primarily to secure transportation for a cooperative person from a mental health center to a hospital. Additionally, counsel may need to address systemic problems with transportation, such as the repeated failure to provide an escort of the same sex as the respondent being taken into custody.

Within a county. Transportation of a respondent for involuntary commitment proceedings within a county is generally provided by either the city or the county. The city must transport a city resident as well as any person taken into custody within the city. The county transports non-city residents and those taken into custody outside city limits. G.S. 122C-251(a).

Between counties. Transportation of a respondent between counties for admission to a facility is generally provided by the county where the respondent was taken into custody. The sheriff is allowed to cross county lines for the purpose of assuming custody pursuant to a petition and for the purpose of transporting a patient to a facility. *See* G.S. 122C-261(e). The county where the petition was initiated must transport a respondent who requests a change of venue back to the initiating county for the district court hearing. G.S. 122C-251(b). The county of the respondent's residence must provide transportation between counties upon the respondent's discharge from the facility, although the respondent may arrange for private transportation and assume any expense thereof. *Id.*

Other provisions. Counties and cities may use their own vehicles or may contract to use private vehicles. Law enforcement officers are to wear plain clothes and drive unmarked vehicles "[t]o the extent feasible." G.S. 122C-251(c). They also must advise respondents being taken into custody, "to the extent possible," that they are being taken for treatment for the safety of themselves and others and are not being arrested and have not committed a crime. *Id.* The city or county must provide either a driver or attendant of the same sex as the respondent, unless a family member is allowed to accompany the respondent. G.S. 122C-251(d).

In addition to using law enforcement personnel, cities and counties may use trained volunteers and personnel from public and private agencies, including private hospital staff, to provide all or part of the transportation required. The training must ensure the safety and protection of both the public and the respondent. G.S. 122C-251(g).

Costs. The county of the respondent's residence is generally responsible for the costs of transportation and must reimburse the state, another county, or a city that has transported the respondent pursuant to the commitment statutes. The county of residence, after giving proper notice and opportunity to object, may seek reimbursement from: 1) a non-indigent respondent; 2) a person or entity with sufficient assets who is legally liable for the respondent's support; 3) a person or entity that is contractually responsible for the cost; or 4) any person or entity otherwise liable for the cost under federal, state, or local law. G.S. 122C-251(h).

Qualified immunity for law enforcement officers. Law enforcement officers providing transportation are allowed to use "reasonable force to restrain the respondent" for the safety of the respondent and others. G.S. 122C-251(e). If "reasonable measures" are employed, the law enforcement officer cannot be held criminally or civilly liable for assault, false imprisonment, or other torts or crimes in carrying out statutory duties. *Id.*

D. Custody and Transport to First Examination

The law enforcement officer or other authorized person is to take the respondent into custody within twenty-four hours after the order is issued. G.S. 122C-261(e). A new custody order must be obtained if the time expires without custody being assumed. The law enforcement officer has no authority to assume custody after the order expires, and a respondent taken into custody without a valid order would have grounds to move to dismiss the petition.

After being taken into custody, the respondent must be transported to an area facility for a first examination by a physician or eligible psychologist. G.S. 122C-263(a). After the magistrate's review of the affidavit, the first examination is the next opportunity available for the respondent to be released from involuntary detention during the commitment process. If there is no physician or eligible psychologist at the area facility available to perform the examination, the respondent may be taken to any physician or eligible psychologist in the local area. Occasionally, neither a physician nor an eligible psychologist is immediately available, in which case the respondent may be temporarily detained pending examination. Temporary detention is allowed in an area facility if available, in the respondent's home under appropriate supervision, in a private hospital or clinic, in a general hospital, or in a state facility for the mentally ill. The statute specifically provides that the temporary detention may not be in a jail or other penal facility. *Id.*

E. First Examination Requirements

Factors to be evaluated. The physician or eligible psychologist must perform the examination as soon as possible and no later than twenty-four hours after the respondent's arrival. G.S. 122C-263(c).

The examiner must evaluate four factors:

> "(1) Current and previous mental illness and mental retardation including, if available, previous treatment history;
> (2) Dangerousness to self . . . or others . . . ;
> (3) Ability to survive safely without inpatient commitment, including the availability of supervision from family, friends or others; and
> (4) Capacity to make an informed decision concerning treatment."

Id.; *see infra* Appendix A, Form DMH 5-72-01.

Criteria for inpatient commitment. The examiner must find that the respondent is mentally ill and dangerous to self or others in order to recommend inpatient commitment. G.S. 122C-263(d)(2).

Criteria for outpatient commitment. The examiner must make the following determinations for recommendation of outpatient commitment:

> "a. The respondent is mentally ill;
> b. The respondent is capable of surviving safely in the community with available supervision from family, friends, or others;
> c. Based on the respondent's psychiatric history, the respondent is in need of treatment in order to prevent further disability or deterioration that would predictably result in dangerousness as defined by G.S. 122C-3(11); and
> d. The respondent's current mental status or the nature of respondent's illness limits or negates the respondent's ability to make an informed decision to seek voluntarily or comply with recommended treatment."

G.S. 122C-263(d)(1).

Temporary waiver of requirement for physician or eligible psychologist to perform first examination. A bill effective July 1, 2003, S.L. 2003-178, and extended periodically allows the Secretary of Health and Human Services, on the request of a local management entity (LME), to waive temporarily the statutory requirement that either a physician or eligible psychologist perform the initial examination. Session Law 2010-119 continues this program until October 1, 2012. The waiver applies only on a "pilot-program basis" upon request and if certain criteria are met. A maximum number of twenty programs may receive a waiver, which would allow the first examination to be performed by a licensed clinical social worker, a masters level psychiatric nurse, or a masters level certified clinical addictions specialist.

F. First Examination via Telemedicine

G.S. 122C-263(c) provides that when the first examination is performed by a physician or eligible psychologist, the respondent either may be in the physical presence of the physician or eligible psychologist or may be examined using telemedicine equipment and procedures. For the purpose of this part of the statute, "telemedicine" is "two-way real-time interactive audio and video between places of lesser and greater medical capability or expertise . . . when distance separates participants who are in different geographical locations." G.S. 122C-263(c). The examiner "must be satisfied to a reasonable medical certainty that the determinations made . . . would not be different" if done face to face. *Id.* If not so satisfied, the examiner must indicate that in writing on the first examination report. The respondent then must be transported for a face-to-face examination. The statute does not expand the twenty-four hour limitation provided for the first examination to occur.

If these conditions are met, G.S. 122C-263(c) supersedes *McLean v. Sale,* 54 N.C. App. 538 (1981), in which the North Carolina Court of Appeals held that the examiner has an affirmative duty to personally examine the respondent prior to forming and putting in writing a recommendation.

If the respondent reports that the professional who signed the examination report did not perform an examination—whether face-to-face or via telemedicine—counsel should discuss the pros and cons of moving to dismiss, discussed *supra* under the case law portion of § 2.3A. Counsel should also advise the respondent of the need to seek private counsel if the respondent plans to bring a cause of action for breach of the examiner's affirmative duty.

G. Determination by Physician or Eligible Psychologist

At the conclusion of the first examination, the physician or eligible psychologist must determine whether the respondent meets the criteria for inpatient commitment, outpatient commitment, or neither, in which case the respondent must be released. G.S. 122C-263(d).

Inpatient. If the examiner determines that the respondent is mentally ill and dangerous to self or others and cannot be treated on an outpatient basis, inpatient commitment must be recommended and noted on the examination report. If inpatient commitment is recommended, the law enforcement officer or other designated person must transport the respondent to a 24-hour facility for the custody and treatment of involuntary clients pending a district court hearing or, if there is no such 24-hour facility and if the respondent is unable to pay for care at a private 24-hour facility, to a state facility for the mentally ill for "custody, observation, and treatment and immediately notify the clerk of superior court of this action." G.S. 122C-263(d)(2).

Outpatient. If the examiner finds that the respondent can be treated on an outpatient basis, this must be recorded and recommended on the examination report. The examiner must show on the report the name, address, and telephone number of the proposed outpatient physician or treatment center. The law enforcement officer or other designated person must take the respondent home, or with the consent of all, to the residence of an individual located in the county where the petition was filed. G.S. 122C-263(d)(1).

If the examiner is not the proposed outpatient provider, the respondent must be given in writing the name, address, and telephone number of the proposed outpatient treatment physician or center. The respondent also must receive a written notice listing the date and time to appear for an appointment with the proposed treatment provider. The examiner is required to telephone the proposed treatment provider prior to the appointment date, as well as send a copy of the notice and examination report. G.S. 122C-263(f).

H. Alternative Procedure to Petition Before Clerk or Magistrate: Affidavit by Physician or Eligible Psychologist

Rather than going before a clerk or magistrate to file a petition, a physician or eligible psychologist may perform an examination of the respondent in compliance with the criteria discussed *supra* in § 2.3E, and then appear before "any official authorized to administer oaths," including a notary public, to execute an affidavit. G.S. 122C-261(d); *see infra* Appendix A, Forms DMH 5-72-01-A and DMH 5-72-01-B.

The affidavit may be transmitted via fax to the clerk or magistrate as long as the original is mailed to that official within five days. The clerk or magistrate reviews the affidavit and, if the commitment criteria are met, issues a custody order for the respondent to be transported to a 24-hour facility. The examination and affidavit of the physician or eligible psychologist substitute for both the petition before a clerk or magistrate and the statutorily-mandated first examination after a petition is filed.

I. Transport to 24-Hour Facility for Inpatient Treatment

If the physician or eligible psychologist who performed the first examination determines that the individual meets the criteria for inpatient commitment, the law enforcement officer or other designated person must then transport the respondent to a 24-hour facility pending the hearing to review the commitment. An area 24-hour facility is the preferred placement, with a private hospital being the next choice if the respondent is able to pay. If there is no area facility and the respondent is indigent, the respondent is taken to a state facility for the mentally ill. The clerk of superior court is to be notified immediately by the law enforcement officer or other designated person of the admission to a state facility. G.S. 122C-263(d)(2).

J. First Examination Detention Limited to Seven Days

According to G.S. 122C-263(d)(2), the respondent may be "temporarily detained" at the place of the first examination while waiting for transport to the 24-hour facility. Until the revision of G.S. 122C-263(d)(2) in 2009, temporary detention had not been defined, nor had there been a statutory remedy when the detention appeared excessive. According to the new version of G.S. 122C-263(d)(2), if the respondent is temporarily detained and a 24-hour facility is not available or medically appropriate seven days after issuance of the custody order, a physician or eligible psychologist must report this to the clerk and the proceedings must be terminated.

Termination of the proceedings does not necessarily preclude initiation of new involuntary commitment proceedings. However, re-petitioning for commitment is only allowed on certain conditions that preserve a modicum of rights for the respondent. A new petition is allowed only if subsequent supporting affidavits are based on a new examination of the respondent and do not contain any of the information relied on in the previous filing. Bear in mind that 122C-270(a) provides counsel only for initial hearings, rehearings, and supplemental hearings. Generally, counsel is appointed after the respondent's admission to the 24-hour facility. *See supra* § 2.1 (right to counsel). Therefore, the respondent may not have benefit of counsel during this potentially lengthy prehearing detention. Procedural relief for respondents at this juncture would require extraordinary measures, e.g., a writ of habeas corpus.

Practice note: A new filing could potentially result in an additional seven-day waiting period for bed space at a 24-hour facility. Once appointed, respondents' counsel should ask clients about the length of time they were held in the hospital waiting for a bed at the 24-hour facility. Violations of the statute warrant dismissal. In addition, attorneys who regularly represent respondents in commitment proceedings should ask commitment clerks to notify them when a first examiner terminates a commitment and then re-files new commitment papers based on the seven-day rule. If so notified by the clerk's office, respondents' counsel should bring any violation of a respondent's due process rights to the attention of the commitment court through appropriate motion. In addition, a respondent's attorney should address any chronic systemic problems with successive seven-day holds with their supervisor or with the chief district court judge.

K. Second Examination by Physician

A physician must perform a second examination within twenty-four hours of the respondent's arrival at a 24-hour facility. The examiner cannot be the physician who performed the first examination or an eligible psychologist. The second examination provides another opportunity prior to the ten-day hearing at which the respondent may be released from involuntary detention. As with the initial examination, the respondent must be assessed to determine if the criteria for inpatient or outpatient commitment are present. Again, if the criteria for neither are present, the respondent must be released. G.S. 122C-266(a); *see infra* Appendix A, Form DMH 5-72-01.

Inpatient. If the criteria for inpatient commitment are met, the respondent is held at the 24-hour facility pending the district court hearing. G.S. 122C-266(a)(1). The treating physician may release the respondent at any time during the process if the respondent no longer meets the criteria for commitment, except for certain cases referred through the criminal justice system. G.S. 122C-266(a)(3); *see also infra* Chapters 7, 8, and 9.

Outpatient. If the criteria for outpatient commitment are met, the respondent must be released pending the district court hearing. The examiner must provide the respondent, and show on the written examination report, the name, address and telephone number of the proposed outpatient treatment physician or center. In addition, the respondent must be given the date and time for the first outpatient appointment. It is the examiner's responsibility to send a copy of the examination report to the proposed outpatient treatment physician or center, as well as to notify the physician or center by telephone. G.S. 122C-266(a)(2).

Case law: The failure to obtain a second physician examination requires that the commitment order be vacated.

In re Barnhill, 72 N.C. App. 530 (1985). Failure to obtain a second examination by a physician is a fatal procedural error requiring that the commitment order be vacated. In *Barnhill,* a physician petitioned for the issuance of a custody order under former statute G.S. 122-58.3. The North Carolina Court of Appeals noted that the record contained no evidence that a second examination was performed as required under the former statute, a requirement now codified in G.S. 122C-261(d) and 122C-266. The court held that the statutory requirements must be followed diligently and vacated the order of commitment for failure to comply. 72 N.C. App. at 532.

L. Outpatient Commitment: Examination and Treatment Pending Hearing

Prehearing examination. When outpatient commitment is recommended by an examiner and the respondent is released pending the district court hearing, the respondent is required to attend an appointment with the proposed outpatient treatment provider. If the respondent does not appear as scheduled, the proposed treatment provider must notify the clerk of superior court. The clerk is required to issue an order for a law enforcement officer or other designated person to take the respondent into custody and transport the respondent for an evaluation. G.S. 122C-265(a); *see infra* Appendix A, Form AOC-SP-224.

Treatment. The proposed outpatient treatment provider may prescribe appropriate medications but may not physically force the respondent to take the medications. Other appropriate treatment may also be prescribed, but the respondent may not be forcibly detained for purpose of treatment. G.S. 122C-265(b), (c).

Change of recommendation. If the outpatient physician or center determines before the district court hearing that the respondent no longer meets the criteria for outpatient commitment, the respondent must be released and the clerk of court notified of the action. The outpatient proceedings are then terminated. G.S. 122C-265(d).

If the outpatient physician or center determines that the respondent now meets the criteria for inpatient commitment, new proceedings must be initiated by petition or by affidavit of physician or eligible psychologist. G.S. 122C-265(e). Upon initiation of proceedings for inpatient commitment, the clerk in the county where the respondent is being held must send notice to the clerk in the county where the outpatient commitment was initiated, if the counties are different. The outpatient commitment proceeding is then terminated. G.S. 122C-265(f).

M. Duties of Clerk of Superior Court

Inpatient commitment. The clerk of court in the county where the 24-hour facility is located must calendar the district court hearing on receipt of a recommendation from a physician or eligible psychologist for inpatient commitment. G.S. 122C-264(b). The hearing must be held within ten days of the date the respondent was taken into the custody of law enforcement. G.S. 122C-268(a). If the clerk or magistrate determined at the time the custody order was issued that a respondent at a non-state facility is indigent, counsel must be appointed. *See* G.S. 122C-268(d). For respondents at the state psychiatric hospitals, indigency is determined by Special Counsel in accordance with G.S. 7A-450(a), although it is subject to redetermination by the court. G.S. 122C-270(a).

Notice of the hearing is to be provided by the clerk to the respondent, the respondent's counsel, and the petitioner. The petitioner may waive notice by filing a written waiver with the clerk. G.S. 122C-264(b).

Outpatient commitment. The clerk in the county where the petition is initiated must calendar the district court hearing on receipt of a recommendation by a physician or eligible psychologist for outpatient commitment. The clerk is to provide notice of the time and place of the hearing to the respondent, the proposed outpatient treatment physician or center, and the petitioner. The petitioner is allowed to waive notice by filing a written waiver with the clerk of court. G.S. 122C-264(a).

There is no statutory provision for notice to counsel for the petitioner, as there is no requirement that the petitioner be represented.

List of outpatient commitments. The clerk in the county where the outpatient commitment is supervised is required to keep a list of outpatient commitments. The statute also requires the clerk to make a quarterly report listing all active cases, the "assigned supervisor" (which is not defined), and the disposition of all hearings, supplemental hearings, and rehearings. G.S. 122C-264(e). There is no direction as to who is to receive this report. Confidentiality requirements would mandate that this not be a public document.

N. Special Provisions for Mentally Retarded Individuals

It is state public policy that individuals with mental retardation not be treated in state facilities for the mentally ill, if possible. *See* G.S. 122C-263(d)(2) (second paragraph).

"Mental retardation" is defined in 122C-3(22) as significant "subaverage general intellectual functioning existing concurrently with deficits in adaptive behavior and manifested before age 22." "Significantly subaverage general intellectual functioning" is generally identified as an intelligence quotient of less than seventy according to *In re LaRue,* 113 N.C. App. 807 (1994).

Throughout the statutes, there are provisions for the petitioner, clerk, magistrate, and examiners to note if a respondent is known or suspected to be mentally retarded. Those individuals are to be diverted to facilities designed for the treatment of people with mental retardation. *See* G.S. 122C-241.

Chapter 122C specifies exceptions that may be made to this policy:

- Any person charged with a violent crime and found incapable of proceeding must be taken to a state facility. G.S. 122C-263(d)(2)a., 122C-266(b).
- Any person who is committed as a result of being found not guilty by reason of insanity must be taken to a state facility. G.S. 122C-263(d)(2)b., 15A-1321.
- A person for whom a waiver is granted by the Director of the Division of Mental Health, Developmental Disabilities, and Substance Abuse Services or his or her designee, because the individual is "extremely dangerous" so as to be a threat both to the community and to other patients in a non-state facility setting, may be admitted to a state facility. G.S. 122C-263(d)(2)c.
- A person for whom a waiver is granted by the Director of the Division of Mental Health, Developmental Disabilities, and Substance Abuse Services or his or her designee because the individual is "so gravely disabled by both multiple disorders and medical fragility or multiple disorders and deafness that alternative care is inappropriate" may be admitted to a state facility. G.S. 122C-263(d)(2)d.

2.4 Outpatient Commitment Recommended by Physician or Eligible Psychologist Affiant

An involuntary commitment proceeding can begin as a request for outpatient commitment only when a physician or eligible psychologist initiates the process by affidavit. *See supra* § 2.3.H and *infra* Appendix A, Form AOC-SP-305. Under that procedure, the physician or eligible psychologist performs an examination in compliance with the requirements for the first examination under G.S. 122C-263(c) prior to filing the affidavit. The physician or eligible psychologist must provide the respondent with written notice of any scheduled appointment and the name, address, and telephone number of the proposed outpatient treatment physician or center. G.S. 122C-261(d).

The clerk or magistrate must review the affidavit and determine if there is "probable cause to believe that the respondent meets the criteria for outpatient commitment." If so, an order must issue directing that a district court hearing be held to determine whether the respondent will be involuntarily committed to outpatient treatment. G.S. 122C-261(d).

2.5   Attorney Representation

There are two primary parties in an involuntary commitment case: the petitioner and the respondent. The respondent is the subject of the petition and is represented by an attorney. The petitioner has the burden of proving the allegations of mental illness and dangerousness by clear, cogent and convincing evidence, yet is often unrepresented.

To prove the allegation of mental illness, various expert witnesses may be required to testify. Psychologists, psychiatrists, social workers, or other mental health workers may be called to testify. These experts are typically employees of the psychiatric hospital where the respondent is being held and treated pending the district court hearing. When further involuntary inpatient treatment is recommended by such experts, the facility holding and treating the respondent has a corresponding interest in maintaining the respondent on involuntary commitment.

In spite of their substantial roles in proving the allegations in support of involuntary commitment, the petitioner and the treatment facility are often without counsel. These participants often lack knowledge of the substantive and procedural rules that apply during the district court hearing. This places an additional burden on the presiding judge and respondent's attorney to ensure that the respondent receives a full and fair hearing before an impartial fact finder.

A. Attorney for Respondent

Inpatient. An indigent respondent, as defined by G.S. 7A-450, is represented by counsel appointed according to the rules of the Office of Indigent Defense Services (IDS). G.S. 122C-268(d). How counsel is appointed depends first on whether the respondent is at a state facility or elsewhere. Special Counsel represents indigent respondents at state facilities "at all hearings, rehearings, and supplemental hearings held at the State facility." G.S. 122C-270(a). The state facility must provide office space for Special Counsel to meet with clients. G.S. 122C-270(b). Because of time and staff limitations, it may be more common for counsel to meet with clients in whatever private space is available in the ward at the time of the meeting.

For respondents at non-state facilities, appointment procedures vary. In some counties, one attorney has been designated to represent all respondents not in a state facility. The clerk maintains an appointment list in other counties, with attorneys on the list assigned on rotation. Attorneys in private practice interested in serving as counsel for respondents in non-state facilities should make inquiry of the local clerk of court, the local bar committee on indigent representation, or IDS.

Appointed counsel for a respondent at a non-state facility is responsible for representation until the respondent is either unconditionally discharged, signs in as a voluntary patient, or is transferred to a state facility. Representation otherwise continues through the proceeding at the trial level until the district court orders that counsel is discharged. If the respondent appeals, the Office of the Appellate Defender appoints counsel. G.S. 122C-270(a), (e).

Respondents who are not indigent are entitled to be represented by privately-retained counsel of choice. If a non-indigent respondent refuses to hire counsel, however, the statute provides for appointment of counsel pursuant to IDS rules. G.S. 122C-268(d). As of this writing, IDS has not adopted specific rules on appointment of counsel in these circumstances, and attorneys are appointed in each county according to local practice.

For more on the role and responsibilities of counsel, see *infra* Appendix C, "Working with Clients."

Outpatient. There is no statutory requirement that an indigent respondent be represented by counsel at a hearing resulting from an affidavit of a physician or eligible psychologist requesting outpatient commitment. The court may appoint counsel if it

> "determines that the legal or factual issues raised are of such complexity that the assistance of counsel is necessary for an adequate presentation of the merits or that the respondent is unable to speak for himself . . . ."

G.S. 122C-267(d); *see also infra* Appendix A, Form AOC-SP-904M.

B. Attorney for Petitioner

Inpatient. The member of the Attorney General's staff assigned to a state facility or to the psychiatric service of the University of North Carolina Hospitals at Chapel Hill represents the state's interest at all hearings held at the facility. G.S. 122C-268(b). The Attorney General also has discretion to assign a staff attorney to represent the state's interest at hearings held at places other than a state facility. *Id.* The Attorney General may provide representation if venue is transferred for a respondent at a state facility and the hearing is held in the county where the petition was initiated. The Attorney General does not provide representation in cases in which the respondent is not admitted to a state facility. In those cases, the private facility or the petitioner is responsible for hiring an attorney to appear at the hearing or may choose to be unrepresented.

There are non-state facilities, such as general hospitals with psychiatric wings, private psychiatric hospitals, or local mental health inpatient facilities, that do not have representation at the commitment hearings. This affords the respondent's counsel the benefit of presenting evidence without objection and arguing the client's case without response from opposing counsel.

However, having no opposing counsel can be a detriment to the respondent if the judge assumes the role of questioning the petitioner and the petitioner's witnesses or otherwise conducts the hearing in a less formal manner. This makes it difficult for the respondent's counsel to make objections and may result in violations of the respondent's substantive and procedural due process rights. When the respondent's counsel is confronted with the prospect of such violations occurring, counsel should enter appropriate and timely objections in order to preserve the respondent's right to appeal.

Case law: No prejudice to the respondent was found where the petitioner was not represented and the judge questioned witnesses.

In re Jackson, 60 N.C. App. 581 (1983). In *Jackson,* the hearing for a Dorothea Dix patient was held in Cumberland County. The respondent alleged that the lack of counsel for the petitioner in her involuntary commitment proceeding violated her constitutional rights to due process, equal protection, and a fair and impartial hearing. First, she challenged the constitutionality of G.S. 122-58.7(b) and 122-58.24, former statutes that provided that the state would be represented at hearings held at four regional psychiatric centers in North Carolina but did not guarantee counsel for the state or the petitioner in hearings held in other places. (As noted above, the current statute, G.S. 122C-268(b), gives the Attorney General discretion to provide attorney representation at hearings held outside the state facilities). Second, she alleged that the involuntary commitment statutes were unconstitutional in that they permitted a trial judge to question witnesses at an involuntary commitment hearing at which the judge was presiding. The court of appeals determined that the respondent had suffered no prejudice due to the challenged portions of the involuntary commitment statute and therefore had no standing to challenge their constitutionality.

See also In re Perkins, 60 N.C. App. 592 (1983). In rejecting the same arguments as presented in *Jackson,* the court in *Perkins* explained that it was

> "aware of no *per se* constitutional right to opposing counsel. Nothing in the record indicates language or conduct by the court which conceivably could be construed as advocacy in relation to petitioner or as adversarial in relation to respondent. Respondent thus fails to show that he has been

adversely affected by the involuntary commitment statutes as applied, and he therefore has no standing to challenge their constitutionality."

Id. at 594.

Jackson and *Perkins* reinforce that counsel for the respondent must make a record of how the respondent was prejudiced by the lack of counsel for the petitioner and the way in which the hearing was conducted. Lack of representation for the petitioner and greater participation by the judge in the proceedings do not themselves establish prejudice.

Outpatient. There is no statutory mandate for representation of a petitioner who initially requests only outpatient commitment. If the proceeding begins as an inpatient commitment and the respondent is admitted to a state facility but is released pending hearing on an outpatient commitment, the statute provides for representation by the Attorney General staff member assigned to the facility. G.S. 122C-268(b). Additionally, the Attorney General has discretion to assign a member of the staff to represent "the State's interest" at any commitment hearing or subsequent hearing held at a place other than a state facility. *Id.* A county or city attorney could appear to represent the interest of an outpatient treatment provider who is employed by the governmental entity, but such representation is not required by statute.

The statute states that the petitioner "*may* be present and *may* provide testimony." G.S. 122C-267(b) (emphasis added). There is no mention of an attorney for the petitioner in the section on outpatient commitment, and no procedural guidelines are provided for conducting the hearing without either a petitioner or a petitioner's attorney. *See* G.S. 122C-267. In some instances the court has reviewed documents on its own motion and questioned the unrepresented respondent. This scenario puts the court in the position of potentially identifying with the interests of the petitioner. If the petitioner does not appear and present testimony, an objection to hearsay could be made as well as a motion to dismiss for failure to prosecute.

2.6   Initial Hearing

A. Time Limit for Hearing

A hearing must be held in district court within ten days of the respondent being taken into custody. G.S. 122C-268(a). For additional discussion of issues pertaining to hearings, see *infra* Appendix C, "Working with Clients."

Case law: A hearing held on the following weekday is within the time limit when the tenth day falls on a Saturday, Sunday, or legal holiday.

In re Underwood, 38 N.C. App. 344 (1978). In *Underwood,* the respondent was taken into custody on August 4, 1977, with the tenth day following being a Sunday. The involuntary commitment hearing was held on Monday, the eleventh day.

The North Carolina Court of Appeals noted that involuntary commitment proceedings are of a civil nature and thus are governed by the pertinent rules of the North Carolina Rules of Civil Procedure. Rule 6(a) provides that when the last day of a time prescribed by statute falls on a Saturday, Sunday, or legal holiday, the period runs to the next day that is not a Saturday, Sunday, or legal holiday. The court held that the hearing was held in due time under the Rules because the tenth day was a Sunday. 38 N.C. App. at 347.

Statutory amendment of definition of legal holiday. Rule 6 of the North Carolina Rules of Civil Procedure was amended effective October 1, 2003, regarding the definition of "legal holiday" for the purpose of calculating statutory time requirements. The amendment clarifies that the time period is extended only when the last date an action is required falls on a legal holiday *and* the courthouse is closed. If the courthouse is open on a legal holiday, such as Columbus Day, the time is not extended to the next day.

B. Venue and Transfer of Venue

Inpatient. Venue is the judicial district in the state in which a case is properly heard. In the involuntary commitment context, the respondent has a choice of venue when inpatient treatment is requested. The district court hearing is held in the county in which the 24-hour facility is located in all cases where the respondent is held pending hearing. If the respondent objects to venue, the hearing is held in the county where the petition was filed. G.S. 122C-269(a); *see infra* Appendix B, "Notice of Objection to Venue and Order Transferring Venue."

Counsel should inform a client who is in a facility outside the county where the petition was filed of the option of moving to transfer venue. The pros and cons to transfer of venue should be discussed with the respondent. Possible benefits of transfer are increased availability of witnesses favorable to the client and the decreased likelihood of testimony from treatment providers from the out-of-county facility. Possible detriments are the need for appointment of local counsel, delay in the hearing caused by scheduling difficulties and appointment of new counsel, the need for transportation of the respondent to the hearing by law enforcement, increased availability of witnesses who observed the events alleged in the petition, and availability of expert witnesses who may have long-term experience with the client.

Possible benefits of not transferring venue are an earlier hearing date, availability of treatment team members for consultation and negotiation of terms of commitment, continuity of legal representation, and the decreased likelihood of witnesses from the initiating county who observed the events alleged in the petition.

Outpatient. The district court hearing is held in the county in which the petition for outpatient commitment was initiated. G.S. 122C-261(d), 122C-264(a). There is no provision for transfer of venue, as the county of origination is the same county where the proposed outpatient treatment would occur.

There is a provision to change venue for further court proceedings when a respondent who has been held in a 24-hour facility is then committed to outpatient treatment in a different county. The court must order that venue be transferred to the county where the outpatient treatment will be supervised. G.S. 122C-271(b)(4).

C. Place of Hearing

Inpatient. The hearing may be held in "an appropriate room not used for treatment" at the facility if it is located within the district of the presiding judge. Proceedings also may be held in the judge's chambers. If the respondent objects, the hearing may not be held in a regular courtroom, unless the judge determines that no more suitable place is available. G.S. 122C-268(g). Unless the respondent requests that it be open, the hearing is closed to the public. G.S. 122C-268(h).

If the hearing is held outside of the 24-hour facility, counsel should tell the client where the hearing will be held, describe the waiting area and courtroom, and inform the client of transportation arrangements. Respondents going to out-of-county hearings should be advised that law enforcement provides transportation. Private facilities may arrange for transportation and supervision of their patients having hearings outside the treatment facility.

Outpatient. Hearings may be held either at the area facility providing outpatient treatment, if within the judge's district, or in the judge's chambers. As with proceedings for inpatient commitment, the hearing may not be held in a regular courtroom over the respondent's objection, unless the judge determines that no more suitable place is available. G.S. 122C-267(e). The hearing is also closed to the public, unless the respondent requests otherwise. G.S. 122C-267(f).

D. Discharge Pending Hearing

The attending physician must release any respondent who no longer meets the criteria for involuntary inpatient or outpatient commitment, except for certain cases referred through the criminal justice system. *See infra* Chapters 7, 8, and 9. Notice of the release is to be given by the attending physician to the clerk of court, and "the proceedings shall be terminated." G.S. 122C-266(d).

In an effort to obtain a discharge pending hearing, the respondent, through counsel, may consent to a physician recommendation for outpatient commitment. On such an agreement, the attending physician may release the respondent from involuntary inpatient services prior to the district court hearing. To effectuate the respondent's agreement at the district court hearing, counsel would waive the respondent's appearance, stipulate that the conditions for outpatient commitment exist, and consent to an order being entered that requires the respondent to receive outpatient services for mental health treatment.

E. Continuance

Inpatient. A continuance of up to five days may be granted on the motion of the court, the respondent's counsel, or the State. The State must move for a continuance "sufficiently in advance to avoid movement of the respondent." G.S. 122C-268(a).

Outpatient. A continuance of up to five days may be granted on the motion of the court, the respondent, or the proposed outpatient treatment physician. G.S. 122C-267(a).

Factors to consider. Many district courts hold commitment hearings only once a week or on two consecutive days, so a five-day continuance may not be workable. It is common practice for the court to allow a seven-day continuance on consent of the parties.

There are many practical reasons a respondent might benefit from a continuance, though it might seem only to extend the respondent's hospital stay. Some clients are suffering most acutely from symptoms of mental illness in the first week or two of admission. A continuance may allow for improvement of symptoms, leading to more effective communication between attorney and client, better decision-making by the client, and more persuasive presentation by the client at the later hearing. Another benefit can result if the client improves enough to be either discharged or allowed to sign in as a voluntary patient. This may be particularly important to someone who has never been committed, as it may avoid the collateral consequences of commitment, such as the inability to own or possess a gun legally. *See infra* Chapter 12.

Counsel sometimes has to make the decision to ask for a continuance without agreement from a client who is too acutely ill to be able to discuss the issues. The attorney should review the respondent's psychiatric history and talk with treatment providers to determine whether the client is likely to improve enough to participate in the hearing process in the near future or whether the hearing will proceed without meaningful assistance from the client. *See infra* § 2.6F.

In addition, a client who is demanding that venue be transferred to the county from which the petition originated should be advised by counsel of the need for the court transferring venue to continue the case to accommodate the client's request. At the new venue, a delay in excess of seven days may be reasonable given the responsibilities of the clerk in assigning new counsel, in scheduling a judge to hear the matter, in scheduling an appropriate hearing location and hearing time, and in serving notices of the hearing.

Case law: Granting of seven-day continuance over objection of respondent was improper.

In re Jacobs*,* 38 N.C. App. 573 (1978). In *Jacobs,* the court file containing the petition and custody order from the originating county had not been transferred as of the hearing date to the clerk of superior court of the county where the commitment hearing was being held. The lower court therefore continued the respondent's initial commitment hearing on its own motion for seven days, over the respondent's objection. This resulted in the district court hearing being held more than ten days from the date the respondent was taken into custody.

The North Carolina Court of Appeals noted that the State failed to present any evidence on the date the hearing was originally scheduled. The court held that a seven-day continuance under these circumstances constituted a denial of the respondent's right to a hearing within ten days of being taken into custody. *Id.* at 575–76.

Note: This case was decided under the former statute G.S. 122-58.7(a), which provided for a continuance of five days only on motion of the respondent's counsel.

F. Not Contesting/Not Resisting Commitment

Not contesting. There are no statutory provisions for respondents to accept the recommendation of commitment, that is, to "not contest." In practice, however, many respondents are in agreement with their attending physicians on the need for inpatient treatment and do not contest the allegations in the petition. Even so, the attending physician may not allow the respondent to become a voluntary patient because of concerns that the respondent might want to leave prematurely or might stop cooperating with recommended treatment. Counsel may, after advising the respondent of the possible consequences of involuntary commitment, inform the client of the option to "not contest." *See infra* Chapter 12.

By not contesting, the respondent can avoid a hearing with potentially upsetting testimony from family, friends, and the treatment team. An uncontested commitment hearing could proceed with testimony from the petitioner's witnesses or by stipulation of the respondent's counsel. Counsel may stipulate to the facts alleged in the petition and in the Qualified Physician's Examination report (for a definition of this report, see *supra* § 2.2), or stipulate that the information in those documents would be the testimony of the authors.

A respondent who is not contesting may wish to attend the hearing and has the right to do so. Counsel should explain the abbreviated nature of the proceedings so that the respondent will know what to expect. Respondents who are not contesting often prefer not to attend the hearing. A motion for waiver of appearance should be filed so that the respondent is not compelled to attend. *See infra* § 2.6G.

Not resisting. Because involuntary commitment involves allegations of mental illness, it is not unusual to have a client who is manifesting acute symptoms of a mental illness. For example, one respondent might be catatonic and completely unresponsive, while another is manic and unable to stop talking long enough to comprehend or to respond to information presented. There are no statutory provisions to guide counsel when the client is unable to express a decision on whether to contest the commitment.

In these cases, counsel should review the respondent's medical and psychiatric records and consult with the attending physician to better understand the respondent's prognosis. If a respondent has suffered from a disease for a long time with no improvement, or with progressive decline, counsel may determine that there is little chance for future meaningful communication. Because of the nature of involuntary commitment, the inability to communicate effectively with the client is not treated as it is in other types of cases. This problem may be an integral part of the reason the client was committed and is therefore not grounds for the case to be postponed due to the respondent's incapacity.

In cases where there is little or no chance for improvement or for the respondent to prevail at the commitment hearing, counsel may report to the court that the respondent is "not resisting." This means that the respondent is unable to understand and discuss the issues enough to contest the commitment, but is equally unable to decide not to contest. This is in contrast to the client who is able to express in any way a desire whether or not to contest. As with an uncontested case, the hearing may then proceed with testimony from the petitioner's witnesses or by stipulation of the respondent's counsel. Counsel may stipulate to the facts alleged in the petition and in the Qualified Physician's Examination report (for a definition of this report, see *supra* § 2.2), or stipulate that the information in those documents would be the testimony of the authors.

A motion for waiver of appearance is filed in virtually every case of commitment for treatment of mental illness in which a respondent is not resisting. This is because the respondent is also unable to make a decision regarding an appearance and would be unable to understand or to benefit from attending court proceedings.

Note that although the same considerations may exist in a substance abuse commitment proceeding, the substance abuse statutes do not allow a waiver of the respondent's appearance. *See infra* § 3.5D.

Continuance. If a respondent appears likely to improve soon, counsel should continue the case with the hope of having a meaningful discussion of the case. For example, a respondent with a diagnosis of bipolar disease who is acutely manic might have a history of responding quickly to medication. This is a good case to continue, with follow-up on the respondent's progress each week. There are no guidelines on what is a reasonable amount of time to pursue this approach. It is best to err on the side of a continuance if there is some prospect of the respondent recovering enough to participate in the hearing. *See supra* § 2.6E.

G. Waiver of Appearance

Inpatient. Counsel may waive in writing the appearance of the respondent at the hearing, although the court must approve. G.S. 122C-268(e); *see infra* Appendix B, "Waiver of Appearance and Order Allowing Waiver of Appearance."

Some of the same considerations discussed above in deciding whether to request a continuance may be involved in deciding whether to waive the client's appearance. Counsel should advise the respondent of the benefits of appearing at the hearing in a contested case. The judge has an opportunity to observe and hear from the respondent. There can be consultation with the client concerning the testimony of the witnesses for the petitioner and the opportunity to present rebuttal testimony.

Some clients are reluctant to appear at the hearing because of fear of the unknown or past unpleasant experiences in other judicial proceedings. Counsel should advise that the hearing will not be in a regular courtroom and that anyone not directly involved in the case can be excluded from the hearing room. Reassurance that this is not a criminal proceeding and going to jail is not a possibility may be helpful.

Outpatient. The statute provides that the presence of the respondent at the hearing for outpatient commitment may not be waived. It further states that a subpoena "may be issued" to compel the respondent's attendance, but does not specify who is responsible for issuing the subpoena. G.S. 122C-267(b).

H. Criteria for Involuntary Commitment: Inpatient Treatment

The court must "find by clear, cogent, and convincing evidence that the respondent is mentally ill and dangerous to self . . . or dangerous to others." G.S. 122C-268(j). The statutory definitions of "dangerous to self" and "dangerous to others" are listed *supra* in § 2.2. The following case summaries are provided so that counsel may follow the progression of the courts' analysis of the dangerousness standards. As counsel will find from a review of these summaries, the outcome of a commitment case will depend on whether the basis for commitment is dangerousness to self or dangerousness to others and whether specific evidence is presented on the required prongs of the dangerousness definitions.

The cases are arranged in the following order based on their general impact:

- The first three cases—*Hatley, Hogan,* and *Frick*—were decided under the dangerousness definitions in former Chapter 122, but they still offer guidance to practitioners in litigating dangerousness allegations.
- The next cases—*Monroe* and *Crainshaw*—reflect an early emphasis on the need for specific findings on the required prongs of the dangerousness definitions.
- Cases from the next period—*Medlin, Lowrey,* and *Zollicoffer*—reflect a willingness by the courts to tolerate broader and less specific allegations of dangerousness as a basis for commitment. (*Crouse,* which questions *Crainshaw* and is discussed in connection with that decision, is also from this period.)
- Two recent unpublished opinions—*McCray* and *Church*—question the *Medlin* line of decisions and return to a closer interpretation of the statutory requirements.
- The last decision—*Hayes*—addresses one aspect of the dangerousness definition, the meaning of the phrase "in the relevant past."

Case law: Danger to self or others.

In re Hatley, 291 N.C. 693 (1977). The North Carolina Supreme Court in *Hatley* examined the evidence required to support a finding of danger to self or others under former Chapter 122. In *Hatley,* the only witness testifying on behalf of the State was the petitioner, who was the respondent's mother. The court also admitted into evidence, apparently without objection, the sworn affidavit of the first examining physician, Dr. Wilson.

The court noted that the lower court relied in part on the testimony of the respondent's mother, who testified that the respondent went into the house of a neighbor while no one was home, that she had heard that the respondent threatened a relative with a brick, and that she felt that the respondent sometimes drove in an unsafe manner. The respondent's mother admitted that she did not know whether the neighbor was home at the time the respondent went in, that she did not witness an incident in which the respondent threatened someone with a brick, and that she did not know of any instances in which the respondent had an automobile accident or disobeyed traffic laws. 291 N.C. at 696–97.

In finding the testimony of the respondent's mother insufficient to support commitment, the court stated, "We find nothing in the testimony of [the respondent's mother] which would even support a reasonable inference that [the respondent] was imminently dangerous to herself or others." *Id.* at 699. [The standard "imminently dangerous" applied by the court in *Hatley* is no longer valid. The pertinent portion of the current "dangerous to others" standard in G.S. 122C-3(11)b. requires that the respondent have "inflicted or attempted to inflict or threatened to inflict serious bodily harm on another" and that there be "a reasonable probability that this conduct will be repeated." The pertinent portion of the current "dangerous to self" standard in G.S. 122C-3(11)a. requires that the respondent be unable, without supervision, to exercise judgment and discretion in the context of daily responsibilities to satisfy her need for self-protection and safety and that there be a reasonable probability that she will suffer serious physical debilitation within the near future unless adequate treatment is given.]

Although the affidavit of the first examining physician was also admitted into evidence, the court observed that, based on review of the affidavit, the conclusions as to mental illness and danger were merely recitations of the information related by the respondent's mother and were not derived from the examination. The court stated that "insertion of these same facts in a medical report does not give them greater force or dignity than the sworn testimony presented in the District Court." *Id.* at 699.

Note: This case illustrates both the need to object to hearsay and to question the source of the witness's information as well as the sort of testimony that does *not* support a finding of danger to self or others. It is also important to challenge information that comes in solely through an examiner's report (or testimony) without first-hand knowledge of the examiner.

In re Hogan, 32 N.C. App. 429 (1977). The North Carolina Court of Appeals reached a result contrary to *In re Frick,* discussed next. Although the facts of the case do not reveal the respondent's living situation, her behavior was similarly at issue. The court held, however, that the evidence of the respondent's mental illness and bizarre behavior was insufficient to support an involuntary commitment.

In *Hogan,* the State presented as its only evidence an affidavit from the physician who performed the second examination of the respondent, which was admitted over the objection of the respondent. Although the appellate court held that the affidavit should not have been admitted because the respondent did not have the opportunity to confront and cross-examine the physician, the court proceeded to review the record to determine if any evidence supported the findings of the lower court. *Id.* at 432–33.

The respondent presented the testimony of Dr. Russ, the psychiatrist who performed the first examination of the respondent at the local mental health center. Dr. Russ testified that the respondent was preoccupied with religion and preached on the streets of Gastonia without the requisite license, accosting strangers and trying to convert them. He found impaired judgment and lack of insight but did not find her to be aggressive. Dr. Russ instead felt that the danger the respondent posed to herself resulted from possibly inciting others to react aggressively to her because of her preaching. *Id.* at 431.

The appellate court held that this testimony did not support a finding that the respondent was dangerous to herself. Rather, it stated that if this scenario did occur, "it would seem more appropriate to commit her aggressor rather than the respondent." *Id.* at 434. The court further held that findings of fact that she had delusions about the Ku Klux Klan, "that she misinterpreted stimuli, and that she was out of touch with reality," even if they had been supported by the evidence, were not sufficient to support a finding of danger to self or others. *Id.* at 433–34.

Note: This case is useful in arguing cases in which a person exhibits symptoms of mental illness, resulting in bizarre behavior and unusual ideas. The court recognized that the person who reacts to non-aggressive behavior in an aggressive way is the one who poses a danger to the community.

In re Frick, 49 N.C. App. 273 (1980). The North Carolina Court of Appeals addressed the issue of danger to self in this case. The respondent was a homeless woman who was diagnosed with a mental illness. She often stayed in her car until it was impounded after her arrest for trespassing at the home of her former husband. The respondent testified that she sometimes stayed in the motel rooms of men she had just met, and on one occasion agreed to have sex with a man for $20.00, but took the money without performing the sexual act. *Id.* at 273–74.

The respondent argued on appeal that the findings of fact did not support the finding that she was a danger to self. The appellate court disagreed, citing evidence relating to the respondent's mental condition and her inability to formulate a plan for self-care. The court noted that the lower court found that the respondent had exhibited both a thought disorder and a psychotic mood disorder with symptoms of pressured speech, loose associations, tangential thinking, and labile, or unstable, emotions. Her treating physician at Dorothea Dix, where she was committed, testified that she was at risk to decompensate and become psychotically manic if not involuntarily committed for treatment. This evidence was sufficient to support the conclusion that the respondent was a danger to self because of inability to provide basic necessities for herself and the probability of decompensation without inpatient treatment, leading her to place herself in dangerous situations. *Id.* at 276–77.

Note: This case illustrates the difficulty of representing a homeless person with mental illness. Although the respondent had found shelter for herself, and apparently had adequate nutrition, the places and situations she put herself into could have been dangerous. This, along with the diagnosis of mental illness, was sufficient to prove danger to self, without evidence of actual harm.

In re Monroe, 49 N.C. App. 23 (1980). The North Carolina Court of Appeals considered both danger to self and danger to others in this case. The State presented evidence that the respondent was irregular in his sleep routine, getting up three to six times per night, that he had unusual eating habits, fasting at times then eating a whole loaf of bread or a whole chicken, and eating about five pounds of sugar every two days. The court stated that this may be evidence of mental illness and might satisfy the first prong of the definition of "danger to self," an "inability to 'exercise self-control, judgment, and discretion in the conduct of his daily responsibilities.'" The second prong of the test, reasonable probability of serious physical debilitation within the near future without adequate treatment, however, was not met. *Id.* at 29 (relying on G.S. 122-58.2(1)a.1.I., now codified as amended at G.S. 122C-3(11)a.).

The court found that evidence of the respondent's calling out to strangers passing by his home likewise did not meet the test of behavior resulting in harm to himself. 49 N.C. App. at 29–30.

The *Monroe* court then addressed the issue of danger to others. Evidence presented by the State showed that the respondent was off his medication, resulting in behavior that was uncontrollable at times, that he made statements to family members that "I'm gonna get you all yet," that he was suspicious of his family and felt that he had been sexually abused by them, and that he was "ready to fight" if family members attempted to correct his behavior. *Id.* at 31. The court found that these facts supported the lower court's conclusion of law that the respondent was dangerous to others by acting "'in such a manner as to create a substantial risk of serious bodily harm to another.'" *Id.* at 31–32.

In re Crainshaw, 54 N.C. App. 429 (1981). In *Crainshaw,* the State's evidence indicated that the respondent had forgotten to turn off the stove when cooking, causing her to burn pots and pans and a Formica countertop. She also was forgetful, talked to the wall, and appeared unaware of her surroundings. *Id.* at 430. Based on this evidence, the lower court found that the evidence "rais[es] a strong inference that she is unable to care for herself," and concluded as a matter of law that she was mentally ill and dangerous to herself. *Id.* at 430. On the respondent's appeal on the issue of danger to self, the appellate court held that the findings of fact did not support either prong of the test for danger to self. The court added that even if the facts were "indicative of some danger," they still would not support the second prong of the test requiring a reasonable probability of serious physical debilitation within the near future without adequate treatment. *Id.* at 432. [In the *Crainshaw* opinion, the court of appeals stated that the second prong of the dangerous to self test "mandates a specific finding of a probability of serious physical debilitation resulting from the more general finding of lack of self-caring ability." *Id.* at 431. In the later case of *In re Crouse,* 65 N.C. App. 696 (1983), the court of appeals explained that it believed such language was dictum and that only a finding that the respondent was mentally ill and dangerous to self was necessary to support an inpatient commitment order.]

In re Medlin, 59 N.C. App. 33 (1982). The *Medlin* case focused on the two-pronged test of danger to self in upholding the commitment of the respondent.

The respondent was diagnosed with paranoid schizophrenia and psychotic depression on admission to John Umstead Hospital. The respondent's daughter testified at the commitment hearing that her mother had been unemployed for about a year and that she had been living in her car for the past two weeks in cold weather. *Id.* at 34. The court noted that it appeared the only food that the respondent received was brought to her by her daughter and that her daughter feared she would die of carbon monoxide poisoning if she continued to live in the car. *Id.* at 37.

The respondent did not appeal the finding of mental illness but argued that the evidence did not support a finding of danger to self. The court noted that the test for danger to self has two prongs: an inability to provide for one's own basic needs; and "a reasonable probability of serious physical debilitation to him within the near future unless adequate treatment is afforded pursuant to this Article." *Id.* at 36 (citing and quoting G.S. 122-58.2(1), now codified as amended at G.S. 122C-3(11)a.). The court found that the facts of the respondent's living situation supported the first prong of the test and that failure "to properly care for her medical needs, diet, grooming and general affairs would meet the required test of dangerousness to self." *Id.* at 38. The court further noted that the test did not require "a showing that violent danger is threatened by respondent to herself," and that the facts of the case indicated that the respondent was likely to incur death or injury "by uneventful slow degrees or by misadventure" without adequate treatment. *Id.* [In an unpublished opinion, *In re McCray*, ___ N.C. App. ___, 697 S.E.2d 526 (2010), discussed below, the court of appeals questioned its ruling in *Medlin*, explaining that a provision of G.S. 122-58.2(1) cited by the *Medlin* court—namely "[t]he phrase 'dangerous to himself' includes, but is not limited to, those mentally ill or inebriate persons who are unable to provide for their basic needs for food, clothing, or shelter"—has been repealed, with no comparable language in the current statute, and further that the provision had been superseded prior to the *Medlin* decision and thus *Medlin* relied on an obsolete statue.]

In re Lowery, 110 N.C. App. 67 (1993). This case supports the proposition that even though there is evidence that a mentally ill respondent could be treated outside of a hospital setting, inpatient commitment is appropriate if the respondent refuses placement recommended as necessary for outpatient treatment to succeed.

In *Lowery*, the respondent was diagnosed with chronic mental illness and polysubstance abuse. His attending psychiatrist from an immediately prior inpatient commitment to the mental health center testified that he refused anti-psychotic medicines, did not eat properly, could not return to his mother's home, and could not properly care for himself. He further testified that the respondent could receive treatment on an outpatient basis if he were in a rest home, but that the respondent refused such placement. The respondent testified that he had lived alone, that he knew how to use food stamps to buy food, and that he was refusing rest home placement. *Id.* at 68–69.

The court held that the State's evidence was sufficient to support the order of inpatient commitment. Citing *In re Medlin*, discussed above, the court stated, "We have held specifically that the failure of a person to properly care for his/her medical needs, diet, grooming and general affairs meets the test of dangerousness to self." *Id.* at 72. The respondent's refusal to accept placement deemed necessary by his psychiatrist for his safety outside the hospital, coupled with his failure to present a viable alternative placement, defeated his argument that outpatient commitment was appropriate. *Id.* at 72–73. [In an unpublished opinion, *In re McCray*, ___ N.C. App. ___, 697 S.E.2d 526 (2010), discussed below, the court of appeals questioned its ruling in *Lowery*. The court observed in footnote 2 of *McCray* that *Lowery* had been based on *Medlin*, which depended on a definition of "dangerous to self" in G.S. 122-58.2 that was obsolete at the time *Medlin* was decided.]

In re Zollicoffer, 165 N.C. App. 462 (2004). This more recent case upheld the lower court's finding of danger to self, despite the lack of evidence in the record of any actual harm suffered by the respondent.

In *Zollicoffer,* the State's evidence consisted of an affidavit from the respondent's treating psychiatrist, Dr. Soriano, apparently admitted into evidence without objection. Dr. Soriano wrote that the respondent had a history of paranoid schizophrenia, admitted to not taking medicine resulting in "high risk for mental deterioration," did not cooperate with treatment providers, and "requires inpatient rehabilitation to educate him about his illness and prevent mental decline." *Id.* at 469. In upholding the lower court's finding that this evidence supported a finding of danger to self, the court quoted *In re Lowery*, 110 N.C. App. 67, 72 (1993): "'We have held specifically that the failure of a person to properly care for his/her medical needs, diet, grooming and general affairs meets the test of dangerousness to self.'" 165 N.C. App. at 469. [In an unpublished opinion, *In re McCray*, ___ N.C. App. ___, 697 S.E.2d 526 (2010), discussed below, the court of appeals questioned its ruling in *Lowery*. The court observed in footnote 2 of *McCray* that *Lowery* had been based on *Medlin,* which depended on a definition of "dangerous to self" in G.S. 122-58.2 that was obsolete at the time *Medlin* was decided.] The court did not address the failure of the record to reflect that this respondent had neglected any areas of self-care.

This case stands in contrast to *In re Hogan,* above, as it seems to rest solely on evidence of mental illness and the psychiatrist's conclusory statements of danger to self.

In re McCray, ___ N.C. App. ___, 697 S.E.2d 526 (2010) (unpublished). In *McCray*, the court of appeals reviewed the evidence before the trial court that the respondent cocked her fist, poured a pitcher of juice on a nurse, and demonstrated loud and aggressive behavior while being escorted to the "quiet room," i.e., isolation. The court of appeals found the incidents insufficient to find the respondent dangerous to others because there was no evidence supporting a "reasonable probability that the conduct would be repeated" as required by G.S. 122C-3(11)(b). Likewise, the court of appeals found the respondent's refusal of blood pressure, thyroid, and psychotropic medications insufficient to constitute a "reasonable probability of . . . suffering serious physical debilitation within the near future," as required to prove dangerousness to self under G.S. 122C-3(11)(a).

In re Church, ___ N.C. App. ___, 698 S.E.2d 200 (2010) (unpublished). In *Church*, the court reversed a district court order of commitment that lacked sufficient findings in support of its conclusions as to dangerousness to others. The court of appeals was not persuaded that the respondent was dangerous to others by the treating psychiatrist's allegation that the respondent would decompensate and become dangerous if the respondent did not receive treatment. The court made clear that a pending charge of murder, standing alone, is not sufficient to conclude that the respondent is dangerous to others. The murder charge is based on a finding of probable cause, which does not rise to the standard of clear, cogent, and convincing evidence required for a finding of dangerousness in the commitment context.

In re Hayes, 151 N.C. App. 27 (2002). The North Carolina Court of Appeals in *Hayes* addressed the interpretation of the statutory definition of danger to others in G.S. 122C-3(11)(b), particularly the meaning of the phrase "in the relevant past" in regard to past acts of the respondent in assessing current danger to others. In *Hayes*, the respondent was found not guilty by reason of insanity for homicides and felonious assaults committed in July of 1988. The recommitment hearing being reviewed on appeal was held in January 2001. The court of appeals found that the standard of review on appeal is "whether there is competent evidence to support the trial court's factual findings and whether these findings support the court's ultimate conclusion that respondent still has a mental illness and is dangerous to others." 151 N.C. App. at 29–30. Despite the lapse of time between the respondent's acts and the hearing, the appellate court held that competent evidence supported the finding of the lower court that:

> "The four homicides and seven felonious assaults committed by the respondent on July 17, 1988, are episodes of dangerousness to others *in the relevant past* which in combination with his past and present mental condition, his multiple mental illnesses, and his conduct since admission to Dorothea Dix Hospital since 1989, and up to and including his conduct in the hospital during the previous year indicates there is a reasonable probability that the respondent's seriously violent conduct will be repeated and that he will be dangerous to others in the future if unconditionally released with no supervision at this time."

Id. at 31 (emphasis added).

In so holding, the court rejected the respondent's argument that under this interpretation of "in the relevant past," a homicide defendant found not guilty by reason of insanity would never be released from psychiatric inpatient commitment. The court noted that even though the respondent would be "presumed dangerous to others" and that this was a "high hurdle for the respondent to overcome," this burden was proper and the lower court's findings and conclusions must be upheld. *Id.* at 38–39.

Note: When objecting to testimony involving danger to others based on remoteness in time, counsel should be prepared to distinguish *Hayes* from the respondent's case. Although the *Hayes* court did not limit its interpretation of the statutory definition of "danger to others" to cases originating under Chapter 15A, the outcome appears linked to the extraordinary facts. The respondent's acts included seven felonious assaults and caused four deaths, resulting in the court's finding that their occurrence was within the "relevant past." Because "relevant past" is not statutorily defined, counsel can argue that less harmful, remote acts of a respondent are not material in assessing current dangerousness.

I.   Criteria for Involuntary Commitment: Outpatient Treatment

The physician or eligible psychologist must recommend outpatient commitment if the following criteria are present:

> "a.   The respondent is mentally ill;
> b.   The respondent is capable of surviving safely in the community with available supervision from family, friends, or others;
> c.   Based on the respondent's psychiatric history, the respondent is in need of treatment in order to prevent further disability or deterioration that would predictable result in dangerousness . . . ; and
> d.   The respondent's current mental status or the nature of the respondent's illness limits or negates the respondent's ability to make an informed decision to seek voluntarily or comply with recommended treatment."

G.S. 122C-263(d)(1).

J.   Evidence: Inpatient Commitment

Burden of proof. The Attorney General staff member assigned to a state facility or the UNC Hospitals psychiatric services will present evidence on behalf of the State. G.S. 122C-268(b). As noted *supra* in § 2.5B, there is no statutory mandate for representation of the petitioner at other facilities. The burden is on the petitioner, however, to prove by "clear, cogent, and convincing evidence that the respondent is mentally ill and dangerous to self . . . or dangerous to others." G.S. 122C-268(j).

Admissible certified copies. The petitioner is allowed to present "[c]ertified copies of reports and findings of physicians and psychologists and previous and current medical records." G.S. 122C-268(f). A respondent has the right, however, to confront and cross-examine witnesses. *Id.* It is unclear whether a petitioner can initially offer certified documents only, forcing the respondent to object. If so, who is then responsible for subpoenaing the witness? If the petitioner can first offer the documents without the witness, the proceeding will likely have to be continued to give the witness time to appear. This scenario forces the respondent to endure a delay in the hearing to enforce the right to cross-examine.

Inadmissibility of voluntary admission. The statutes specifically prohibit the admission of evidence regarding a voluntary admission in a hearing on involuntary inpatient commitment. G.S. 122C-208.

Case law: The admission of a physician's report when the physician does not appear at the hearing constitutes a denial of the respondent's right to confront and cross-examine the witness.

In re Mackie, 36 N.C. App. 638 (1978). The North Carolina Court of Appeals addressed the issue of admission of a physician's written report without his appearance. In *Mackie*, the petitioner testified at the respondent's rehearing and stated that she had not seen the respondent in almost eight months. The only other evidence presented by the State was the written report of a physician at Broughton Hospital.

The court held that the admission of the physician's report without the physician's appearance at the hearing constituted a denial of the respondent's right to confront and cross-examine witnesses. As the only other evidence presented was the testimony of the petitioner, there was no evidence supporting the lower court's findings of mental illness and danger to self or others, and the order was reversed. *Id.* at 640.

In re Hogan, 32 N.C. App. 429 (1977). In *Hogan*, the State's only evidence was the written report of the physician who performed the second examination of the respondent, admitted over the respondent's objection. The respondent called as a witness the psychiatrist who performed the first examination.

The court stated that because the physician who wrote the report that was admitted into evidence did not appear and testify at the hearing, the respondent was "clearly denied her right to confront and cross-examine him." *Id.* at 432. The court stated that this denial would "at least entitle respondent to a new hearing." *Id.* at 433. The court reversed the order, however, on the ground that the findings of fact in the order did not support the finding that the respondent was imminently dangerous to herself or others (under the old statute) and that there was not any competent evidence to support that finding. *Id.* at 433–34.

Hearsay. Counsel for the respondent must be vigilant in objecting to hearsay testimony. Admission of a written report over the objection of the respondent is grounds for reversal of an order of commitment absent other competent supporting evidence, as illustrated by the above cases.

Other hearsay evidence may be harder to recognize. A staff person may begin to testify to an incident illustrating a danger to self or others without having witnessed the occurrence. The respondent's attorney may have to object when the testimony begins in order to ascertain whether the witness's knowledge is first-hand. A physician may be allowed to testify to hearsay contained in the medical records as part of the basis of a psychiatric diagnosis. Counsel should still object and request that, if the court allows the testimony, it be admitted for the limited purpose of explaining the diagnosis and that it not be considered on the issue of danger.

Witnesses. The respondent's attorney must determine, in consultation with the respondent as appropriate, who to call as a witness and what documents to subpoena. Some of these decisions may depend on the strength of the petitioner's case. For example, if the petitioner presents a weak case, counsel might recommend that the respondent not testify and thus not be subject to cross-examination. Some respondents will feel that their cases have not been fully presented if they have not testified. If the client insists on exercising the right to testify, counsel should make a written note in the file of the advice given not to testify.

K. Evidence: Outpatient Commitment

Burden of proof. As noted *supra* in § 2.5B, the petitioner may be unrepresented or not be present at the hearing. The court still must find by "clear, cogent, and convincing evidence that the respondent meets the criteria specified in G.S. 122C-263(d)(1)." G.S. 122C-267(h).

Certified copies admissible. The statute specifies that "[c]ertified copies of reports and findings of physicians and psychologists and medical records of previous and current treatment are admissible in evidence." G.S. 122C-267(c). Unlike the provisions regarding inpatient commitment, there is no specified right to confront and cross-examine witnesses, and evidence of a voluntary admission may be considered as a part of treatment history. G.S. 122C-208.

Witnesses and hearsay. The statute appears to provide for only a limited judicial review of the physician's recommendation for outpatient commitment. The court may review what would otherwise be hearsay statements in medical records and may hear testimony from only the respondent. If the respondent is unrepresented, the court may need to pose questions to the respondent (and to any other witnesses) and decide what weight, if any, to give hearsay testimony.

2.7   Disposition

A. Dispositional Alternatives: Respondent Held in 24-Hour Facility Pending Hearing

Inpatient. If the court finds that the respondent meets the criteria for inpatient commitment—that is, that the respondent is mentally ill and dangerous to self or others—it may order inpatient treatment in a 24-hour facility for up to ninety days. If the commitment proceeding was initiated as the result of the respondent being charged with a violent crime and found incapable of proceeding, this must be noted on the commitment order. *See infra* Chapter 8. If the respondent is currently under an outpatient commitment order, that commitment is terminated. G.S. 122C-271(b)(2).

The subsection on inpatient commitment specifically provides that "no respondent found to be both mentally retarded and mentally ill may be committed to a State, area or private facility for the mentally retarded." G.S. 122C-271(b)(2). There are limited circumstances in which an individual with mental retardation can be committed to a state facility for the mentally ill. G.S. 122C-263(d)(2); *see also supra* § 2.3.N.

Outpatient. If the court finds that the respondent meets the criteria for outpatient commitment, it may order outpatient commitment for up to ninety days. G.S. 122C-271(b)(1); *see supra* § 2.6I. The court also may order that a respondent being held at a 24-hour facility pending hearing be held by the facility up to seventy-two hours to allow the facility time to notify the outpatient physician or center of the treatment needs of the respondent. G.S. 122C-271(b)(4). If the court orders outpatient commitment in excess of the initial ninety days allowed by statute, the order is voidable, not void ab initio, and must be honored until vacated or corrected. *In re Webber*, ___ N.C. App. ___, 689 S.E.2d 468 (2009). The proper remedy in such a case is for the respondent to appeal the erroneous order or request a supplemental hearing pursuant to G.S. 122C-274(e). *Webber*, 689 S.E.2d at 476. The statute requires that if the commitment petition was filed as the result of the respondent being charged with a violent crime, and the respondent was found incapable of proceeding, this must be noted on the commitment order. G.S. 122C-271(b)(1); *see also infra* § 8.10.

The court must make a specific finding of availability of services before ordering outpatient commitment. In addition, the name of the outpatient treatment physician or center responsible for the respondent's treatment must be shown on the order. G.S. 122C-271(b)(4).

Inpatient/outpatient. The statute also allows the court to commit the respondent to a combination of inpatient and outpatient treatment for up to ninety days. G.S. 122C-271(b)(2). For example, the judge may order up to forty-five days of inpatient treatment, followed by up to forty-five days of outpatient treatment. The outpatient commitment begins on the respondent's release from the inpatient facility. In this example, if the respondent is released on the thirtieth day of inpatient treatment, the forty-five days of outpatient commitment begins then.

The court may feel more comfortable with an earlier release from a facility if an outpatient commitment is ordered. Although a contesting client may object to *any* commitment, counsel may suggest to the client proposing to the court a lesser amount of recommended inpatient time followed by an outpatient commitment, or simply an outpatient commitment.

As with an inpatient order alone, the court must note on the order whether the commitment proceedings were initiated as a result of the respondent being charged with a violent crime. Likewise, any inpatient period of commitment terminates a prior outpatient commitment. G.S. 122C-271(b)(2).

Discharge. If the court does not find that the criteria for either inpatient or outpatient criteria are met, the respondent must be discharged. G.S. 122C-271(b)(3).

B. Dispositional Alternatives: Outpatient Recommendation, Respondent Released Pending Hearing

There are only two possible dispositional alternatives when the affiant physician or eligible psychologist has recommended outpatient commitment and the respondent has been released pending hearing. The court may order an outpatient commitment of up to 90 days if the criteria for outpatient commitment are found by clear, cogent, and convincing evidence. G.S. 122C-271(a)(1). If the court does not find that the outpatient criteria are met, the respondent must be discharged. G.S. 122C-271(a)(2).

C. Order

Inpatient. The court must find by clear, cogent, and convincing evidence that the respondent is mentally ill and dangerous to self or others. The underlying facts supporting these findings must be set out in the order. G.S. 122C-268(j); *see infra* Appendix A, Form AOC-SP-203. The trial court's duty to record facts in support of its findings is "mandatory," and failure to do so requires reversal of the order without regard to the evidence elicited at hearing. *In re Booker*, 193 N.C. App. 433 (2008).

Outpatient. The court must find by clear, cogent, and convincing evidence that the criteria for outpatient commitment are present. G.S. 122C-271(b)(1). The court also must make findings of fact regarding the availability of outpatient treatment and show on the order the name of the supervising outpatient physician or center. If the respondent was held in a 24-hour facility pending the hearing, the court may order that the respondent be held by the facility for up to seventy-two hours to notify the outpatient treatment provider of the respondent's treatment needs. G.S. 122C-271(b)(4). The form used for an inpatient commitment, AOC-SP-203, is also used for an outpatient commitment. *See infra* Appendix A.

D. Duties of Physician for Follow-Up on Inpatient Commitment Order

General duties. There is only a brief statutory paragraph regarding duties for follow-up on an inpatient commitment order. The statute directs that the attending physician "may administer to the respondent reasonable and appropriate medication and treatment that are consistent with accepted medical standards." G.S. 122C-273(d).

Release and conditional release. Subject to exceptions concerning patients involved with the criminal justice system, the attending physician must discharge any respondent held pursuant to an inpatient commitment order upon determination that the criteria for inpatient treatment are no longer met. If the criteria for outpatient treatment are met, the attending physician may file a request with the clerk for a supplemental hearing on the issue of outpatient commitment. G.S. 122C-277(a).

The attending physician also may conditionally release a respondent for up to thirty days on "medically appropriate conditions." G.S. 122C-277(a). Conditional release is used for patients who have improved but still meet the commitment criteria. Often called a "trial visit," a conditional release affords the respondent an opportunity to demonstrate the ability to function safely in the community while still under the commitment order. The use of a trial visit has decreased recently because of concerns about hospital and physician liability for a respondent's acts while out of the facility.

Conditions imposed on the release may include taking medicine as prescribed, attending outpatient appointments, and abstaining from dangerous behaviors. The conditional release can range from a visit of a few hours outside the hospital with family or friends, to an overnight or weekend visit home, to the full thirty-day period of conditional release to home. Successful completion of a trial visit should result in unconditional discharge.

If a conditionally released respondent violates the specified conditions, the attending physician may request a law enforcement officer to take the respondent into custody for return to the facility. G.S. 122C-277(a); *see infra* Appendix A, Forms DMH 5-82-02 and DMH 5-83-01.

Notice of discharge or conditional release is to be provided to both the clerk of court in the county where the petition for commitment was originally filed and in the county where the facility is located. G.S. 122C-277(a).

E. Duties of Physician or Center for Follow-Up on Outpatient Commitment Order

Medication and treatment. An outpatient physician may prescribe or administer or an outpatient center may administer "reasonable and appropriate medication and treatment that are consistent with accepted medical standards." G.S. 122C-273(a). Note, however, the respondent may not be physically forced to take medication or be forcibly detained for treatment except in the case of immediate danger to self or others. Forced treatment or detention may only be undertaken in conjunction with the initiation of inpatient commitment proceedings. G.S. 122C-273(a)(3). There is also a mandate for LMEs that no individual may be refused services because of an inability to pay. G.S. 122C-146(a).

Failure to comply or clearly refuses to comply. The treating outpatient physician or center must make "all reasonable effort [sic]" to obtain the respondent's cooperation with treatment. G.S. 122C-273(a)(1). If the respondent "fails to comply or clearly refuses to comply" with treatment recommendations, the treatment provider *must* report the efforts made, along with a request for a supplemental hearing. *Id.; see infra* Appendix A, Form AOC-SP-221. The form is filed with the clerk of superior court, who is responsible for calendaring the supplemental hearing.

Failure to comply, but does not clearly refuse to comply. The treatment provider must make reasonable efforts to engage the respondent in prescribed treatment. If the respondent does not comply, but does not clearly refuse prescribed treatment, the treatment provider *may* request that the respondent be taken into custody for the purpose of examination. G.S. 122C-273(a)(2); *see infra* Appendix A, Form AOC-SP-220. The form is filed with the clerk of superior court, not a magistrate, who *must* issue an order (included on the request form) for a law enforcement officer to take the respondent into custody for transport to the outpatient physician or center for examination. G.S. 122C-273(a)(2).

After examination, the outpatient treatment provider must release the respondent unless inpatient commitment proceedings are instituted. If inpatient commitment proceedings are instituted, the examination substitutes for the first examination ordinarily required for commitment. The clerk or magistrate must issue a custody order within six hours of the examination if this procedure is pursued. G.S. 122C-273(a)(2).

This provision allows the treatment provider to use law enforcement to force the respondent to submit to an examination. Unlike the procedure for a respondent who clearly refuses to comply, however, there is no concurrent request for and scheduling of a supplemental hearing.

Respondent no longer meets outpatient commitment criteria. At any time that the respondent no longer meets the criteria for outpatient commitment, the court must be notified and the case terminated. There is an exception for a respondent first committed as a result of being charged with a violent crime and found incapable of proceeding. In that case, the treatment provider must notify the clerk that discharge is recommended. The clerk must schedule a supplemental hearing for the court to determine whether the respondent is to be released from outpatient commitment. G.S. 122C-273(a)(4); *see infra* § 8.12.

Respondent moves to another state or to unknown location. The clerk of superior court of the county supervising outpatient treatment must be notified by the treatment provider if the respondent moves to another state or to an unknown location. The outpatient commitment is then terminated. G.S. 122C-273(c).

Respondent becomes dangerous to self or others. Anyone who has knowledge that a person under outpatient commitment has become dangerous to self or others may initiate a petition for inpatient commitment. If the respondent is committed on an inpatient basis, the prior outpatient commitment is terminated. G.S. 122C-273(a)(5).

2.8   Outpatient Commitment Supplemental Hearings

A. Request for Supplemental Hearing

Supplemental hearing distinguished from rehearing. A supplemental hearing is held during the term of an outpatient commitment if the respondent fails to comply or clearly refuses to comply with treatment, or if the respondent moves or intends to move to another county within the state. These are matters concerning the terms of the existing commitment.

A rehearing is held on a request to *extend* the current outpatient commitment. For example, a rehearing may be held on request of the attending physician for an additional ninety days of outpatient commitment following a ninety-day commitment.

There is no statutory definition for either "supplemental hearing" or "rehearing."

Mandatory requests. A supplemental hearing must be requested by the treatment provider in the following instances:

- when the respondent "fails to comply or clearly refuses to comply" with recommended treatment (G.S. 122C-273(a)(1); *see infra* Appendix A, Form AOC-SP-221); or
- when the respondent moves or intends to move to another county within the state. G.S. 122C-273(b).

Discretionary requests. A supplemental hearing may be requested:

- by the treatment provider if the respondent "fails to comply, but does not clearly refuse to comply" with recommended treatment (G.S. 122C-273(a)(2), 122C-274; *see infra* Appendix A, Form AOC-SP-220); or
- by the respondent at any time in writing seeking discharge from outpatient commitment. G.S. 122C-274(e).

An attending physician for an inpatient respondent may request a supplemental hearing for the purpose of transferring the respondent to an outpatient commitment. G.S. 122C-277(a). There are no separate statutory provisions for a supplemental hearing for inpatient commitment.

B. Calendaring of Supplemental Hearing and Notice

The clerk of superior court of the county supervising the outpatient commitment must calendar a supplemental hearing within fourteen days of receipt of a request. Notice to the petitioner, the respondent's attorney, if any, and the designated outpatient treatment provider must be given by the clerk by first-class mail, postage prepaid, at least seventy-two hours prior to the hearing. The respondent must be personally served with an order to appear at least seventy-two hours before the hearing. G.S. 122C-274(a).

C. Supplemental Hearing Procedures

The supplemental hearing is held in district court pursuant to the procedures provided for the initial outpatient commitment hearing. G.S. 122C-274(b); *see also* G.S. 122C-267. As with the initial hearing, the appearance of the respondent may not be waived, and the court may consider certified medical documents that would otherwise be considered hearsay evidence.

D. Disposition

Alleged failure to comply. The court must first determine whether the respondent has failed to comply with outpatient treatment. If the respondent is in compliance, presumably the proceeding is terminated and the original outpatient commitment continues, although this is not stated in the statute. *See* G.S. 122C-274(c).

If the respondent is found not to be in compliance, the court may order one of three alternatives:

- if the court finds "probable cause to believe that the respondent is mentally ill and dangerous to himself . . . or others . . . ," it may order an examination by the outpatient or other physician or an eligible psychologist to determine the need for continued outpatient commitment or for inpatient commitment;
- it may reissue or change the outpatient commitment order in accordance with

the initial dispositional criteria and order outpatient commitment of up to ninety days; or

- it may discharge the respondent from outpatient commitment and dismiss the case.

G.S. 122C-274(c)(1)–(3); *see infra* Appendix A, Form AOC-SP-206.

Respondent has moved or intends to move. The court is required to determine first whether the respondent continues to meet the criteria for outpatient commitment, even though the supplemental hearing has been requested pursuant to a move or planned move. If the respondent continues to meet the criteria, the court must continue in effect the outpatient commitment and designate a treatment provider in the new county of residence to supervise the outpatient treatment. The court must order that the respondent appear at the address provided for the new treatment provider for continued outpatient treatment. In addition, the court is required to transfer venue of the case to the county of the provider supervising the outpatient treatment. G.S. 122C-274(d); *see infra* Appendix A, Form AOC-SP-206.

Respondent's request for discharge. On the respondent's request for a supplemental hearing, the court must "determine whether the respondent continues to meet the criteria specified in G.S. 122C-263(d)(1) [outpatient commitment]. The court may either reissue or change the commitment order or discharge the respondent and dismiss the case." G.S. 122C-274(e); *see infra* Appendix A, Form AOC-SP-206.

Attending physician's request to transfer respondent from inpatient to outpatient commitment. The court is first required to determine whether the respondent continues to meet the criteria for inpatient commitment. If so, it must order that the original inpatient commitment be continued. If the court finds that the respondent meets the criteria for outpatient commitment, it must order outpatient commitment of up to ninety days. The respondent must be discharged and the case dismissed if the respondent does not meet the criteria for either type of commitment. G.S. 122C-274(f).

2.9   Rehearings for Inpatient Commitment

A. Notice to Clerk by Facility

If the attending physician determines that an additional period of inpatient treatment will be required, notice of the need for a rehearing must be provided to the clerk at least fifteen days before the end of the commitment. This notice is given to the clerk of the county where the facility is located. G.S. 122C-276(a); *see infra* Appendix A, Form DMH 5-76-01.

B. Scheduling of Hearing and Notice

The clerk is to calendar the rehearing at least ten days before the end of the inpatient commitment hearing. Except for respondents committed as a result of being charged with a violent crime, discussed *infra* in § 8.11, notice is to be provided in accord with the requirements for the initial hearing. G.S. 122C-276(d); *see infra* Appendix A. Form AOC-SP-301.

C. Hearing Procedures

Rehearings for inpatient commitment are held in accord with the procedures set forth for the initial hearing. The respondent is afforded the same rights, including the right to appeal. G.S. 122C-276(d), (f); *see supra* § 2.6. The North Carolina Court of Appeals has held that G.S. 122C-276(d) does not require that the respondent be examined by a second physician, as required for the initial commitment proceeding. The examination of the attending physician who requested the rehearing is sufficient to satisfy statutory requirements. *In re Lowery,* 110 N.C. App. 67, 70 (1993).

D. Disposition

At the first rehearing, the court has the same dispositional alternatives as at the initial hearing, except that a second period of inpatient commitment may be for up to 180 days. G.S. 122C-276(e); *see also* G.S. 122C-271(b). Additionally, if the court finds that the criteria for outpatient commitment are met, an outpatient commitment of up to 180 days may be ordered. G.S. 122C-276(g). The court may also commit a respondent for a combination of both inpatient and outpatient days, i.e. a "split commitment." However, the total number of days committed cannot exceed 180 days.

At second and subsequent rehearings, if the court finds that the criteria are met, it may order inpatient commitment for up to one year. G.S. 122C-276(f). The court may also order outpatient commitment of up to 180 days at any subsequent rehearing. G.S. 122C-276(g). The court also may combine inpatient and outpatient commitment days for a total maximum of 365 days, although this is rarely, if ever, done.

In re Hayes, ___ N.C. App. ___, 681 S.E.2d 395 (2009), is one in a lengthy series of cases regarding the possible discharge of Michael Hayes, a defendant found not guilty by reason of insanity. *See supra* § 2.6H (discussing the underlying facts of the case). Although the case is specific to G.S. 122C as it relates to individuals who are found not guilty by reason of insanity, the case is also important for its discussion of the court's disposition options at a rehearing. Essentially, the case holds that the trial court on rehearing may order any disposition allowed by Chapter 122C regardless of the specific relief requested by the treating physician. Therefore, commitment counsel would be well advised to be creative in making recommendations that provide the least restriction on the respondent's liberty as long as the recommendations are within the dispositional alternatives allowed by statute. As always, counsel should advise the respondent of the alternatives available and obtain the respondent's consent before offering dispositional alternatives to the court.

E. Respondent's Waiver of Right to Second and Subsequent Rehearings

The attending physician must notify the respondent, the respondent's counsel, and the clerk in the county where the facility is located, if inpatient treatment beyond the second inpatient commitment is recommended. The respondent may file with the clerk, through counsel, a written waiver of the right to a rehearing. G.S. 122C-276(f).

2.10 Rehearings for Outpatient Commitment

A. Notice to Clerk by Treatment Provider

The outpatient treatment physician or center must notify the clerk of superior court at least fifteen days before the end of initial or subsequent outpatient treatment if an additional period of outpatient commitment is required. Additionally, the treatment provider must notify the clerk if a respondent no longer meets the criteria for outpatient commitment. The clerk must then dismiss the case, unless the respondent was committed as a result of being charged with a violent crime and being found incapable of proceeding. In that case, the clerk also must schedule a hearing before the district court. G.S. 122C-275(a). This procedure is discussed *infra* in § 8.12.

B. Scheduling of Hearing and Notice

The clerk must calendar the hearing at least ten days before the end of the outpatient commitment period. Notice is to be provided in accord with the requirements for the initial hearing. G.S. 122C-275(a), (b); *see also supra* § 2.3M.

C. Hearing Procedures

Rehearings for outpatient commitment are held in accord with the procedures set forth for the initial hearing. The respondent is afforded the same rights, including the right to appeal. G.S. 122C-275(b).

D. Disposition

The court has two dispositional alternatives at a rehearing on an outpatient commitment. First, if the court finds that the respondent no longer meets the criteria for outpatient commitment, the respondent must be unconditionally discharged. The clerk must transmit a copy of the discharge order to the outpatient treatment provider. G.S. 122C-275(c).

If the court finds that the respondent continues to meet the criteria for outpatient commitment, it may order outpatient commitment to continue for up to 180 days at each rehearing. G.S. 122C-275(c).

2.11 Special Emergency Procedure

A. Transportation for Examination for Immediate Hospitalization

A person in need of immediate inpatient commitment to prevent harm to self or others may be transported by anyone with knowledge of the circumstances, including a law enforcement officer, for examination by a physician or eligible psychologist. The individual may be taken to an area facility or other place, including a state facility for the mentally ill, for this examination. G.S. 122C-262(a).

B. Certification by Examiner of Need for Immediate Hospitalization

If the physician or eligible psychologist finds after examination that the individual meets the criteria for immediate hospitalization, the examiner must so certify in writing before an officer authorized to administer oaths. The certificate must state the reasons immediate hospitalization is necessary, as well as any information regarding whether the person is mentally retarded. G.S. 122C-262(b); *see infra* Appendix A, Forms DMH 5-72-01-A and DMH 5-72-01-B.

C. No Appearance Before Magistrate

The certification of need for immediate hospitalization obviates the need for an appearance by the physician or eligible psychologist before a magistrate. A copy of the certificate must be sent by the physician or eligible psychologist to the clerk "by the most reliable and expeditious means." If it appears that the certificate will not be delivered within twenty-four hours, the findings also must be communicated to the clerk by telephone. G.S. 122C-262(c).

D. Transportation to 24-Hour Facility Pending Hearing

The certificate of the physician or eligible psychologist serves as the custody order for the person to be transported to a 24-hour facility. Pending the district court hearing, the individual may be transported by anyone, including a law enforcement officer, to the facility. If there is no area 24-hour facility, and the respondent is indigent and cannot pay for care at a private facility, the respondent may be transported to a state facility for the mentally ill. G.S. 122C-262(d).

E. Chief District Court Judge to Examine Certificate

The clerk of superior court must submit the certificate of the physician or eligible psychologist immediately upon receipt to the chief district court judge for review. The chief district court judge reviews the certificate under the same standard used by the clerk or magistrate reviewing a petition under G.S. 122C-261(b)—that is, that there are "reasonable grounds to believe that the facts alleged in the affidavit are true and that the respondent is probably mentally ill and either (i) dangerous to self . . . or dangerous to others . . . or (ii) in need of treatment in order to prevent further disability or deterioration that would predictably result in dangerousness." G.S. 122C-261(b), 122C-264(b1).

The judicial review of the certificate is to occur within twenty-four hours, excluding Saturdays, Sundays, and holidays. The clerk must then notify the treatment facility of the findings of the court by telephone. G.S. 122C-264(b1). If the court does not find that reasonable grounds exist, presumably the respondent must be released.

F. Further Proceedings

Upon determination by the court that reasonable grounds exist for immediate hospitalization, the clerk proceeds as in a case initiated by petition or physician's affidavit. G.S. 122C-264(b1). Procedures for further examination and court hearings are also in accord with cases initiated by petition or affidavit. G.S. 122C-262(e); *see also supra* § 2.3H.

2.12 Appeal

A. Appeal to North Carolina Court of Appeals

The district court has exclusive original jurisdiction over civil commitments and admissions requiring judicial review. Appeal from a district court order is directly to the North Carolina Court of Appeals. An appeal does not stay the order of the district court, which retains jurisdiction to hear all reviews, rehearings, or supplemental hearings allowed or required by statute. G.S. 122C-272.

It is important for counsel to stress to the respondent that appealing does not result in immediate release from the hospital. In most cases, the respondent will be either discharged or recommitted prior to issuance of an opinion from the court of appeals. Although discharge of the client does not render the appeal moot (*see infra* § 2.12E), if the client is recommitted pending resolution of the appeal, winning the appeal does not result in discharge from the current commitment.

B. Who May Appeal

The statute allows the state or "any party on the record as in civil cases" to appeal. G.S. 122C-272. It is not specified who, other than the respondent, would be a party of record. There is no case law on this point.

C. Representation of Respondent

Chapter 122C provides for attorney representation of a respondent through any appellate proceedings. G.S. 122C-270. Appeal by the respondent's counsel is at the direction of the respondent. Pursuant to G.S. 122C-270(a) and (e), assigned counsel represents respondents through all proceedings in the district court. Presumably, this covers notice of appeal, which is required to be given at the district court level. Counsel appointed by the Office of the Appellate Defender represent respondents through the conclusion of any appeal. G.S. 122C-270(e).

D. Confidentiality on Appeal

There is no provision in the North Carolina Rules of Appellate Procedure for using the initials of a respondent in appellate documents to preserve patient confidentiality. Recent amendments to the Rules, however, mandate the use of initials for most records in juvenile proceedings, which also are confidential proceedings. Counsel should consider filing a motion with the court requesting to be allowed to use initials, citing the rule for juvenile cases as analogous. If the motion is granted, the respondent's name would be redacted from *all* records designated by the court, including the transcript and all exhibits.

Counsel should advise a client who is considering an appeal that confidentiality of the proceeding may be sacrificed as a consequence of appealing. This might be an important factor to some clients.

E. Appeal Not Moot

An appeal is not rendered moot by the discharge of the respondent pending the resolution of the appeal.

Case law: An appeal is not moot if the respondent is discharged or the term of commitment has expired.

In re Hatley, 291 N.C. 693 (1977). An appeal is not rendered moot because the term of commitment ordered by the lower court has expired. In *Hatley*, the North Carolina Supreme Court considered the possible consequences of being adjudged mentally ill, such as the finding or order being used adversely against the respondent in future civil or criminal proceedings. The court also noted that in the instant case, the lower court based its order in part on the respondent's record of prior commitments. Because there were possible collateral legal consequences, the court held that the respondent's appeal was not moot. *Id.* at 694–95.

In re Hogan, 32 N.C. App. 429 (1977). In *Hogan*, the North Carolina Court of Appeals stated that even though the record contained a certificate indicating that the respondent had been unconditionally discharged from the order of commitment, the appeal was not moot, citing *In re Hatley*, discussed above, and other cases. The court of appeals did not discuss the facts of the case or possible collateral legal consequences. *Id.* at 432.

In re Benton, 26 N.C. App. 294 (1975). The North Carolina Court of Appeals held in *Benton* that the respondent's appeal was not moot even though the commitment period of sixty days had expired. The court did not discuss the facts of the case or possible collateral legal consequences in reaching its holding. *Id.* at 295.

Appendix 2-1
Involuntary Commitment for Mental Health Treatment:
Checklist for Respondents' Attorneys

This checklist applies after Special Counsel or the appointed attorney receives notice of the patient's admission. Consult the indicated forms as necessary.

Receipt and Review of Documents

- ❏ Receive the petition or affidavit of the physician or eligible psychologist, accompanied by the affidavit(s) of the examiner. This will occur by different methods depending on local practice. Counsel should inquire of the clerk of court and the records clerk of the facility to determine local practice.
- ❏ Review documents for compliance with statutory requirements.

Affidavit and Petition for Involuntary Commitment (Form AOC-SP-300)

- ❏ Is the petition signed and sworn before an authorized officer? G.S. 122C-261(a).
- ❏ Was the petition properly clocked in with a date and time stamp?
- ❏ Is box 1, alleging mental illness and danger to self or others, checked?
- ❏ Do the allegations in the petition support on their face a finding of reasonable grounds to believe that the respondent is mentally ill and either dangerous to self or others or in need of treatment to prevent further disability or deterioration that would predictably result in dangerousness?
- ❏ Who does the petition indicate are witnesses to the behaviors and actions alleged in the petition?

Findings and Custody Order Involuntary Commitment (Form AOC-SP-302)

- ❏ Is the custody order properly signed and dated with the time noted by the appropriate court official?
- ❏ Is box 1, alleging mental illness and danger to self or others under "Findings," checked?
- ❏ Is box 1 and/or 2 checked under "Custody Order"?
- ❏ Does the "Return of Service" on the back indicate that the respondent was taken into custody within 24 hours of issuance of the custody order?
- ❏ Did the law enforcement officer complete either Section A, B, C, or D appropriately on the back of the custody order?

Affidavit of Examining Physician or Eligible Psychologist—First Examination Report (Form DMH 5-72-01, Examination and Recommendation to Determine Necessity for Involuntary Commitment)

- ❏ Was the examination performed within 24 hours of the time the respondent was taken into the custody of the law enforcement officer?

❑ Was the first examination performed by either a physician or eligible psychologist?

❑ Is the examination report properly signed?

❑ Does the examination report indicate that the examiner performed a personal examination and did not merely repeat the allegations of the petition? If the examination was via "telemedicine" and not in the examiner's physical presence, did it comply with the requirements of G.S. 122C-263(c)?

❑ Do the findings of the examiner support the conclusion of a diagnosis of mental illness?

❑ Do the findings of the examiner support the conclusion of a finding of danger to self or others?

❑ Does the examiner's report recommend inpatient commitment?
Recommendation: _____

❑ Was the respondent detained 7 days or less while awaiting transport to a 24-hour facility? If the respondent was detained more than 7 days, was a new commitment petition filed in accordance with the requirements of G.S. 122C-263(d)(2)?

Affidavit of Physician—Second Examination Report (Form DMH 5-72-01, Examination and Recommendation to Determine Necessity for Involuntary Commitment)

❑ Was the examination performed within 24 hours of admission to a 24-hour facility?

❑ Was the examination performed by a physician?

❑ Is the examination report properly signed?

❑ Does the examination report indicate that the examiner performed a personal examination and did not merely repeat the allegations of the petition?

❑ Do the findings of the examiner support the conclusion of a diagnosis of mental illness?

❑ Do the findings of the examiner support the conclusion of a finding of danger to self or others?

❑ Does the examiner's report recommend inpatient commitment?
Recommendation: _____

Medical Records Review

❑ Review records in the patient's chart(s) at the 24-hour facility

❑ Do Progress Notes contain staff observations of manifestation of symptoms of mental illness?

_____

❑ Do Progress Notes contain staff observations of dangerous behavior toward self or to others? _____

❑ Results of drug testing:

_____

❑ Current medications: _____

❏   Psychological examination or other special examinations or reports?

_____

❏   Any pending criminal charges noted in the record?

_____

Interview with Client

Attorney role:

❏   Meet with client as soon as possible
❏   Explain you represent client, no one else
❏   Inform client that he or she may retain private attorney (explain time parameters, request that retained attorney call you, request to be on stand-by in event retained attorney does not appear)
❏   Explain that representation for commitment proceeding only

Explanation of proceeding:

❏   Special proceeding reviewing hospitalization, jail not a possibility
❏   Hearing before judge, but not in regular courtroom (describe hearing room)
❏   Confidential proceeding, hearing, and court file
❏   Time and date of hearing
❏   Venue—right to transfer if petition initiated in another county and possible need for continuance to facilitate hearing in originating county
❏   Waiver of appearance—importance of appearance if contesting
❏   Witnesses for State and for client may be called
❏   Continuance may be requested by client, by State, or on motion of court

Discussion of case:

❏   Review allegations of petition—get client's side of events
❏   Discuss medical evidence
❏   Ask what treating psychiatrist or social worker has told client about treatment team recommendation on length of stay
❏   Ask client if there are prior commitments or other information on mental illness or danger that might be raised by State's witnesses
❏   Explain consequences of involuntary commitment: ____firearms ____ military
❏   Does client have alternative plan to inpatient care (housing, job, outpatient care, day program, etc.)?
❏   Client states would agree to (sign as voluntary, shorter stay, continuance if early discharge pending, etc.) _____
❏   Discuss possible witnesses; obtain client consent to contact/subpoena
❏   Advise of possible technical motions (e.g., motion to dismiss for failure of petition to be signed but possibility of new petition)

Explanation of hearing procedures:

- ❑ Attorney for State or petitioner to call witnesses—possibly petitioner, psychiatrist, social worker, staff, or family
- ❑ Witnesses for client—discuss allegations, likely witnesses, advisability of client testifying
- ❑ Courtroom demeanor—not get upset, not speak unless testifying, stay seated unless called to testify, whisper quietly or write note if need to communicate with attorney
- ❑ Closing arguments—client should not react or speak during

Client's position:

_____ Contest   _____ Not contest

_____ Agrees to venue   _____ Requests change of venue

_____ Agrees to: (sign in as voluntary patient, shorter inpatient stay, outpatient commitment, continuance, etc.): _____

_____ Appear   _____ Not appear

_____ Move to continue   Reason: _____

Follow-up to Client Interview

- ❑ Notify opposing counsel, appropriate court personnel of result (contest/not contest, appear/not appear)
- ❑ Negotiate with opposing counsel or psychiatrist as appropriate for desired client result (what client would agree to)
- ❑ Contact witnesses to discuss case
- ❑ Subpoena witnesses as necessary
- ❑ Meet with client as necessary to discuss results of negotiation, information from witnesses
- ❑ Prepare for hearing: motions, questions, relevant case law

Action needed:

_____ Motion to dismiss   Reason: _____

_____ Motion to continue   Reason: _____

_____ Contested hearing: _____ Client appear

                             _____ Not appear   _____ Motion to Waive Appearance

_____ Not contested: _____ Client appear

                          _____ Not appear   _____ Motion to Waive Appearance

Client agrees to:

_____ Inpatient
_____ Outpatient
_____ Split: _____ Inpatient   _____ Outpatient
_____ Client signed voluntary
_____ Client was discharged

Follow-up to Hearing When Client Committed

- ❏ Discuss order with client, reiterate that amount of days committed is *maximum* inpatient stay without a rehearing and that can be discharged sooner
- ❏ Explain outpatient commitment, if any, importance of attending appointments, and consequences of failure to comply
- ❏ Explain that representation continues for duration of commitment and through any appeal
- ❏ Advise of appeal right, discuss limitations (length of time to appeal, likely discharge or rehearing well before appeal decided)

Appendix 2-2
Memorandum to Magistrates[*]

The shortage of suitable 24-hour facilities for persons in need of mental health evaluation and treatment has received significant attention in recent months. The purpose of this memo is to inform magistrates about recent legislation enacted to address one aspect of this problem, and to caution magistrates to avoid a practice, currently relied upon in some parts of the State, that is not authorized by law.

New Law

Session Law 2009-340 (House Bill 243), effective October 1, 2009, is a legislative acknowledgement that many persons who are found mentally ill and dangerous to self or others at the first commitment examination are not proceeding to the next step in the commitment process in a timely manner. Statutory law requires that these persons (known as "respondents") be taken to a 24-hour psychiatric facility for a second examination and treatment pending a commitment hearing in district court. This hearing must take place within 10 days from the time the respondent was taken into law enforcement custody at the beginning of the commitment process. Because the state-operated psychiatric hospitals do not have sufficient bed space, many respondents are kept waiting in community hospital emergency rooms for several days. By the time some of these respondents arrive at a state hospital, the clerk of court does not even have time to calendar a hearing within the 10-day time frame.

This 10-day hearing requirement is one of North Carolina's statutory mechanisms for assuring that a respondent is not deprived of liberty without the due process guaranteed by the U.S. Constitution. The new law is a response to the concern that delays in transporting respondents to psychiatric inpatient facilities may deprive some respondents of statutory and constitutional due process. S.L. 2009-340 amends G.S. 122C-261(d) and -263(d) to provide that, with respect to respondents who have been found to meet the inpatient commitment criteria, if a 24-hour facility is not immediately available or medically appropriate seven days after issuance of the custody order, a physician or psychologist must report this fact to the clerk of superior court and the proceedings must be terminated. If this happens, a new commitment proceeding may be initiated, but affidavits filed and examinations conducted as part of the previous commitment proceeding may not be used to support a new commitment. Certainly, some of the facts considered by the magistrate in deciding to issue the first custody order may be relevant in making the new determination, but any papers filed and examinations conducted in support of a new proceeding must also be new.

In situations where a respondent is temporarily detained at the site of first examination because a 24-hour facility is not immediately available or medically appropriate, S.L. 2009-340 also permits a physician or psychologist to terminate the inpatient commitment proceeding and discharge the respondent (or recommend outpatient commitment), upon finding that the respondent's condition has improved to the point that he or she no longer meets the criteria for inpatient commitment. Any such finding must be documented in writing and reported to the clerk of superior court.

---

* This memorandum was written by UNC School of Government faculty member Mark F. Botts, on November 15, 2009.

A Practice to be Avoided

It is not at all surprising that legal and medical professionals confronted with the current crisis presented by a shortage of available 24-hour facilities craft creative responses in an effort to improve the way the system responds to citizens in need of help. One practice currently being employed by some magistrates, however, is inconsistent with the law and presents significant problems for other participants in the system. This practice consists of holding a commitment petition and not issuing a custody order until the availability of a particular 24-hour facility has been confirmed. The result is that the facility performing the first evaluation must hold a respondent for the period—sometimes days, as discussed above—**without this hold being authorized by a custody order.** Without a custody order, this hold is without legal authority (subject to an exception not relevant to magistrates), raising serious issues about the due process rights of the respondent as well as questions about the potential liability of the facility exerting custodial control over the respondent. Accordingly, magistrates should not engage in this modification of the statutory procedure. When a magistrate receives a petition and makes a determination that reasonable grounds exist to believe that an individual meets the statutory criteria for commitment, the law is clear that a magistrate <u>must</u> issue a custody and transportation order. The commitment statutes do not authorize a magistrate to delay issuance of a custody order pending the receipt of other information. Nor do the statutes permit a magistrate to make his or her decision subject to criteria not identified in the commitment statutes. In the space on the custody order for designating a 24-hour facility, the magistrate should enter the name of the facility normally used by the jurisdiction, followed by the words "or any state-approved facility." This allows the commitment process to proceed without delay and permits the involuntary detention of the respondent throughout all phases of the commitment process, including during the time it takes following the first examination to identify an available 24-hour facility. Moreover, some 24-hour facilities will not agree to accept an involuntary patient until *after* a custody order has been issued. The magistrate's role in this process is critically important, and it is absolutely essential that magistrates follow the statutory procedure in carrying out their responsibilities.

If you have questions or concerns about any of the information in this memo, contact the School of Government faculty member specializing in mental health law, Mark Botts. Mark can be reached by telephone (919-962-8204) or email (botts@sog.unc.edu).

Chapter 3
Involuntary Commitment of Adults and Minors for Substance Abuse Treatment

---

3.1   Substance Abuse Commitment

Involuntary commitment for substance abuse treatment is the judicial procedure to compel a substance abuser to submit to treatment. While many of the procedures are the same as or similar to those for involuntary commitment for mental health treatment, there are differences in the statutes allowing treating professionals to tailor treatment for substance abusers. This chapter will focus on the statutes applicable specifically to substance abuse commitment, while noting procedures that parallel those for mental health commitment.

The major substantive difference between substance abuse commitment and commitment for mental health treatment is that the respondent in a substance abuse proceeding is committed to the care of the area authority or a physician, rather than to a 24-hour facility. The commitment term may be up to 180 days, during which treatment may be either on an inpatient or outpatient basis, as determined by the area authority or physician. The area authority or physician must, however, request a supplemental hearing for court review of any proposed inpatient treatment period exceeding forty-five consecutive days.

A substance abuse commitment, unlike a mental health commitment, must be reported to the North Carolina Department of Motor Vehicles. *See infra* § 3.6C. This can result in the client's loss of driving privileges, a collateral consequence that threatens the client's future ability to maintain employment, maintain a household, and maintain appointments with a community treatment provider. It is important that this information be provided to a client facing a substance abuse commitment.

3.2   Terminology Used in this Chapter

"Area authority" is the area mental health, developmental disabilities, and substance abuse authority. N.C. GEN. STAT. § 122C-3(1) (hereinafter G.S.). The area authority is a statutory creation that is the "locus of coordination among public services for clients of its catchment area." G.S. 122C-101. The catchment area may be a single county, which is referred to as a "county program," or a combination of two or more counties. *See* G.S. 122C-3(5), (10a). The term "local management entity" or LME is also used to describe an area authority or county program. LME is a collective term that refers to functional responsibilities rather than governance structure. G.S. 122C-3(20b). The area authority or LME is charged with implementing and monitoring community-based mental health and substance abuse services as well as coordinating the care of individual clients to ensure care is appropriate. *See* G.S. 122C-115.4, 122C-117.

"Dangerous to self" and "dangerous to others." *See supra* § 2.2.

"Eligible psychologist" is a licensed psychologist with at least two years' clinical experience who "holds permanent licensure and certification as a health services provider psychologist issued by the North Carolina Psychology Board." G.S. 122C-3(13d).

"Qualified professional" is "any individual with appropriate training or experience as specified by the General Statutes or by rule of the Commission [for Mental Health, Developmental Disabilities, and Substance Abuse Services] in the fields of mental health or developmental disabilities or substance abuse treatment or habilitation, including physicians, psychologists, psychological associates, educators, social workers, registered nurses, certified fee-based practicing pastoral counselors, and certified counselors." G.S. 122C-3(31).

"Responsible professional" is "an individual within a facility who is designated by the facility director to be responsible for the care, treatment, habilitation, or rehabilitation of a specific client and who is eligible to provide care, treatment, habilitation, or rehabilitation relative to the client's disability." G.S. 122C-3(32).

"Substance abuse" is "the pathological use or abuse of alcohol or other drugs in a way or to a degree that produces an impairment in personal, social, or occupational functioning. 'Substance abuse' may include a pattern of tolerance and withdrawal." G.S. 122C-3(36).

"Substance abuser" is "an individual who engages in substance abuse." G.S. 122C-3(37).

"24-hour facility" is a "facility that provides a structured living environment and services for a period of 24 consecutive hours or more." G.S. 122C-3(14)g.

3.3   Involuntary Substance Abuse Commitment

A. Affidavit and Petition Before Clerk or Magistrate

Involuntary substance abuse commitment begins with an individual appearing before either the clerk of superior court or a magistrate to petition by affidavit for a person believed to be a substance abuser and dangerous to self or others to be taken into custody for an examination. The affidavit must include the facts on which the affiant's opinion is based. G.S. 122C-281(a).

This statute tracks the provisions for mental health commitment in G.S. 122C-261(a), except that there is no requirement that the affiant state whether the respondent is believed to be mentally retarded. G.S. 122C-281(a); see *infra* Appendix A, Form AOC-SP-300. Counsel should review the treatment provider's justification for maintaining a client with mental retardation on any type of involuntary commitment. When the justification does not meet the legal standard for a waiver or other exception allowing involuntary commitment, counsel should seek to have the client removed from involuntary status. For a discussion of commitment of individuals with mental retardation, see *supra* § 2.3N.

Case law: An unsworn petition and a petition without facts supporting conclusory statements are grounds for dismissal.

In re Ingram, 74 N.C. App. 579 (1985). The *Ingram* case contains two important holdings concerning the sufficiency of the affidavit and petition:

- failure of the petition to be sworn to under oath is ground for dismissal of the petition; and

- failure of the petition to state sufficient facts supporting the allegations that the respondent is mentally ill and dangerous to self or others is ground for dismissal of the petition.

For a more complete discussion of the case, see *supra* § 2.3A.

B. Custody Order for Examination

The clerk or magistrate must review the petition to determine if there are "reasonable grounds to believe that the facts alleged in the affidavit are true and that the respondent is probably a substance abuser and dangerous to himself or others." G.S. 122C-281(b). If so, the clerk or magistrate must issue an order to a law enforcement officer or other authorized person to take the respondent into custody for examination by a physician or eligible psychologist. *Id; see infra* Appendix A, Form AOC-SP-302. The clerk has no duty to contact the area authority regarding a respondent who might be mentally retarded. *But cf. infra* Appendix A, Form AOC-SP-302 (indicating that the area authority must be contacted if a respondent who is mentally ill is also mentally retarded).

C. Transportation Procedures

The general provisions for transportation of respondents in involuntary substance abuse proceedings are the same as the transportation provisions applicable to mental health commitment proceedings discussed *supra* in § 2.3C. *See* G.S. 122C-251.

D. Custody and Transport to First Examination

Procedures for a law enforcement officer or other authorized individual to assume custody of and transport a substance abuse respondent for examination are contained in G.S. 122C-281(e) and 122C-283(a) and generally mirror the procedures governing mental health commitments found in G.S. 122C-261(e) and 122C-263(a). *See supra* § 2.3D. Unlike the mental health statute, the substance abuse statute does not provide for temporary detention in a state facility for the mentally ill pending the first examination. *Compare* G.S. 122C-283(a) (substance abuse statute) *with* G.S. 122C-263(a) (mental health statute).

E. First Examination Requirements

Factors to be evaluated. The physician or eligible psychologist must perform the examination as soon as possible, and no later than twenty-four hours after the respondent's arrival.

The examiner must assess the following:

"(1)   Current and previous substance abuse including, if available, previous treatment history; and

(2)   Dangerousness to himself or others . . . ."

G.S. 122C-283(c).

Although substance abuse commitment usually involves outpatient treatment, the substance abuse statute does not require the determination that "the respondent is in need of treatment in order to prevent further disability or deterioration that would predictably result in dangerousness," which is necessary for a mental health outpatient commitment. *See* G.S. 122C-263(d)(1)c. (mental health statute); *see also supra* § 2.3E. In addition, for a substance abuse commitment, there is no provision for first examination via telemedicine. *See supra* § 2.3F.

Recommendation. If the examiner finds that the respondent is a substance abuser and is dangerous to self or others, commitment must be recommended. Unlike mental health commitment procedures, there is then an additional determination. The examiner must recommend whether the respondent should be released or held at a 24-hour facility pending hearing. G.S. 122C-283(d); *see infra* Appendix A, Form DMH 5-72-01, Section III. If the examiner recommends that the respondent be held, the law enforcement officer or other designated individual must transport the respondent to a 24-hour facility. G.S. 122C-283(d). This detention at the facility pending hearing is distinguished from the substance abuse commitment itself; substance abuse commitment is not commitment to a facility, but rather to the care of the area authority or a physician.

If the examiner does not recommend that the respondent be held at a 24-hour facility pending hearing, the respondent must be released pending the hearing. G.S. 122C-283(d)(1).

If the examiner finds that the respondent is not a substance abuser and dangerous to self or others, the respondent must be released and the proceedings terminated. G.S. 122C-283(d)(2).

Temporary waiver of requirement of physician or eligible psychologist to perform first examination. A bill enacted on July 1, 2003, S.L. 2003-178, and extended periodically allows the Secretary of Health and Human Services, on the request of a LME, to waive temporarily the statutory requirement that either a physician or eligible psychologist perform the initial examination. Session Law 2010-119 continues this program until October 1, 2012. The waiver applies only on a "pilot program basis" on request and if certain criteria are met. A maximum of twenty programs may receive a waiver, which would allow the first examination to be performed by a licensed clinical social worker, a masters level psychiatric nurse, or a masters level certified clinical addictions specialist.

Note: If recommending commitment, the examiner is not required to recommend either inpatient or outpatient commitment. A substance abuse commitment is to the physician or area authority that will be supervising and managing treatment and determining what portion of the treatment, if any, will be in a 24-hour facility. The examiner recommends only whether the respondent will be held in a 24-hour facility pending hearing.

F. Alternative Procedure: Affidavit by Physician or Eligible Psychologist

As in the mental health commitment procedures, a physician or eligible psychologist who has examined the respondent may petition for substance abuse commitment without appearing before the clerk or a magistrate. *See supra* § 2.3H. The physician or eligible psychologist must conduct the examination in compliance with the requirements of the first examination described *supra* in § 3.3E and then execute the affidavit before any official authorized to administer oaths. G.S. 122C-281(d).

The legislature has not amended this statute to allow filing of the affidavit with the clerk or magistrate by facsimile transmission as of this writing. The parallel section in the mental health commitment section, G.S. 122C-261(d), was amended in 2005 to allow filing by facsimile transmission.

G. Second Examination

A second examination is required only when substance abuse commitment is recommended by the first examiner *and* the respondent is held in a 24-hour facility pending hearing. This examination must occur within twenty-four hours of the respondent's arrival at the facility. G.S. 122C-285(a). If the first examination occurred at the "same facility in which the respondent is held, the second examination must occur not later than the following regular working day." G.S. 122C-285(b).

The second examination must be performed by a physician if the first examination was conducted by an eligible psychologist. If a physician performed the first examination, however, the second examination may be conducted by a "qualified professional," which includes a wide range of professionals. G.S. 122C-285(a); *see supra* § 3.2.

The examiner must use the same assessment criteria used for the initial examination. If the examiner finds that the respondent is a substance abuser and is dangerous to self or others, the examiner must hold the respondent for treatment pending a hearing. The examiner has the option of either holding the respondent at the 24-hour facility or designating other treatment pending the hearing. G.S. 122C-285(a).

If the second examiner does not find that the criteria for substance abuse commitment exist, the respondent must be released and the proceeding terminated. The individual who transported the respondent to the facility must return the respondent to the originating county. The examiner is required to report the reasons for the release in writing to the clerk of court of the county in which the custody order originated. G.S. 122C-285(a).

H. Duties of the Clerk of Superior Court

On receipt of a recommendation of substance abuse commitment from a physician or eligible psychologist, the clerk, on direction of a district court judge, must assign counsel, calendar the case for hearing, and give notice to the respondent, the respondent's counsel, and the petitioner of the time and place of the hearing. As in mental health commitment proceedings, the petitioner may file a written waiver of the right to notice of the hearing. G.S. 122C-284(a).

If the respondent was released pending hearing, the clerk of the county where the petition originated is responsible for these duties. If the respondent is held in a 24-hour facility pending hearing, the clerk of the county where the facility is located is responsible. *Id.*

3.4   Attorney Representation

A. Attorney for Respondent

Representation of respondents in substance abuse proceedings is generally provided under G.S. 122C-270, under Chapter 122C, Article 5, Part 7 of the North Carolina General Statutes concerning mentally ill individuals, although there are some specific provisions in Chapter 122C, Article 5, Part 8 applicable only to substance abuse commitments. There is statutory provision for representation of all respondents throughout the substance abuse commitment process regardless of whether they are currently being treated in a 24-hour facility because they *may* be treated on an inpatient basis at any time during the commitment.

Special Counsel represents all indigent respondents at a state facility. *See generally* 122C-270(a). Although this section addresses representation of the mentally ill, it presumably applies to representation of substance abusers admitted to these state facilities.

Appointment of counsel for indigent respondents must be made in accordance with rules adopted by the Office of Indigent Defense Services. G.S. 122C-286(d). No specific rules have been adopted by IDS as of this writing, and attorney appointments are made pursuant to local rules or practice. The clerk of court generally assigns counsel for respondents not represented by Special Counsel. The clerk of court, on direction of a district court judge, must assign counsel on receipt of a recommendation for substance abuse commitment from a physician or eligible psychologist. G.S. 122C-284(a). If the respondent is held pending hearing in a 24-hour facility that is not a state facility, counsel is assigned by the clerk of the county where the facility is located. If the respondent was released pending hearing, counsel is assigned by the clerk of the county in which the petition originated. *Id.*

Respondents who are not indigent are entitled to be represented by privately-retained counsel of choice. G.S. 122C-286(d). Presumably a non-indigent respondent who refuses to hire counsel will be appointed counsel pursuant to the statute in Article 5, Part 7 of Chapter 122C. *See* G.S. 122C-268(d). An indigent respondent may also arrange for private representation.

For more on the role and responsibilities of counsel, see *infra* Appendix C, "Working with Clients."

B. Attorney for Petitioner

The attorney from the Attorney General's staff assigned to a state facility or to the psychiatric service of the University of North Carolina Hospitals at Chapel Hill is specifically designated to represent the state's interest at all commitment hearings held at the facility. G.S. 122C-270(f). Although it appears that the Attorney General's office *may* represent the state's interest in substance abuse proceedings held outside the state facilities (*see* G.S. 122C-268(b)), the office does not have sufficient staff to represent the state's interest, if any, at hearings outside the state facilities. Because a county agency may be the substance abuse treatment provider, an attorney from the District Attorney's office or the County Attorney's office may choose to represent the petitioner's interest.

Private substance abuse treatment facilities generally retain an attorney to provide representation in support of commitment.

There are no other statutory provisions for representation of either the state or the petitioner in Article 5, Part 8 of Chapter 122C concerning substance abuse proceedings. For a further discussion of the question of representation of the petitioner's interest, see *supra* § 2.5B.

3.5   Hearings

A. Time Limit for Hearing

A hearing must be held in district court within ten days of the respondent being taken into custody if substance abuse commitment is recommended. G.S. 122C-286(a). The hearing must occur regardless of whether the respondent is in a 24-hour facility or released pending hearing. The time limitation for the district court hearing is the same as that for involuntary mental health commitment.

For a further discussion of issues pertaining to hearings, see *infra* Appendix C, "Working with Clients."

B. Venue and Transfer of Venue

Respondent held pending hearing. When the respondent is held pending hearing, the hearing is held in the county where the 24-hour facility is located. On the respondent's objection, the hearing must be held in the county where the petition originated. G.S. 122C-286.1(a).

Respondent released pending hearing. When the respondent is released pending hearing, the hearing is held in the county where the petition originated. G.S. 122C-284(a).

C. Continuance

A continuance of up to five days may be granted on motion of the court, the respondent, or the State. In addition, the "responsible professional" may also move for a continuance. G.S. 122C-286(a). Because many district courts hold commitment hearings only once a week or on two consecutive days, a five-day continuance is unworkable. It is common practice for the court to allow a seven-day continuance on consent of the parties. For a discussion of potential benefits of continuing the case, see *supra* § 2.6E.

D. No Waiver of Respondent's Appearance

The respondent's appearance at the hearing may *not* be waived. G.S. 122C-286(b). The statute provides that a subpoena may be issued to compel the respondent's appearance, but it does not specify who is responsible for obtaining the issuance of the subpoena. *Id.*

This mandatory appearance potentially creates a problem for a respondent when the treating physician recommending substance abuse commitment arranges a discharge before the respondent's court date. The respondent may obtain release before the court date because bed space is available at a rehabilitation facility or because the respondent's condition has stabilized. Often, a respondent who has been released from involuntary inpatient care will either refuse or be unable to attend a future court hearing in spite of the mandatory appearance requirement.

In these circumstances, counsel for respondents have sometimes agreed to a waiver of the respondent's appearance in negotiating the respondent's release before the commitment hearing, and courts have allowed the waiver and entered a substance abuse commitment when later sought by the physician. No appellate decisions have yet addressed this practice. Before considering such a waiver, counsel should advise the respondent of the statutory appearance requirement, the collateral consequences of a substance abuse commitment, and the respondent's obligations if served with a subpoena for a future court date. Counsel should document these efforts in the office case file for future reference.

E. Not Contesting/Not Resisting Commitment

Not contesting. There are no statutory provisions for respondents to accept the recommendation of substance abuse commitment or to "not contest." In practice, however, many respondents are in agreement with their attending physicians on the need for substance abuse treatment and do not contest the allegations in the petition. Counsel may, after advising the client of the possible consequences of substance abuse commitment, inform the client of the option to "not contest." *See infra* § 3.6C (discussing potential license consequences) and Chapter 12 (discussing various collateral consequences of commitment). An alternative possibility with a cooperative respondent, if the attending physician agrees, is not contesting an involuntary mental health commitment. This would allow a period of inpatient treatment without incurring the possible consequences of a substance abuse commitment.

By not contesting, the respondent can avoid an adversarial hearing. Although the respondent's appearance cannot be waived in a substance abuse commitment proceeding, the hearing could proceed by abbreviated testimony or by stipulation of the respondent's counsel. Counsel may stipulate to the facts alleged in the petition and in the Qualified Physician's Examination report (for a definition of this report, see *supra* § 2.2), or stipulate that the information in those documents would be the testimony of the authors.

Not resisting. In substance abuse cases, a period of detoxification may be necessary before the respondent is able to understand the issues involved in a substance abuse commitment. A short-term continuance could address this problem.

The respondent may, however, exhibit serious symptoms resulting from long-term substance abuse or of a concurrently existing mental illness that interfere with the ability to express a decision whether to contest the commitment. There are no statutory provisions to guide counsel when the client is unable to express a decision on whether to contest. In these cases, counsel should review the respondent's medical and psychiatric records and consult with the attending physician to better understand the respondent's prognosis.

In the cases where the client has not expressed a desire to contest and there is little or no chance for improvement or of the respondent prevailing at the commitment hearing, counsel may report to the court that the respondent is "not resisting." This means that the respondent is unable to understand and discuss the issues enough to contest the commitment, but is equally unable to decide not to contest. As with an uncontested case, the hearing may then proceed with abbreviated testimony from the petitioner's witnesses or by stipulation of the respondent's counsel. Counsel may stipulate to the facts alleged in the petition and in the Qualified Physician's Examination report (for a definition of this report, see *supra* § 2.2), or stipulate that the information in those documents would be the testimony of the authors.

F. Criteria for Commitment

To order commitment, the court must find "by clear, cogent, and convincing evidence that the respondent is a substance abuser and is dangerous to himself or others." G.S. 122C-287(1).

There are no North Carolina appellate opinions addressing the evidence necessary to support a finding that the respondent is a substance abuser.

For a discussion of cases addressing the courts' interpretation of the standard of danger to self or others, see *supra* § 2.6H.

G. Evidence

Admissible certified copies. "Certified copies of reports and findings of physicians and psychologists and medical records of previous and current treatment are admissible in evidence . . . ." G.S. 122C-286(c). As with mental health commitments, the respondent retains the right to confront and cross-examine witnesses. *Id.* For a discussion of the issues involved in this provision, see *supra* § 2.6J.

Burden of proof. The court must find that the respondent is a substance abuser and is dangerous to self or others by clear, cogent, and convincing evidence. G.S. 122C-287(1).

There are no North Carolina appellate cases addressing the evidence necessary to support a finding that a respondent is a substance abuser. Depending on the evidence presented, counsel may be able to make an argument that even if there is evidence of substance use, it does not support a finding that the respondent suffers from "an impairment in personal, social, or occupational functioning," as required by the statutory definition. *See* G.S. 122C-3(36).

As with some mental health commitments, the petitioner may not be present or may be unrepresented at the hearing. For a discussion of the challenges in handling such hearings, see *supra* § 2.5B.

Witnesses and hearsay. See supra § 2.6J.

3.6   Disposition

A. Dispositional Alternatives

Recommendation for substance abuse commitment. If the court finds that the respondent is a substance abuser and dangerous to self or others, it may order up to 180 days commitment to and treatment by an area authority or physician. The area authority or physician is responsible for the management and supervision of the respondent's treatment during the term of the substance abuse commitment. G.S. 122C-287(1).

During the term of commitment, the area authority or physician may prescribe or administer reasonable and appropriate treatment on either an inpatient or outpatient basis, with the proviso that a supplemental hearing must be requested if inpatient treatment is to exceed forty-five consecutive days. G.S. 122C-290(a), (b). There is no case law or formal opinion from the Attorney General concerning intermittent inpatient treatment within the same substance abuse commitment of 180 days.

If the court finds that the respondent does not meet the commitment criteria, the respondent must be discharged and the facility at which the respondent was last treated must be notified of the discharge. G.S. 122C-287(2). The statute does not specify who must provide this notice, but presumably it would be the clerk of superior court of the county in which the hearing was held.

Negotiating outpatient mental health commitment as an alternative. Because of the possible collateral consequence of loss of driving privileges resulting from a substance abuse commitment discussed *infra* in § 3.6C, counsel may advise the client to agree instead to a mental health outpatient commitment. If the client is agreeable, counsel may approach the attending physician or opposing counsel, as appropriate, to negotiate an agreement to present to the court.

Outpatient commitment will give the treating physician authority to compel treatment without endangering the client's driver's license. If the attending physician believes that the respondent requires further inpatient treatment, there are two possibilities. First, if the respondent consents, a continuance may be requested. This would allow the inpatient treatment to be received pending the hearing, without subjecting the client to a substance abuse commitment. Second, as part of the outpatient commitment order, the court may allow the treating physician to hold the respondent at the facility for seventy-two hours while outpatient treatment is arranged. G.S. 122C-271(b)(4).

B. Order

To order commitment, the court must find by "clear, cogent, and convincing evidence that the respondent is a substance abuser and is dangerous to himself or others." G.S. 122C-287(1). The underlying facts supporting these findings must be set forth in the order. Additionally, the order must identify the area authority or physician responsible for the management and supervision of the respondent's treatment. G.S. 122C-286(h); *see infra* Appendix A, Form AOC-SP-306.

Case law: The respondent must meet the criteria for substance abuse commitment for treatment to be ordered.

In re Royal, 128 N.C. App. 645 (1998). The *Royal* case presents the unusual instance of the State appealing from an order requiring inpatient treatment for substance abuse. In this case, the respondent had complained to the district court that he was not provided adequate inpatient treatment before being discharged. He asserted that the past practice of the hospital had been to transport him to the Alcohol Treatment Center for evaluation prior to the hearing and before he received treatment. He stated further that he would then be placed on a waiting list and released without treatment. *Id.* at 646.

The North Carolina Court of Appeals considered the appeal of the State from the trial court's order that required the 24-hour facility to "provide [the respondent] appropriate treatment until such time as other more appropriate, less restrictive, long-term residential treatment is arranged and ready for [the respondent]." *Id.* at 646. The court did not directly address the issue raised by the respondent— whether a facility can be compelled to provide substance abuse treatment rather than to transfer or discharge a patient. The court instead focused on the failure of the district court to include in the order the condition that the respondent must continue to meet the criteria for substance abuse commitment. The court of appeals vacated the order on this ground, although it stated that the district court had authority to order treatment "while [the respondent] was lawfully committed to the facility." *Id.* at 647.

C. Report of Substance Abuse Commitment to Department of Motor Vehicles

The North Carolina statutes require that a report of an involuntary commitment for "treatment of alcoholism or drug addiction" be made to the North Carolina Division of Motor Vehicles (DMV). G.S. 20-17.1(b). The clerk of court in the county of adjudication must send a certified copy of an abstract of the order to the DMV. *Id.* Note that these provisions appear in Chapter 20, the chapter of the North Carolina General Statutes dealing with motor vehicle laws, rather than in Chapter 122C.

On receipt of this notice, it is the duty of the DMV Commissioner to investigate whether the person is competent to drive. The person's license must be revoked unless the Commissioner is "satisfied" that the person is a fit driver. G.S. 20-17.1(a). On receipt of notice of revocation, the person may file a written request for a hearing and is allowed to keep the license pending the hearing. If the license is revoked after a hearing, an appeal may be filed with the review board of the DMV. *Id.*

It appears that the DMV may revoke the license on receipt of the notice of commitment and, in effect, require the respondent to file a request for a hearing and prove fitness to drive.

See infra Chapter 12 (discussing various collateral consequences of commitment).

D. Follow-Up on Commitment Order

Ongoing treatment. The area authority or physician to whom the respondent is committed is required to be closely involved with the respondent's treatment. The area authority or physician is responsible for the management and supervision of the respondent's treatment when treatment is received in a 24-hour facility and when it is provided on an outpatient basis. "Reasonable and appropriate treatment" must be prescribed and administered throughout the term of commitment. G.S. 122C-290(a). This differs from a mental health commitment in that a respondent released and committed to outpatient treatment is no longer the responsibility of the treatment provider at the 24-hour facility.

Failure to comply, escape, or breach of conditions. The area authority or physician may request the clerk or magistrate to issue an order for the respondent to be taken into custody for an examination if:

- the respondent "fails to comply with all or part of the prescribed [outpatient] treatment after reasonable effort to solicit the respondent's compliance";
- the respondent has been discharged from a 24-hour facility after escaping; or
- the respondent breaches the conditions of release from a 24-hour facility and does not return to the 24-hour facility.

G.S. 122C-290(b), 122C-205.1(b); *see infra* Appendix A, Form AOC-SP-223.

On receipt of this request, the clerk or magistrate must issue an order to a law enforcement officer to assume custody of the respondent. G.S. 122C-290(b); *see infra* Appendix A, Form AOC-SP-223. Upon assuming custody the law enforcement officer must deliver the respondent to the area authority or physician to conduct an examination. The examiner will determine whether to release the respondent or to have the respondent taken to a 24-hour facility. G.S. 122C-290(b). There is no requirement that a new substance abuse commitment proceeding be instituted if the respondent is taken to a 24-hour facility. A request for a supplemental hearing must be made, however, if it appears that the respondent will need treatment in a 24-hour facility for more than forty-five consecutive days. *Id.*

Treatment in 24-hour facility to exceed forty-five consecutive days. A supplemental hearing *must* be requested if the area authority or physician determines that the respondent requires treatment for more than forty-five consecutive days in a 24-hour facility. G.S. 122C-290(b). The area authority or physician must notify the clerk of court by the thirtieth day of the inpatient stay and request a supplemental hearing. *Id.*; *see infra* § 3.7.

Respondent intends to move or moves to another county within the state. If the respondent intends to move or has moved to another county within the state, the area authority or physician *must* notify the clerk of court in the county where the commitment is being supervised and request a supplemental hearing. G.S. 122C-290(c); *see infra* § 3.7.

Respondent moves to another state or to an unknown location. The clerk of court of the county where the commitment is supervised must be notified by the treatment supervisor if the respondent moves to another state or to an unknown location. The substance abuse commitment is then terminated. G.S. 122C-290(d).

Respondent no longer meets commitment criteria. At any time a committed respondent no longer meets the criteria for substance abuse commitment, the area authority or physician supervising treatment must unconditionally discharge the respondent. The clerk of court must be given notice of the discharge and receive a written report stating the reasons for release. G.S. 122C-293.

3.7   Supplemental Hearings

A. Requests for Supplemental Hearings

Supplemental hearing distinguished from rehearing. A supplemental hearing is held during the term of a substance abuse commitment if the respondent has moved to another county, out of state, or to an unknown location or the respondent is in need of treatment exceeding forty-five consecutive days at a 24-hour facility. These are matters concerning the terms of the existing commitment.

A rehearing is held on a request to *extend* the current substance abuse commitment. For example, a rehearing may be held on request of the attending physician for an additional forty-five days of substance abuse commitment following a 180-day commitment.

A respondent may seek discharge from a substance abuse commitment by filing a written application for a supplemental hearing with the clerk of court. G.S. 122C-291(d). There is no AOC form for the respondent's use.

There is no statutory definition of either "supplemental hearing" or "rehearing."

Mandatory requests. The area authority or physician *must* request a supplemental hearing if the respondent intends to move or has moved to another county within the state. G.S. 122C-290(c).

Additionally, the area authority or physician *must* request a supplemental hearing if inpatient treatment in a 24-hour facility will exceed forty-five consecutive days. The clerk must be notified by the thirtieth day of the inpatient treatment of the need for the supplemental hearing. G.S. 122C-290(b).

B. Scheduling of Supplemental Hearing and Notice

On receipt of a request for a supplemental hearing, the clerk must calendar a hearing to be held within fourteen days. The clerk must also give notice at least seventy-two hours before the hearing to the petitioner, the respondent, the respondent's attorney, if any, and the area authority or physician. G.S. 122C-291(a).

The statute requires that the respondent be served with notice as provided in Rule 4(j) of the North Carolina Rules of Civil Procedure (principally, by personal delivery or leaving at the respondent's "usual place of abode with some person of suitable age and discretion then residing therein," by delivery to an authorized agent, or by mailing a copy by registered or certified mail, return receipt requested). All others are to receive notice by first-class mail, postage prepaid. G.S. 122C-291(a), 122C-284(a).

C. Supplemental Hearing Procedures

The supplemental hearing is held in district court pursuant to the procedures for the initial substance abuse commitment hearing. G.S. 122C-291(a); *see also* G.S. 122C-286. As with the initial hearing, the respondent's appearance may not be waived.

D. Disposition

Respondent's request for discharge. The statute provides that the court is to determine whether the respondent continues to meet the criteria for commitment. G.S. 122C-291(d). The statute does not state whether the burden of proof is on the moving respondent. It presumably would be up to the respondent to prove that the criteria for substance abuse commitment are no longer present because the supplemental hearing is held during the term of the existing commitment.

Respondent has moved or intends to move to another county within the state. The court must determine first whether the respondent continues to meet the criteria for commitment. If not, the respondent must be discharged and the case dismissed. If the respondent continues to meet the commitment criteria, the court must continue the commitment but designate an area authority or physician within the respondent's new county of residence to provide treatment. Venue for further court proceedings is changed to the new county providing supervision of treatment. The clerk of court in the original county must transfer the records to the clerk of the county to which venue has been transferred. G.S. 122C-291(b).

Inpatient treatment to exceed forty-five consecutive days. The court must first determine whether the respondent continues to meet the criteria for substance abuse commitment. If not, the respondent must be released and the case dismissed. G.S. 122C-291(c). If the respondent continues to meet the commitment criteria, the court must determine whether further treatment in the 24-hour facility is necessary. If so, the court may order continued inpatient treatment for up to ninety days. If the court finds that the respondent continues to meet the commitment criteria, but is not in need of continued inpatient treatment, it may continue the commitment but order the release of the respondent from the 24-hour facility. G.S. 122C-291(c).

Order. *See infra* Appendix A, Form AOC-SP-206.

3.8   Rehearings

A. Rehearing Distinguished from Supplemental Hearing

See supra § 3.7A.

B. Notice to Clerk by Facility

The area authority or physician must send a request for a rehearing to the clerk at least fifteen days before the end of the commitment period. This notice is sent to the clerk of the county where the respondent's treatment is being supervised. G.S. 122C-292(a).

C. Calendaring of Hearing Notice

The clerk must calendar the hearing at least ten days before the end of the commitment period. Notice is to be provided in accord with the requirements for the initial hearing. G.S. 122C-292(a), (b); *see infra* Appendix A, Form AOC-SP-301.

D. Hearing Procedures

Rehearings for substance abuse commitment are held in accord with the procedures for the initial hearing. The respondent is afforded the same rights, including the right to appeal. G.S. 122C-292(b); *see supra* §§ 3.5, 3.6.

E. Disposition

At any rehearing, if the court determines that the respondent continues to meet the criteria, it may order commitment for up to 365 days. If the court finds that the respondent no longer meets the criteria, it must order unconditional discharge. G.S. 122C-292(c).

F. No Waiver by Respondent of Right to Rehearing

The respondent is not allowed to waive the right to a rehearing in a substance abuse commitment proceeding. G.S. 122C-286(b), 122C-292(b). This differs from a mental health commitment, in which the respondent may waive the right to second and subsequent rehearings. *See* G.S. 122C-276(f).

3.9 Discharge by Area Authority or Physician

The area authority or physician must discharge a respondent unconditionally from a substance abuse commitment at any time the criteria for commitment no longer exist. G.S. 122C-293.

3.10 Emergency Procedure for Violent Individuals

A. Custody by Law Enforcement Officer

A law enforcement officer may take into custody a person who meets the criteria for substance abuse commitment *and* is violent and requires restraint. This procedure may be used only when the delay in taking the person for examination would be likely to endanger life or property. The law enforcement officer must immediately take the respondent before a magistrate or clerk to execute the affidavit required to initiate a substance abuse commitment. G.S. 122C-282; *see infra* Appendix A, Form AOC-SP-909M. The affidavit must include the facts concerning violence, need for restraint, and the danger posed by the delay. G.S. 122C-282.

Substance abuse emergency procedure distinguished from mental health emergency procedure. The substance abuse emergency procedure differs from the mental health emergency procedure in that the mental health procedure may be initiated by anyone with knowledge of the facts supporting the affidavit rather than only by a law enforcement officer. In addition, the mental health emergency procedure bypasses the clerk or magistrate and authorizes the initiating person to take the respondent directly to an examiner.

B. Determination by Clerk or Magistrate

The clerk or magistrate must determine by clear, cogent, and convincing evidence if the allegations in the affidavit are true, the respondent is violent and requires restraint, and the delay caused by taking the respondent to a physician or eligible psychologist for examination would endanger life or property. On making these findings, the clerk or magistrate must order the law enforcement officer to transport the respondent directly to a 24-hour facility. G.S. 122C-282; *see infra* Appendix A, Form AOC-SP-909M (back).

The statute does not address the alternatives if the clerk or magistrate finds that the criteria for the emergency procedure are not met. It appears that the law enforcement officer could proceed as if filing a regular petition and request a custody order for transport for an examination by a physician or eligible psychologist. The clerk or magistrate could issue the custody and transport order or could find the allegations insufficient and terminate the proceeding.

C. Duties of 24-Hour Facility

A respondent transported to a 24-hour facility pursuant to an order of the clerk or magistrate is to be examined pursuant to the procedures for a regular substance abuse commitment, discussed *supra* in § 3.3E. G.S. 122C-282.

3.11 Appeal

A. Statutory Provision

The section on appeal in substance abuse proceedings tracks nearly verbatim the provisions for appeal in mental health proceedings. G.S. 122C-288; *see also supra* § 2.12. Appeal is to the North Carolina Court of Appeals.

B. Representation of Respondent

Any party on the record may appeal as in civil cases. Appeal by the respondent's counsel is at the direction of the respondent. Pursuant to G.S. 122C-289, assigned counsel represents respondents through all proceedings in the district court. Presumably, this covers notice of appeal, which is required to be given at the district court level. Counsel appointed by the Office of the Appellate Defender represent respondents through the conclusion of any appeal. G.S. 122C-289.

C. Confidentiality on Appeal

There is no provision in the North Carolina Rules of Appellate Procedure for using the initials of a respondent in appellate documents to preserve patient confidentiality. Recent amendments to the Rules, however, mandate the use of initials for most records in juvenile proceedings, which are also confidential proceedings. *See* N.C. R. App. P. 3.1(b). Counsel should consider filing a motion with the court requesting to be allowed to use initials, citing the rule for juvenile cases as analogous. If the motion is granted, the respondent's name must be redacted from *all* records designated by the court, including the transcript and all exhibits.

Counsel should advise a client who is considering an appeal that confidentiality of the proceeding may be sacrificed as a consequence of appealing. This might be an important factor to some clients.

D. Rehearing or Discharge

Although an appeal is not rendered moot by the respondent's subsequent discharge, counsel should advise the client of the time generally required to receive an opinion from the North Carolina Court of Appeals. The client should be informed of the likelihood of discharge from the substance abuse commitment before an appellate decision is handed down.

A rehearing must be held before the end of substance abuse commitment being appealed if the respondent has not been discharged. This would usually occur before the appeal is decided. If recommitted, the respondent would not be released except by the attending physician or the district court judge even if victorious on appeal.

Case law: An appeal is not moot if the respondent is discharged or the term of commitment has expired.

See supra § 2.12E.

3.12 Public Intoxication

A. Alternatives for Law Enforcement Officers to Address Public Intoxication

"Public Intoxication," Chapter 122C, Article 5, Part 9, provides a variety of alternatives for law enforcement officers dealing with an intoxicated individual, including substance abuse commitment. G.S. 122C-301(a). In addition to substance abuse commitment, other publicly-funded programs might include a voluntary residential treatment facility, provision of counseling and group programs, and referral to group programs such as Alcoholics Anonymous and Narcotics Anonymous. Private counseling and residential treatment programs are available to those able to pay. The public intoxication statutes provide options for law enforcement officers dealing with the immediate problems resulting from public intoxication and are directed toward providing emergency medical care and a place to sober up rather than ongoing treatment.

B. Substance Abuse Commitment

Law enforcement officers may initiate substance abuse commitment proceedings for those who meet the commitment criteria. G.S. 122C-301(a)(5). The right to appointment of counsel under Chapter 122C attaches only after a substance abuse commitment petition is filed and commitment has been recommended.

C. 24-Hour Detention by Shelter or Medical Facility

The law enforcement officer may transport an intoxicated person in need of food, clothing, or shelter, but not in need of immediate medical care, to a private or public shelter. An intoxicated person in need of immediate medical care may be transported to an area facility, hospital, physician's office, or other appropriate health care facility until sober or for a maximum of twenty-four hours. G.S. 122C-301. Counsel should be aware of this legally allowed detention without process because a distressed potential client might call while being detained.

D. Use of Jail

An officer may transport an intoxicated individual to a city or county jail in limited circumstances, which can never be done during a mental health commitment. The person must be in need of food, clothing, or shelter, but not in need of immediate medical care, and no other facility is "readily available." G.S. 122C-303. Again, the person may be detained only until sober or for a maximum of twenty-four hours. *Id.*

Appendix 3-1
Involuntary Commitment for Substance Abuse Treatment:
Checklist for Respondents' Attorneys

This checklist applies after Special Counsel or the appointed attorney receives notice of the patient's admission. Consult the indicated forms as necessary.

Receipt and Review of Documents

❑ Receive the petition or affidavit from the physician or eligible psychologist, accompanied by the affidavit(s) of the examiner. This will occur by different methods depending on local practice. Counsel should inquire of the clerk of court and the records clerk of the facility to determine local practice.

❑ Review documents for compliance with statutory requirements.

Affidavit and Petition for Involuntary Commitment (Form AOC-SP-300)

❑ Is the petition signed and sworn before an authorized officer? G.S. 122C-281(a).

❑ Was the petition properly clocked in with a date and time stamp?

❑ Is box 2, alleging substance abuse and danger to self or others, checked?

❑ Do the allegations in the petition support on their face a finding of reasonable grounds to believe that the respondent is a substance abuser and is dangerous to self or others?

❑ Who does the petition indicate are witnesses to the behaviors and actions alleged in the petition?

Findings and Custody Order Involuntary Commitment (Form AOC-SP-302)

❑ Is the custody order properly signed and dated with the time noted by the appropriate court official?

❑ Is box 2, alleging substance abuse and danger to self or others under "Findings," checked?

❑ Is either box 1 and/or 2 checked under "Custody Order"?

❑ Does the "Return of Service" on the back indicate that the respondent was taken into custody within 24 hours of issuance of the custody order?

❑ Did the law enforcement officer complete either Section A, B, C, or D appropriately on the back of the custody order?

Affidavit of Examining Physician or Eligible Psychologist—First Examination Report (Form DMH 5-72-01, Examination and Recommendation to Determine Necessity for Involuntary Commitment)

❑ Was the examination performed within 24 hours of the time the respondent was taken into custody by a law enforcement officer?

❑ Was the first examination performed by either a physician or eligible psychologist?

❑ Is the examination report properly signed?

❑ Does the examination report indicate that the examiner performed a personal examination, and does not merely repeat the allegations of the petition?

❑ Do the findings of the examiner support the conclusion of a diagnosis of substance abuse?

❑ Do the findings of the examiner support the conclusion of a finding of danger to self or others?

❑ Does the examiner's report recommend substance abuse commitment? Recommendation: _____

❑ Did the examiner recommend that the respondent be held at a 24-hour facility pending hearing? _____ yes _____ no

Affidavit of Physician When Respondent Held Pending Hearing—Second Examination Report (Form DMH 5-72-01, Examination and Recommendation to Determine Necessity for Involuntary Commitment)

❑ Was the examination performed within 24 hours of admission to a 24-hour facility?

❑ Was the examination performed by a physician?

❑ Is the examination report properly signed?

❑ Does the examination report indicate that the examiner performed a personal examination and did not merely repeat the allegations of the petition?

❑ Do the findings of the examiner support the conclusion of a diagnosis of substance abuse?

❑ Do the findings of the examiner support the conclusion of a finding of danger to self or others?

❑ Does the examiner's report recommend substance abuse commitment? Recommendation: _____

Medical Records Review: Respondent Held Pending Hearing

❑ Review records in the patient's chart(s) at the 24-hour facility.

❑ Do Progress Notes contain staff observations of manifestation of symptoms of substance abuse?

_____

❑ Do Progress Notes contain staff observations of dangerous behavior toward self or to others? _____

❑ Results of drug testing:

_____

❑ Current medications: _____

❑ Psychological examination or other special examinations or reports?

_____

❑ Any pending criminal charges or past convictions noted in the record?

_____

Medical Records Review: Respondent Released Pending Hearing

- ❏ Consult with client regarding existence of treatment records and obtain client's consent to review or copy records.
- ❏ Contact medical records clerk and arrange to review or copy records.
- ❏ Results of drug testing: _____
- ❏ Current medications:_____
- ❏ Psychological examination or other special examinations or reports?
  _____
- ❏ Any pending criminal charges or past convictions noted in record?
  _____

Interview with Client

Attorney role:

- ❏ Meet with client as soon as possible; contact client to arrange appointment if released pending hearing
- ❏ Explain you represent client, no one else
- ❏ Inform client that he or she may retain private attorney (explain time parameters, request that retained attorney call you, request to be on stand-by in event retained attorney does not appear)
- ❏ Explain that representation for commitment proceeding only

Explanation of proceeding:

- ❏ Special proceeding reviewing hospitalization, jail not a possibility
- ❏ Hearing before judge, but not in regular courtroom (describe hearing room)
- ❏ Confidential proceeding, hearing, and court file
- ❏ Time and date of hearing
- ❏ Venue—right to transfer if respondent held in 24-hour facility pending hearing and petition initiated in another county
- ❏ No waiver of appearance
- ❏ Witnesses for State and for client may be called
- ❏ Continuance may be requested by client, State, or responsible professional, or may be on motion of the court

Discussion of case:

- ❏ Review allegations of petition—get client's side of events (attach interview notes)
- ❏ Discuss medical evidence
- ❏ Ask what treating treatment provider has told client about treatment recommendation
- ❏ Ask client if there are prior commitments or other information on substance abuse or danger that might be raised by State's witnesses

❑ Explain consequences of substance abuse commitment: ____ driver's license ____ firearms ____ military

❑ Does client have alternative plan to substance abuse commitment (voluntary treatment program, attendance at AA or NA meetings, etc.)?

❑ Client states would agree to (sign as voluntary, continuance if pending unconditional discharge, etc.) _____

❑ Discuss possible witnesses; obtain client consent to contact/subpoena

❑ Advise of possible technical motions (e.g., motion to dismiss for failure of petition to be signed but possibility of new petition)

Explanation of hearing procedures:

❑ Attorney for State or petitioner to call witnesses—possibly petitioner, psychiatrist, social worker, staff, or family

❑ Witnesses for client—discuss allegations, likely witnesses, advisability of client testifying

❑ Courtroom demeanor—not get upset, not speak unless testifying, stay seated unless called to testify, whisper quietly or write note if need to communicate with attorney

❑ Closing arguments—client should not react or speak during

Client's position:

____ Contest   ____ Not contest

____ Agrees to venue   ____ Requests change of venue (if held pending hearing)

____ Agrees to (sign in as voluntary patient, shorter inpatient stay, outpatient commitment, continuance, etc.): _____

____ Move to continue   Reason: _____

Follow-up to Client Interview

❑ Notify opposing counsel, appropriate court personnel of result (contest/not contest)

❑ Negotiate with opposing counsel or psychiatrist as appropriate for desired client result (what client would agree to)

❑ Contact witnesses to discuss case

❑ Subpoena witnesses as necessary

❑ Meet with client as necessary to discuss results of negotiation, information from witnesses

❑ Prepare for hearing: motions, questions, relevant case law

Action needed:

_____ Motion to dismiss   Reason: _____

_____ Motion to continue   Reason: _____

_____ Contested hearing: _____ Client appear

                                         _____ Not appear

_____ Not contested: _____ Client appear

                                         _____ Not appear

Client agrees to:

_____ Inpatient
_____ Outpatient
_____ Split: _____ Inpatient stay   _____ Outpatient
_____ Client signed voluntary
_____ Client was discharged

Follow-up to Hearing When Client Committed

❏ Discuss order with client, reiterate that amount of days committed is *maximum* substance abuse commitment without rehearing and that can be discharged from commitment sooner
❏ Commitment is to treatment of area authority or physician, not facility—importance of cooperation
❏ Maximum of 45 consecutive days of inpatient treatment without supplemental hearing
❏ Representation continues for duration of commitment and through any appeal
❏ Advise of appeal right, discuss limitations (length of time to appeal, likely discharge or rehearing well before appeal decided)

Chapter 4
Voluntary Admission of Adults for Substance Abuse Treatment

4.1   Voluntary Admission for Substance Abuse Treatment

A competent adult may voluntarily seek admission to a facility for substance abuse treatment pursuant to the same procedures set forth for mental health admissions in sections 122C-211 and 122C-212 of the North Carolina General Statutes (hereinafter G.S.). *See infra* Chapter 10. This chapter will address provisions applicable solely to a voluntary substance abuse admission. Counsel should be aware of these specific provisions in order to advise clients facing an involuntary commitment of the possible option of a voluntary admission.

An important distinction from an *involuntary* substance abuse commitment is that a "family unit" may be voluntarily admitted to a facility providing substance abuse treatment. This might be a crucial factor for a parent who does not want to separate from a young child during treatment.

4.2   Terminology Used in this Chapter

"Family unit" is "a parent and the parent's dependent children under the age of three years." G.S. 122C-211(g).

"Incapable adult" is a person who, "in the opinion of a physician or eligible psychologist, . . . currently lacks sufficient understanding or capacity to make and communicate mental health treatment decisions." G.S. 122C-72(4).

"Incompetent adult" is "an adult individual adjudicated incompetent." G.S. 122C-3(17). The procedures for an incompetency proceeding are set forth in Chapter 35A of the North Carolina General Statutes and are beyond the scope of this manual.

"Legally responsible person" is the legally-appointed guardian for an adult who has been adjudicated incompetent. G.S. 122C-3(20)(i).

4.3 Admission and Treatment of Family Unit

A family unit may be admitted to a 24-hour substance abuse treatment facility upon the parent's application if the facility is able to provide services that will address the needs of the family unit, in addition to the needs of the parent. The statute specifies these services as "gender-specific substance abuse treatment, habilitation, or rehabilitation for the parent as well as assessment, well-child care, and, as needed, early intervention services for the child." G.S. 122C-211(f). The facility must determine whether it can provide services for the family unit. If the family unit is denied admission, the facility is required to provide a referral to another facility or facilities that may be able to provide adequate treatment. *Id.*

This provision seeks to address the needs of a parent who requires treatment but who is reluctant or unable to leave a young child or children during inpatient treatment. Additionally, it is directed at early assessment and intervention for developmental problems frequently seen in children of parents, particularly mothers, who are substance abusers.

4.4 Voluntary Admission of Incompetent Adult

An incompetent adult may be admitted pursuant to the procedures for voluntary admission of a competent adult set forth in G.S. 122C-211, with the legally responsible person acting for the individual. The procedures for judicial review of these admissions are set forth *infra* in Chapter 5.

An incompetent person may also be the subject of an involuntary substance abuse commitment proceeding. *See supra* Chapter 3.

4.5 No Admission by Advance Instruction

The statute allowing admission of an incapable person by advance instruction to a facility for "the care or treatment of mental illness" does not include a similar provision for substance abuse treatment. *See* G.S. 122C-73(c1).

A person deemed incapable of making and communicating treatment decisions may be the subject of an involuntary substance abuse commitment proceeding. *See supra* Chapter 3.

4.6   No Admission by Health Care Power of Attorney

The statute granting the power to a health care agent appointed pursuant to a health care power of attorney to "authorize the giving or withholding of mental health treatment" does not include a similar provision for substance abuse treatment. *See* G.S. 32A-19(a). Likewise, the statutory form for a health care power of attorney, although broad, does not grant authority to consent to substance abuse treatment. *See* G.S. 32A-25.1. A health care agent could consent to medical treatment required as a result of substance abuse, subject to any limitations in the health care power of attorney placed on the authority of the agent to consent to medical care.

A person who lacks sufficient understanding or capacity to make or communicate decisions regarding treatment may be the subject of an involuntary substance abuse commitment proceeding. *See supra* Chapter 3.

4.7   Negotiating a Voluntary Admission When Substance Abuse Commitment Recommended

After discussing the strength (or weakness) of the case for involuntary substance commitment with the client, along with the collateral consequences of substance abuse commitment, counsel should explore the client's willingness to agree to accept treatment voluntarily. A voluntary admission will allow the client to avoid the possibility of being committed and perhaps to have more control over the treatment. These factors are less important if the client has prior substance abuse commitments and has already lost driving privileges.

Counsel should contact the attorney representing the state or the petitioner, if any, if necessary to obtain permission to talk directly with the attending physician or other treatment provider. Discussion points include the client's willingness to follow through with substance abuse treatment, progress the client has made pending the hearing, the statutory preference for voluntary treatment, and the availability of outside support for the client. It might also be persuasive to inform the attending physician of the likely loss of the client's driving privileges, and the effect of that on the client's job and home life, as well as the ability to get to outpatient treatment.

Chapter 5
Voluntary Admission of Incompetent Adults

5.1 Overview

The North Carolina General Statutes provide for the voluntary admission of an adjudicated incompetent adult to facilities for the mentally ill and substance abusers. Procedures for the voluntary admission of competent adults generally apply. *See supra* Chapter 4 and *infra* Chapter 10. The exception is that the acts required of the competent adult in applying for admission and consenting to treatment are performed by the legally responsible person, in this instance the guardian of the person or general guardian. As the admission is not a voluntary act by the person admitted, the statutes provide for appointment of counsel and judicial review of these admissions.

5.2 Terminology Used in this Chapter

"General guardian" means "a guardian of both the estate and the person." N.C. GEN. STAT. § 35A-1202(7) (hereinafter G.S.). A general guardian has authority to make health care decisions, including decisions concerning mental health and substance abuse treatment, unless limited by the order of the clerk of superior court appointing the guardian.

"Guardian," for the purposes of Chapter 122C of the North Carolina General Statutes, is the "person appointed as a guardian of the person or general guardian by the court under Chapters 7A or 35A or former Chapters 33 or 35 of the General Statutes." G.S. 122C-3(15). Because a guardian of the estate (see below) cannot make mental health or substance abuse treatment decisions for the ward, that type of guardian is not referenced in Chapter 122C.

"Guardian of the estate" is "a guardian appointed solely for the purpose of managing the property, estate, and business affairs of a ward." G.S. 35A-1202(9). A guardian of the estate does not have the authority to make health care decisions, which include decisions concerning mental health and substance abuse treatment, for the ward.

"Guardian of the person" is "a guardian appointed solely for the purpose of performing duties relating to the care, custody, and control of a ward." G.S. 35A-1202(10). A guardian of the person has authority to make health care decisions, including decisions concerning mental health and substance abuse treatment, unless limited by the order of the clerk of superior court appointing the guardian.

"Incompetent adult" as defined in Chapter 35A, "Incompetency and Guardianship," is "an adult or emancipated minor who lacks sufficient capacity to manage the adult's own affairs or to make or communicate important decisions concerning the adult's person, family, or property whether the lack of capacity is due to mental illness, mental retardation, epilepsy, cerebral palsy, autism, inebriety, senility, disease, injury, or similar cause or condition." G.S. 35A-1101(7). The term "incompetent adult" as used in Chapter 122C means "an adult individual adjudicated incompetent." G.S. 122C-3(17).

"Incompetent child" is "a minor who is at least 17 1/2 years of age and who, other than by reason of minority, lacks sufficient capacity to make or communicate important decisions concerning the child's person, family, or property whether the lack of capacity is due to mental illness, mental retardation, epilepsy, cerebral palsy, autism, inebriety, disease, injury, or similar cause or condition." G.S. 35A-1101(8).

"Incompetent person" is "a person who has been adjudicated to be an 'incompetent adult' or 'incompetent child' as defined in G.S. 35A-1101(7) or (8)." G.S. 35A-1202(11).

"Interim guardian" is "a guardian, appointed prior to adjudication of incompetence and for a temporary period, for a person who requires immediate intervention to address conditions that constitute imminent or foreseeable risk of harm to the person's physical well-being or to the person's estate." G.S. 35A-1101(11). An interim guardian has authority to make decisions regarding mental health or substance abuse treatment only if specifically granted by the order of the clerk of superior court appointing the interim guardian.

"Legally responsible person" is "(i) when applied to an adult, who has been adjudicated incompetent, a guardian." G.S. 122C-3(20). The term is used in the statutes governing voluntary admission of incompetent adults, and therefore is used in this chapter, although a legally responsible person for an incompetent adult is the guardian.

"Limited guardianship" is a guardianship limited to the specific areas of decision-making determined by the clerk of superior court to be beyond the ward's capacity. The ward retains the right to make all decisions in matters not encompassed by the limited guardianship. G.S. 35A-1212(a), 35A-1215(b). For example, a guardianship may be limited to medical decision-making. The ward would retain the right to make all decisions except those related to health care.

"Ward" is "a person who has been adjudicated incompetent or an adult or minor for whom a guardian has been appointed by a court of competent jurisdiction." G.S. 35A-1202(15).

5.3 Admission by Consent of Guardian

A. By Application of Guardian of the Person or General Guardian

A person previously adjudicated incompetent pursuant to Chapter 35A or former Chapters 33 or 35 of the General Statutes may be voluntarily admitted to a 24-hour facility by application of the guardian of the person or the general guardian. *See* G.S. 122C-231, 35A-1241. A petition for involuntary commitment is not required. G.S. 122C-232(b).

A guardian of the estate alone does not have authority to make medical decisions for a ward. For powers of the guardian of the estate, see G.S. 35A-1251. When appointing a guardian of the person or a general guardian, the clerk of superior court may also make findings of fact regarding the "nature and extent" of the ward's incompetence and order that the ward retain specific legal rights by ordering a limited guardianship. G.S. 35A-1215(b). As the ward could retain the right to make mental health or substance abuse treatment decisions, the guardianship order must be examined to determine if either has been retained.

These provisions do not apply to a person who is de facto incompetent but who has not been so adjudicated. Involuntary commitment procedures must then be followed (*see supra* Chapters 2 and 3), unless the person has executed an applicable advance instruction or health care power of attorney. *See infra* Chapter 11.

B. Guardian Acts for Respondent

The provisions of G.S. 122C-211 regarding the voluntary admission of competent adults (*see infra* Chapter 10) apply to the voluntary admission of an incompetent adult, with the guardian of the person or general guardian acting in place of the individual. G.S. 122C-231. The guardian so acting makes treatment decisions in the best interest of the ward unless the ward executed advance instructions for mental health treatment while competent. If advance instructions exist, the guardian shall follow those instructions in consenting to or refusing treatment, "consistent with G.S. 35A-1201(a)(5)." 122C-73(e). This statute instructs the guardian to allow the ward an opportunity to participate in decision-making "within his comprehension and judgment, allowing for the possibility of error to the same degree as is allowed to persons who are not incompetent." G.S. 35A-1201(a)(5).

5.4 Evaluation for Admission

Voluntary admission of an incompetent adult is generally pursuant to G.S. 122C-211, the statute governing the voluntary admission of a competent adult, with the legally responsible person acting on behalf of the individual. G.S. 122C-231. Under G.S. 122C-211(a), an individual applying for voluntary admission must be evaluated to "determine whether the individual is in need of care, treatment, habilitation or rehabilitation for mental illness or substance abuse or further evaluation by the facility." The incompetent adult must therefore be evaluated under this standard prior to admission. *See infra* Appendix A, Form DMH 5-73-01.

5.5 Attorney Representation

A. Appointment of Counsel

The statute requiring judicial review of a voluntary admission of an incompetent adult provides that, "[u]nless otherwise provided in this Part, the hearing . . ., including the provisions for representation of indigent incompetent adults," and all related proceedings are governed by the procedures for involuntary commitment. G.S. 122C-232(c); *see supra* § 2.5A.

For more on the role and responsibilities of counsel, see *infra* Appendix C, "Working with Clients."

B. Ethical Considerations

There are challenges in representing a person who has already been adjudicated incompetent. The statutory section on admissions states that the legally responsible person shall act for the person admitted, including "giving or receiving any legal notice." G.S. 122C-231. The hearing procedures, however, are designed to protect the due process rights of the *respondent*. Counsel is ethically required to explain the hearing procedures and dispositional alternatives to the respondent. Although the incompetent respondent does not have the legal capacity to sign in to the facility voluntarily, the respondent may contest the admission at the district court hearing or may decide not to contest. The attorney should determine how the respondent wishes to proceed. If the respondent is contesting, counsel must prepare the case as any other, reviewing records, talking with witnesses, and issuing subpoenas as appropriate.

Effective communication, given the disability of the client, is a concern. A prior review of records, as well as talking with the treatment team after obtaining any required consent by opposing counsel, may offer guidance on how best to approach the client interview.

See infra Appendix C, "Working with Clients."

5.6 Hearings

A. Venue

All hearings are held in the district court in the county in which the 24-hour facility is located. G.S. 122C-232(a).

B. Application of Involuntary Commitment Procedures

Except when otherwise specified in the sections dealing with voluntary admission of incompetent adults, the required initial hearing and any subsequent proceedings are governed by the provisions for involuntary commitments in Article 5, Part 7 of Chapter 122C. G.S. 122C-232(c). These procedures are discussed *supra* in Chapter 2.

C. Duties of Clerk of Superior Court

Calendaring of hearing. The procedures and notice required for involuntary adult commitment proceedings apply to hearings for the voluntary admission of an incompetent person. The process begins with the written application for admission rather than with a petition. G.S. 122C-231. The clerk of superior court in the county where the facility is located must calendar the hearing within 10 days of the admission. G.S. 122C-268(a).

Notice to respondent. Notice is given by the clerk to the respondent according to Rule 4(j) of the North Carolina Rules of Civil Procedure at least seventy-two hours before the hearing. G.S. 122C-264(b), (c). Rule 4(j) requires service on the respondent by, among other methods, personal service or certified mail (with proof of service on the respondent). Rule 4(j)(2)b. provides for separate service on the guardian.

It is doubtful that service on the respondent is actually being done given the time limitations of the hearing and the notice requirements. The respondent's counsel could make a motion to dismiss for lack of service, but rather than being released, the respondent could be readmitted by a new application of the guardian. The ward might remain in the facility while the process begins anew, delaying the time before the respondent is afforded a hearing.

Notice to others. The clerk is also to provide notice to the respondent's counsel and to the legally responsible person, who is the guardian. G.S. 122C-232(d). This notice is to be sent at least seventy-two hours before the hearing by first-class mail, postage prepaid. G.S. 122C-264(c). Although the legally responsible person may file a written waiver with the clerk of the right to receive notice, there is no provision for waiver by the respondent's counsel. G.S. 122C-232(c), (d).

Due to the time constraints and volume of cases, it is unclear whether the notices are given as required by Rule 4(j) and the statutes. Again, the respondent's counsel could make a motion to dismiss for lack of service, but this might result in delay of the hearing to allow proper service rather than the respondent's release.

D. Continuance

A continuance of the hearing of up to five days may be granted on motion of the court, the respondent's counsel, or the responsible professional, who is the person named by the facility director to oversee the respondent's care. G.S. 122C-232(a), 122C-3(32). As many district courts hold hearings for commitments and admissions only once a week or on two consecutive days, a five-day continuance will not suffice. It is common practice for the court to allow a seven-day continuance upon consent of the parties.

E. Criteria for Judicial Review of Admission

The court must determine whether the respondent "is mentally ill or a substance abuser and is in need of further treatment at the facility." G.S. 122C-232(b). The court must find that these requirements have been met by clear, cogent, and convincing evidence and that treatment cannot be provided in a less restrictive manner. If these requirements are not met, the respondent is to be released. *Id.* An important distinction between these "voluntary" proceedings and involuntary commitment hearings is that there is no requirement of a finding of danger to self or others.

F. Dispositional Alternatives

The dispositional alternatives for the voluntary admission of an incompetent adult are either concurrence with the inpatient admission or discharge. G.S. 122C-232(b). If the treatment provider is recommending outpatient treatment, an involuntary commitment proceeding for outpatient commitment must be initiated.

G. Discharge Pending Hearing

Prior to the initial court hearing, the respondent is to be discharged on request of the legally responsible person, who is the guardian, subject to the right of the facility to hold the respondent for up to seventy-two hours to initiate involuntary commitment proceedings. G.S. 122C-233(a), 122C-211(b).

H. Discharge After Hearing

After the court has concurred in the admission, only the court or the facility may release the respondent. The legally responsible person may apply to the court to review a request for discharge if the facility refuses to release the respondent when the legally responsible person believes release is in the best interest of the respondent. G.S. 122C-233(b). There is no provision for appointed counsel for the legally responsible person. Special Counsel or appointed counsel continues to represent the respondent until unconditional discharge or through proceedings at the trial level. G.S. 122C-270(a), (e).

5.7 Appeal

Appeal is directly to the North Carolina Court of Appeals. G.S. 122C-272. The statute provides that any party on the record may appeal as in civil cases. *Id.* It is unclear how this would apply to the voluntary admission of an incompetent person.

It seems clear that the incompetent adult could appeal as the person whose rights are protected by the judicial review of the admission. It is less clear whether the legally responsible person can appeal as the person acting on behalf of the incompetent adult. There is no case law on this point, but it could be argued that the legally responsible person is a party.

Chapter 122C provides for attorney representation of an incompetent person through any appellate proceedings. G.S. 122C-232(c), 122C-270. Appeal by the respondent's counsel is therefore at the direction of the respondent. In determining who is responsible for providing notice of appeal, the only guidance from 122C-232 (c) is that "all subsequent proceedings, . . . are governed by the involuntary commitment procedures of Part 7 of this Article [Article 5 of Chapter 122C]." Part 7 regulates involuntary commitment of the mentally ill. Appeals under Part 7 are taken by respondents. Pursuant to 122C-270, assigned counsel represents respondents through all proceedings in the district court. Presumably, this covers notice of appeal, which is required to be given at the district court level. These specific statutory provisions take precedence over the North Carolina Rules of Civil Procedure, which provide that an incompetent person can appear or appeal in civil cases only through a guardian ad litem or general guardian. N.C. R. CIV. P. 17.

Attorneys assigned by the North Carolina Office of the Appellate Defender are responsible for representing the respondent following the filing of appeal. G.S. 122C-232(c), 122C-270(a), (e).

Chapter 6
Voluntary Admission of Minors

6.1 Overview

The legally responsible person may voluntarily admit a minor to a 24-hour facility by written application. Judicial review and concurrence is required to ensure that the admission is appropriate, as the minor does not have capacity to consent to the admission. Procedures for the voluntary admission of a competent adult generally apply, with the legally responsible person giving or refusing consent as necessary. The provision for keeping the minor up to fifteen days in the facility prior to a hearing and the lack of a requirement for the court to find danger to self or others in order to concur in the admission are important differences from the involuntary commitment procedures.

6.2 Terminology Used in this Chapter

"Legally responsible person" for a minor is "a parent, guardian, a person standing in loco parentis, or a legal custodian other than a parent who has been granted specific authority by law or in a custody order to consent for medical care, including psychiatric treatment." N.C. Gen. Stat. § 122C-3(20)(ii) (hereinafter G.S.).

"Mental illness" as defined for a minor is "a mental condition, other than mental retardation alone, that so impairs the youth's capacity to exercise age adequate self-control or judgment in the conduct of his activities and social relationships so that he is in need of treatment." G.S. 122C-3(21).

"Qualified Physician's Examination report (QPE)" is the term commonly used to refer to the Department of Health and Human Services form completed by an examining physician when prepared for use in court. *See infra* Appendix A, DMH form 5-73-01. It is forwarded to the clerk of court when involuntary commitment is recommended following the filing of a petition or when a rehearing on commitment is requested by the attending physician.

"Responsible professional" is the "individual within a facility who is designated by the facility director to be responsible for the care, treatment, habilitation, or rehabilitation of a specific client and who is eligible to provide care, treatment, habilitation, or rehabilitation relative to the client's disability." G.S. 122C-3(32).

"Substance abuse" is "the pathological use or abuse of alcohol or other drugs in a way or to a degree that produces an impairment in personal, social, or occupational functioning. 'Substance abuse' may include a pattern of tolerance and withdrawal." G.S. 122C-3(36). There is no separate statutory definition of substance abuse applicable only to minors.

"Substance abuser" is "an individual who engages in substance abuse." G.S. 122C-3(37).

"24-hour facility" is "a facility that provides a structured living environment and services for a period of 24 consecutive hours or more and includes hospitals that are facilities under [Chapter 122C of the North Carolina General Statutes]." G.S. 122C-3(14)g. A 24-hour facility includes by statutory definition a "'residential facility', which is a 24-hour facility that is not a hospital, including a group home." G.S. 122C-3(14)e.

6.3 Procedures for Admission and Discharge

A. Application for Admission

The provisions governing the voluntary admission of competent adults apply to the voluntary admission of minors unless otherwise specified. G.S. 122C-221(a); *see infra* Chapter 10. The legally responsible person may seek to admit a minor by appearing at the 24-hour facility with the minor and signing a written application for admission. G.S. 122C-221(a), 122C-211(a). An evaluation must be conducted to determine if the minor is in need of treatment or further evaluation for mental illness or substance abuse at the facility. *Id.*; *see infra* Appendix A, Form DMH 5-73-01.

A private physician or facility is not required to accept the minor for treatment or evaluation. G.S. 122C-209. A voluntary application for admission of a minor can be denied in the discretion of the physician or facility.

B. Notice of Provision for 72-Hour Hold Upon Request for Discharge

The admitting facility must give written information setting forth the procedures for judicial review and discharge to both the legally responsible person and the minor before admission. G.S. 122C-224(b). This information must include that the minor may be held for up to seventy-two hours after a written request for discharge by the legally responsible person to allow the facility to initiate involuntary commitment procedures. *Id.*

C. Notice to Clerk of Superior Court of Admission

The clerk of superior court in the county where the facility is located must be notified within twenty-four hours of the admission of the minor. G.S. 122C-224(c). The notice must request that a judicial hearing be scheduled and must supply the names and addresses of the legally responsible person and the responsible professional. *Id.*

6.4 Duties of Clerk of Superior Court

A. Schedule Hearing

The clerk must schedule a hearing for judicial review upon receipt of notice of the minor's admission. G.S. 122C-224.1(b). The hearing must be held within fifteen days of date of admission. *Id.* This is in contrast to the requirement of a hearing within *ten* days of the date a respondent is taken into custody for an involuntary commitment.

B. Appoint Attorney

Within forty-eight hours of receipt of notice of the admission, an attorney shall be appointed in accord with the rules of the Office of Indigent Defense Services. G.S. 122C-224.1(a). Typically, the clerk has made the appointments. If the minor is in a state facility, Special Counsel serves as the minor's attorney. All minors are presumed to be indigent. *Id.*; *see infra* Appendix A, Form AOC-SP-912M.

The Attorney General issued an opinion that only the legally responsible person can choose or engage an attorney for a minor. *See* Opinion of Attorney General to C. Robin Britt, Sr., Secretary, Department of Human Resources, Attorney Access to Minors in State Hospitals and Attorney General Opinion (December 20, 1995), *available at* www.ncdoj.com/About-DOJ/Legal-Services/Legal-Opinions/Opinions/Attorney-Access-to-Minors-in-State-Hospitals-and-A.aspx. The opinion also states that the minor's rights are protected during commitment proceedings by G.S. 122C-224.1 and 122C-270, which provide for representation of the minor by Special Counsel or appointed counsel. Presumably, this is acknowledgement that an attorney selected by the legally responsible person, who signed the application for the voluntary admission of the minor before the court, would have an inherent conflict of interest in representing the minor in the judicial proceeding. Appointed counsel's responsibilities for a minor continue until counsel is discharged by the court. G.S. 122C-224.2(c); *see also infra* § 6.5E.

C. Give Notice

Upon calendaring of the hearing, the clerk must give notice of the time and place of the hearing to the minor's attorney on behalf of the minor. G.S. 122C-224.1(b). The notice must be given as soon as possible but not later than seventy-two hours before the hearing, pursuant to Rule 4(j) of the North Carolina Rules of Civil Procedure. *Id.* Rule 4(j) requires personal service, service by certified mail, or other designated methods of service.

The clerk also must send notice as soon as possible but not later than seventy-two hours before the hearing, by first-class mail, postage prepaid, to the legally responsible person and to the responsible professional. G.S. 122C-224.1(b).

6.5   Duties of Attorney for Minor

A. Meet with Client

By statute, the attorney must meet with the minor within ten days of appointment and not later than forty-eight hours before the hearing. G.S. 122C-224.2(a); *see infra* Appendix C, "Working with Clients."

B. Deliver Notice of Hearing

The attorney must deliver a copy of the notice of the time and place of hearing to the minor no later than forty-eight hours before the hearing. G.S. 122C-224.2(a). As the attorney must be served with the notice no later than seventy-two hours before the hearing, it is possible that the attorney will have only twenty-four hours in which to deliver the notice.

C. Advise Minor on Hearing Procedure

It is the duty of the attorney to explain the hearing procedures to the minor. The attorney may want to review the records and talk with the treatment team to learn about the minor's level of understanding. Especially with very young children, the attorney may need to use non-legal terms to help the minor better understand the proceeding.

If the minor is contesting the admission, the attorney should explain about evidence and testimony and explore potential witnesses for the petitioner and for the minor. Evidence supporting admission should be discussed, along with the judicial standard of review. The minor should be advised that counsel might need to contact other people in preparation for the hearing. If the minor objects to communication, for example with parents, counsel should explain the reasons contact might benefit the case and explore the basis for the objection. If the minor continues to object, it is better practice to follow the minor's wishes. Counsel should make a note in the office case file of the advice given and the minor's position.

Minors may equate "contesting" with "going home." The attorney should explain that the judge makes the decision after hearing all the evidence and that contesting does not necessarily mean that the minor will be released. A realistic assessment of the merits of the case may help the minor make a good decision regarding whether to contest.

The statute provides that minors have the right to be present at the hearing, as well as the separate right to testify even if otherwise not in attendance at the hearing. G.S. 122C-224.3(b); *see infra* § 6.6E. The attorney should explain that the minor may appear at the hearing whether or not the admission is contested. If the minor is not contesting, an appearance will have no effect on the outcome on the case. The minor still may be interested in being present at the proceeding. Some minors may look at the hearing as a chance for an outing. Counsel might gently discourage this but ultimately must leave the decision to the client.

Even if the minor does not wish to appear at the hearing, the minor still has the right to testify. G.S. 122C-224.3(b). For example, the minor might not want to be present in the hearing room to hear the testimony of the petitioner's witnesses, yet might want to testify. If the minor is contesting, counsel should explore the possible testimony of the minor. Counsel must assess whether the minor's testimony will aid or hinder the minor's position.

Note that the motions for waiver of appearance and the waiver of right to testify must be filed separately and in writing. G.S. 122C-224.2(b). This is presumably to ensure that the minor has the opportunity to testify, if desired, without having to sit through the entire hearing, which may be daunting to a minor.

D. Advise Minor on Potential Effects of Admission

Generally. The attorney should explain that the minor may be kept as a patient in the facility as long as the court concurs in the admission and the facility determines that the minor continues to be in need of treatment that could not be received in a less restrictive manner. Other matters that arise only after reaching the age of majority are more difficult to explain meaningfully. For example, in applying for college or employment, if asked whether the client has ever been committed, must the client answer in the affirmative? There is a good argument that a voluntary admission is not a commitment and does not have to be disclosed. It is also a confidential proceeding and is not a public record. *See infra* Chapter 12.

Federal gun laws. Federal gun laws prohibit ownership or possession of a gun by someone who has been committed to a psychiatric institution. Again, there is an argument that these laws do not apply to a voluntary admission. It is difficult to explain these legal concepts to a young person, especially when they might not become a real concern for years. *See infra* § 12.3.

Expunction of records. There is a statutory procedure for expunction of a minor's records of admission or commitment to a 24-hour facility. G.S. 122C-54(e). Either the legally responsible person or the former patient may request that the records be expunged after the minor reaches adulthood and has been released from the facility. *Id.* The statute provides that the court is to inform the legally responsible person and the minor in writing of the right to expunge records. This notice is to be given at the time the application for admission is filed. *Id.* It is unclear how the court would provide this information. It appears that only the facility staff would be in a position to provide this information at the time of admission. *See infra* § 12.6.

E. Represent Minor Until Relieved by Court

The statute provides that counsel for the minor shall continue the representation until relieved by the court. G.S. 122C-224.2(c). Presumably, representation also ends when the minor is unconditionally discharged or when the minor reaches the age of majority.

6.6 Hearings

A. Venue

The statute provides for the hearing for judicial review of the minor's admission to be held at the 24-hour facility if located within the judge's district. G.S. 122C-224.3(a). The hearing may be held elsewhere, however, if the judge determines that holding the hearing at the facility would be disruptive to the court calendar. *Id.* In that case, the hearing may be held in another location, including the judge's chambers. The hearing may not be held in a regular courtroom over the minor's objection if a more suitable place is available. *Id.*

There is no statutory provision for change of venue.

B. Preparation

Counsel should review the medical and psychiatric records from this and any prior psychiatric admissions. Additionally, any available school records and psychological reports or testing should be reviewed. The treatment team should be consulted, after obtaining any necessary consent, to learn the recommended length of stay and to explore the possibility of an agreement between the client and the treatment team on the length of the admission.

As with any other client, the minor's attorney should obtain the consent of the minor to contact witnesses outside the facility, including the legally responsible person. Counsel should interview possible witnesses and issue subpoenas for documents and witnesses as necessary. Admission papers and court documents should be examined to determine if they comply with statutory and due process requirements. For example, the admission application should be checked to see if it was properly signed by the legally responsible person. If there are irregularities, counsel may consider whether a motion to dismiss is possible and discuss the possible outcomes with the client.

C. Continuance

The hearing is to be held within fifteen days of admission, with statutory provision for one continuance of not more than five days. G.S. 122C-224(a). The statute neither specifies nor limits who may move for the continuance.

As many district courts hold hearings for commitments and admissions only once a week or on two consecutive days, a five-day continuance will not suffice. It is common practice for the court to allow a seven-day continuance upon consent of the parties.

D. Not Contesting/Not Resisting Commitment

Not contesting. There are no statutory provisions for minors to accept the recommendation for continued inpatient treatment or to "not contest." In practice, however, many minors are in agreement with their attending physicians on the need for inpatient treatment and do not want to contest the admission. Counsel may inform the client of the option to "not contest" the voluntary admission.

By not contesting, the minor can avoid a hearing with possibly upsetting testimony from family, friends, and the treatment team. An uncontested hearing on admission could proceed with testimony from witnesses supporting the admission or by stipulation of the respondent's counsel. Counsel may stipulate to the facts alleged in the Qualified Physician's Examination report (for a definition of this report, see *supra* § 6.2) or stipulate that the information in that document would be the testimony of the author.

A minor who is not contesting may wish to attend the hearing and has the right to do so. Counsel should explain the abbreviated nature of the proceedings so that the minor will know what to expect. Minors who are not contesting often prefer not to attend the hearing. A motion for waiver of appearance should be filed so that the minor is not compelled to attend. *See infra* § 6.6E.

Not resisting. The minor's lack of maturity, as well as the acute symptoms of mental illness, may prevent the minor from understanding the nature or import of the proceeding. The minor may be unable to discuss the issues or respond to counsel's questions, even at an elementary level. There are no statutory provisions to guide counsel when the client is unable to express a decision on whether to contest the commitment. For a discussion of these issues in cases involving adults, see *supra* § 2.6F.

If a review of the psychiatric and educational records support counsel's observations of the minor's level of understanding and there is no prospect of the minor being released by the court, counsel may report to the court that the respondent is "not resisting." This means that the minor is unable to understand and discuss the issues enough to contest the admission, but is equally unable to decide not to contest. As with an uncontested case, the hearing may then proceed with testimony from witnesses supporting the admission or by stipulation of the minor's counsel. Counsel may stipulate to the facts alleged in the Qualified Physician's Examination report (for a definition of this report, see *supra* § 6.2) or stipulate that the information in that document would be the testimony of the author.

A motion for waiver of appearance is filed in virtually every voluntary admission case in which the minor is not resisting. The minor is often also unable to make a decision regarding an appearance and is unable to understand or to benefit from attending court proceedings.

E. Waiver of Right to Appear and Waiver of Right to Testify

If the minor client does not want to be present at the hearing, counsel must file a written motion to waive the right to appear. G.S. 122C-224.2(b), 122C-224.3(b). The minor retains the right to testify even if the right to appear is waived. *Id.* If the minor client does not want to testify, counsel must file a *separate* written motion waiving the right to testify. *Id.*

An interesting section of the statute on the minor's testimony provides that the minor may appear "to respond to the judge's questions." G.S. 122C-224.3(b). Although one could infer that this means that only the judge may question the minor, this would appear to be a violation of the minor's due process right to representation by an attorney and the right of the petitioner to cross-examination.

F. Attorney Representation of Legally Responsible Person

There is no provision for representation of the legally responsible person, the person who signed the application for admission of the minor to the 24-hour facility. There is no provision for notice of judicial proceedings to an attorney representing the interests of the legally responsible person or the facility, although the legally responsible person and the responsible professional are among those who must receive notice. G.S. 122C-224.1(b). At state facilities, the attorney from the Attorney General's office may represent the interest of the state in the admission. Private facilities may employ private counsel to represent the interest of the facility in the admission. The legally responsible person could presumably hire an attorney to present evidence supporting the admission, although this is not provided by statute.

G. Hearing Closed to Public

Unless the attorney moves for the hearing to be open, it is closed to the public. G.S. 122C-224.3(d). The attorney is presumably the attorney for the minor, as no other attorney is mentioned in the section on voluntary admissions of minors. It also appears that if the minor's attorney requests that the hearing be open, the judge must grant the request.

H. Evidence

It may be unclear who will present evidence at the hearing to support admission. Counsel for the minor may find that the court is taking judicial notice of documents in the court file. The statute provides that "[c]ertified copies of reports and findings of physicians, psychologists and other responsible professionals as well as previous and current medical records are admissible in evidence." G.S. 122C-224.3(c). Copies of all documents admitted into evidence as well as a transcript of the hearing must be provided by the clerk at the request of the minor's attorney. G.S. 122C-224.3(e).

The minor, through counsel, has the statutory right to confront and cross-examine witnesses. G.S. 122C-224.3(c). If the legally responsible person is not represented at the hearing, who arranges for the appearance of the authors of the documents? The attorney for the minor should not be required to subpoena witnesses adverse to the client. Does the court issue a subpoena, and does this occur after objection to admitting the documentary evidence at hearing? If so, asserting the right to cross-examination will necessarily result in a delay of the hearing.

This may produce the uncomfortable situation of defending against the "empty chair." The court in effect produces or reviews the evidence, creating the appearance that the court is adverse to the minor client.

Counsel for the minor must determine, along with the client, whether to have the minor testify. It is also counsel's responsibility to subpoena any other favorable witnesses or documents.

I. Criteria for Admission

The criteria for the court to concur in the voluntary admission of a minor are less stringent than for an involuntary commitment as there is no need for a finding of danger to self or others. The court must first find that the minor is either mentally ill or a substance abuser. Additionally, the minor must be in need of further treatment at the 24-hour facility. Finally, there must be no less restrictive mode of treatment available. G.S. 122C-224.3(f).

J. Dispositional Order

There are three possible choices for the dispositional order. If the court finds by clear, cogent, and convincing evidence that the criteria for voluntary admission have been met, it must concur in the admission. The court must set the maximum length of stay, up to ninety days. G.S. 122C-224.3(g)(1).

The court may find that there are "reasonable grounds to believe" that the admission criteria exist, but additional evaluation and diagnosis are needed. In that case, it may order a one-time authorization of a stay of up to fifteen more days for such evaluation and diagnosis. G.S. 122C-224.3(g)(2).

Finally, if the court finds that the criteria for admission or additional evaluation have not been met, it must order that the minor be released. G.S. 122C-224.3(g)(3).

See infra Appendix A, Form AOC-SP-913M.

6.7 Treatment

The responsible professional is allowed to administer "reasonable and appropriate medication and treatment that is consistent with accepted medical standards and consistent with Article 3 of this Chapter [Clients' Rights and Advance Instruction]." G.S. 122C-224.6(a). This treatment may be administered both pending hearing and after any judicial concurrence in the admission. *Id.*

6.8 Rehearings

A. Right to Rehearing

A minor admitted to a facility upon concurrence of the court for either further evaluation and diagnosis or for continued treatment, has the right to a rehearing on whether the court authorizes additional time in the facility. G.S. 122C-224.4(a), (b).

B. Notice to Clerk of Superior Court

The responsible professional must notify the clerk at least fifteen days before the end of the approved stay if there is a request for an extension of the admission. G.S. 122C-224.4(c). The clerk is required to schedule a rehearing on the request prior to the expiration of the current admission. *Id.*

These time provisions cannot be met if the initial authorized stay is limited, for example, to one or two weeks. If the responsible professional determines at any time during the admission that additional time is needed, it will be too late to give the fifteen days' notice to the clerk.

C. Notice of Rehearing

Notices are to be sent by the clerk pursuant to the same procedures and time limits as for the initial hearing. G.S. 122C-224.1(c) (requiring clerk to "schedule all hearings and rehearings as required by this Part"). The clerk might not be able to serve and send the required notices within the statutory time periods if the prior admission term was relatively short. Because the minor's interest is not typically to extend the initial admission, counsel may waive timely notice of the rehearing.

D. Rehearing Procedures

Rehearings are to be conducted pursuant to the provisions of the statutes for the initial hearing. G.S. 122C-224.4(b).

E. Length of Authorized Admission Upon Rehearing

The court may authorize up to an additional 180 days' stay in the facility at each rehearing for admission of a minor. G.S. 122C-224.4(b). This is in contrast to the ninety-day maximum stay that may be authorized by the court at an initial hearing.

6.9 Discharge and Conditional Release

A. Conditional Release

The responsible professional is allowed to conditionally release the minor for up to thirty days during the admission. G.S. 122C-224.6(b). This conditional release could be as limited as a day pass to go out with a parent, to as broad as returning home for thirty days. In all cases, the minor must abide by any conditions of the release imposed by the responsible professional. Violation of any conditions of release authorizes the responsible professional to contact a law enforcement officer to take the minor into custody for return to the facility. *Id.*

B. Duty of Responsible Professional to Discharge

If the responsible professional determines that the minor is no longer mentally ill or a substance abuser, or that the minor is no longer in need of treatment at the facility, the minor must be unconditionally discharged. G.S. 122C-224.7(a). This discharge can occur at any time during the admission. It is important to stress this possibility, as the minor client may believe the judicial concurrence in a maximum length of admission is a "sentence" to be served. This belief could hinder cooperation in treatment and thus result in a longer stay.

C. Request of Responsible Person

At any time, the legally responsible person may file a written request for discharge of the minor from the facility. G.S. 122C-224.7(b). The responsible professional must discharge the minor within seventy-two hours, unless it is determined that the minor is either mentally ill or a substance abuser and is a danger to self or others. In that case, the facility may utilize the seventy-two hours in order to initiate involuntary commitment proceedings. *Id.* This option must be explained to both the legally responsible person and the minor at admission. G.S. 122C-224(b); *see supra* § 6.3B.

D. Discharge Within 72 Hours of Reaching Age 18

If the minor reaches the age of eighteen while in the facility and refuses to sign an authorization within seventy-two hours of reaching eighteen, the client either must be discharged or involuntarily committed. 122C-224.7(c). Upon reaching the age of majority, the client could choose to sign in to the facility as a voluntarily admitted adult. If not, the facility must discharge the client, unless it is determined that the criteria for involuntary commitment exist. In that case, the facility may hold the individual for up to seventy-two hours, presumably after the minor has reached the age of eighteen, in order to institute the involuntary commitment procedure.

6.10 Emergency Admission

A minor may be admitted to a 24-hour facility for treatment of mental illness or substance abuse on the minor's own written application in an emergency situation. G.S.122C-223(a). The legally responsible person must be notified by the facility of the admission within twenty-four hours, if possible. G.S. 122C-223(b). If the legally responsible person is not located within seventy-two hours of the admission, the responsible professional must report the juvenile's admission to Child Protective Services in either the minor's county of residence or in the county where the facility is located. 122C-223(c).

Chapter 7
Automatic Commitment—Not Guilty by Reason of Insanity

7.1 Overview

A defendant found not guilty by reason of insanity is not subject to further criminal proceedings related to the charges adjudicated. North Carolina statutes require, however, that a defendant found not guilty by reason of insanity (NGRI) be automatically committed to a state facility for the treatment of mental illness. The defendant, now a respondent in the mental health treatment system, cannot be discharged by either the attending physician or the court during the first fifty days.

Defendants who were charged with a crime *not* involving allegations that the defendant inflicted or attempted to inflict serious injury or death are committed to a state facility for the treatment of mental illness. Defendants charged with a crime involving allegations that the defendant inflicted or attempted to inflict serious injury or death must be committed to a forensic unit operated by the Department of Health and Human Services. The only such facility currently is the forensic unit at Central Regional Hospital (formerly Dorothea Dix Hospital).

Upon the automatic commitment of the defendant by the criminal court, the statutory provisions for involuntary commitment for treatment of mental illness, contained in Chapter 122C of the North Carolina General Statutes (hereinafter G.S.), apply. Procedures under Chapter 122C, including a hearing in district or superior court, determine whether the individual will remain under commitment and, if so, the term of the commitment.

Respondents found not guilty by reason of insanity in criminal district court are represented by Special Counsel. Respondents found not guilty by reason of insanity in criminal superior court are typically represented by assigned counsel in the civil commitment proceedings.

7.2 Terminology Used in this Chapter

"Forensic Unit" means a separate unit within a state facility for treatment of mental illness, reserved exclusively for individuals entering through the criminal justice system. These individuals may include those being evaluated for capacity to stand trial, those found incapable of proceeding to trial, and those found not guilty by reason of insanity. The only forensic unit currently in North Carolina is located at Central Regional Hospital (formerly Dorothea Dix Hospital).

"Not guilty by reason of insanity (NGRI)" is the verdict resulting from a finding that the defendant committed the acts alleged by the state, but is not guilty because the defendant did not know the nature or quality of the act or could not distinguish between right and wrong.

"State 24-hour facility" means a facility operated by the Department of Health and Human Services that "provides a structured living environment and services for a period of 24 consecutive hours or more." G.S. 122C-3(14)f., g.

7.3 Characterization of Offense

A. No Definition by Statute or Case Law

A defendant found not guilty by reason of insanity faces a different statutory disposition if the crime charged alleges that the defendant inflicted or attempted to inflict serious physical injury or death. G.S. 15A-1321. There is, however, no statutory definition or case law outlining which crimes fall into this category. The characterization of the crime is important because more restrictions are placed on an involuntarily committed defendant who has been determined to have committed such an act. These defendants must be committed to a forensic unit of a state facility, rather than to the general population.

No statutory provision exists for commitment counsel to challenge the categorization of the respondent's alleged crime. For example, a defendant may have been charged with armed robbery but did not harm or attempt to harm the victim in any way. The criminal court judge might nevertheless commit the defendant as one who inflicted or attempted to inflict serious physical injury or death.

Counsel for the respondent could raise the issue at the commitment hearing but might be unsuccessful because the initial commitment order was entered by the criminal court judge. Counsel might seek the assistance of the respondent's defense attorney. The defense attorney might be able to make a motion in criminal court that the nature of the crime be re-categorized.

B. Crime Charged Does <u>Not</u> Allege Defendant Inflicted or Attempted to Inflict Serious Physical Injury or Death, and Defendant Found NGRI: Judge Must Order Commitment to State 24-Hour Facility

A defendant who is charged with a crime where it is not alleged that the defendant inflicted or attempted to inflict serious injury or death and who is found not guilty by reason of insanity must be committed by the criminal court judge to a state 24-hour facility. The court also must order the defendant into the custody of a law enforcement officer for transport directly to the facility. All subsequent proceedings are to be conducted pursuant to Chapter 122C, which governs involuntary commitment. G.S. 15A-1321(a); *see infra* Appendix A, Form AOC-SP-910M.

C. Crime Charged <u>Does</u> Allege Defendant Inflicted or Attempted to Inflict Serious Physical Injury or Death, and Defendant Found NGRI: Judge Must Order Commitment to DHHS Forensic Unit

A defendant who is charged with a crime where it is alleged that the defendant inflicted or attempted to inflict serious injury or death and who is found not guilty by reason of insanity must be committed by the criminal court judge to a forensic unit operated by the Department of Health and Human Services. Currently the only such unit is at Central Regional Hospital (formerly Dorothea Dix Hospital).

The court also must order the defendant into the custody of a law enforcement officer for transport directly to the forensic unit. All subsequent proceedings are to be conducted pursuant to Chapter 122C, which governs involuntary commitment. G.S. 15A-1321(b).

7.4 Temporary Restraint Pending 15A-1321 Proceedings

The criminal court judge "may order the respondent be held under appropriate restraint pending proceedings under G.S. 15A-1321" if there are reasonable grounds to believe that the respondent is mentally ill and dangerous to self or others as defined in Chapter 122C. G.S. 15A-1322.

7.5 Commitment Hearing Under Chapter 122C

A. Attorney for Respondent

Entitlement to counsel. If committed following an NGRI verdict, the respondent is entitled to be represented at subsequent commitment proceedings by counsel of choice if financially able. *See supra* § 2.5A. If the respondent is indigent or refuses to retain counsel, the statute provides that counsel is to be appointed in accord with rules adopted by the Office of Indigent Defense Services. G.S. 122C-268.1(d).

The current practice is for Special Counsel to represent respondents for most hearings held at the facility. Assigned counsel represent respondents at hearings held in counties outside the state facilities and for respondents in high-profile criminal cases regardless of where the hearing is held.

Notice of admission. Special Counsel routinely receives notice of the admission of a respondent to the state facility pursuant to an automatic commitment. Special Counsel should receive a copy of the order finding the respondent not guilty by reason of insanity and the order of automatic commitment. Because the statute provides that the commitment hearing must be within fifty days of the date of the custody order (*see* G.S. 122C-268.1(a)) rather than within the ten-day limit for non-NGRI mental health commitments, preparation for the hearing does not have to begin immediately. It is good practice, however, to meet with the client soon after admission to explain the commitment procedure and answer any questions.

Notice of hearing. The respondent's counsel must receive notice of each commitment hearing from the clerk of superior court at least seventy-two hours prior to the hearing. G.S. 122C-264(d1); *see infra* Appendix A, Form AOC-SP-301. Although not required by statute, the practice is for the attending physician to prepare a Qualified Physician's Examination report, which is the Department of Health and Human Services form completed by the attending physician that accompanies a request for a rehearing on commitment in non-NGRI cases. *See supra* § 2.2 (describing a Qualified Physician's Examination report) and *infra* Appendix A, Form DMH 5-72-01. Counsel should receive a copy of the report.

B. Attorney for State

The district attorney in the county in which the respondent was found NGRI may represent the state's interest at the commitment hearing. If the district attorney opts not to represent the state, then the state's interest is represented by the attorney assigned to the state facility or, in the Attorney General's discretion, a staff attorney designated by the Attorney General. G.S. 122C-268.1(b).

C. Trial Division and Venue

The commitment hearing is held in the trial division in which the original criminal trial was held. G.S. 122C-268.1(g). For example, if the criminal trial was held in superior court, the commitment hearing will also take place in superior court.

Venue is initially in the county in which the 24-hour facility is located. If the district attorney chooses to represent the state's interest at the commitment hearing, however, the district attorney may move to change venue to the county in which the respondent was found NGRI. Upon such a motion, the venue for the hearing, rehearings, and supplemental hearings must be moved to that county. G.S. 122C-268.1(b). There is no provision for the respondent to request a change of venue.

D. Waiver of Hearing

An NGRI respondent has the option of waiving the Chapter 122C commitment hearing. G.S. 122C-268.1(a). The current practice is for the court to treat a waiver of hearing as if the respondent is not contesting recommitment. Because the respondent has the burden of proof, this results in an order of recommitment for the maximum statutory term. *See infra* § 7.5I.

E. Not Contesting/Not Resisting

Although not addressed by statute, the respondent may choose not to contest being recommitted. Because the respondent has the burden of proof, choosing not to present evidence will result in recommitment.

A respondent who is too mentally ill to be able to discuss the commitment proceeding or to communicate a decision on how to proceed with counsel may be termed "not resisting." Although unable to state agreement with being recommitted, the respondent is "not resisting" by presenting no evidence supporting release. For a discussion of these issues in non-NGRI involuntary commitment cases, see *supra* § 2.6F.

F. Clerk of Court to Calendar and Give Notice

The commitment hearing under Chapter 122C must occur within fifty days of the date of commitment under G.S. 15A-1321. G.S. 122C-268.1(a). The clerk of superior court is responsible for calendaring the hearing. G.S. 122C-264(d1).

After calendaring the hearing, the clerk must notify the respondent, the respondent's attorney, counsel for the State, and the district attorney involved in the original trial. The respondent must receive notice at least seventy-two hours before the hearing by personal service, by registered or certified mail, return receipt requested, or by other method permitted under Rule 4(j) of the North Carolina Rules of Civil Procedure. The other individuals must receive notice at least seventy-two hours before the hearing by first-class mail, postage prepaid. G.S. 122C-264(d1); *see infra* Appendix A, Form AOC-SP-301.

The district attorney must notify "any persons he deems appropriate," in addition to persons who have filed a request for notification with the district attorney's office. The notice must be sent by first-class mail to the person's last known address. G.S. 122C-264(d1).

G. Waiver of Appearance

The respondent's counsel may waive the respondent's presence with the consent of the court. G.S. 122C-268.1(e). For a discussion of waiver of appearance in non-NGRI cases, see *supra* § 2.6G.

H. Hearing Open to Public

The commitment hearing resulting from the NGRI verdict is open to the public, just as the criminal trial is. G.S. 122C-268.1(g). This means that anyone may attend the commitment hearing.

I. Burden of Proof

The *respondent* has the burden of proving by a preponderance of the evidence that the respondent:

- no longer has a mental illness as defined in G.S. 122C-3(21), *or*
- no longer is dangerous to others as defined in G.S. 122C-3(11)b.

G.S. 122C-268.1(i).

This standard reverses the burden applicable in other commitment proceedings. Ordinarily, the State has to prove mental illness *and* danger to self or others by clear, cogent, and convincing evidence. Note that the respondent's standard is "preponderance of the evidence." Also, the respondent needs to prove only one of the prongs listed above—either lack of mental illness or lack of danger to others.

Case law: Acts committed by a respondent more than a decade earlier could be considered to be "in the relevant past" in determining whether the respondent currently is "dangerous to others."

In re Hayes, 151 N.C. App. 27 (2002). The North Carolina Court of Appeals in *Hayes* addressed the interpretation of the statutory definition of "danger to others" in G.S. 122C-3(11)b., particularly the meaning of the phrase "in the relevant past" in regard to past acts of the respondent in assessing current danger to others. In *Hayes*, the respondent was found not guilty by reason of insanity for homicides and felonious assaults committed in July of 1988. The recommitment hearing being reviewed on appeal was held in January 2001. The court of appeals found that the standard of review on appeal is "whether there is competent evidence to support the trial court's factual findings and whether these findings support the court's ultimate conclusion that respondent still has a mental illness and is dangerous to others." 151 N.C. App. at 29–30. Despite the lapse of time between the respondent's acts and the hearing, the appellate court held that evidence supported the finding of the lower court that:

> "The four homicides and seven felonious assaults committed by the respondent on July 17, 1988, are episodes of dangerousness to others *in the relevant past* which in combination with his past and present mental condition, his multiple mental illnesses, and his conduct since admission to Dorothea Dix Hospital since 1989, and up to and including his conduct in the hospital during the previous year indicates there is a reasonable probability that the respondent's seriously violent conduct will be repeated and that he will be dangerous to others in the future if unconditionally released with no supervision at this time."

Id. at 31 (emphasis added).

In so holding, the court rejected the respondent's argument that under this interpretation of "in the relevant past," a homicide defendant found not guilty by reason of insanity would never be released from psychiatric inpatient commitment. The court noted that even though the respondent would be "presumed dangerous to others" and that this was a "high hurdle for the respondent to overcome," this burden was proper and the lower court's findings and conclusions must be upheld. *Id.* at 38–39.

J. Evidence

Certified copies of reports and findings of physicians and psychologists, as well as previous and current medical records, are admissible in evidence. The respondent, however, retains the right to confront and cross-examine witnesses. G.S. 122C-268.1(f). This may require counsel to object when documents are offered by the State without the testimony of the authors or other qualified witnesses.

The respondent has the right to employ an independent expert to conduct an examination. G.S. 122C-62(a)(2). This is at the respondent's expense and will not be paid by the state unless counsel has obtained a prior court order approving the expenditure.

K. Preparation for Hearing

Because of the interrelationship between the criminal trial and the commitment proceeding, it might be helpful for the respondent's attorney to contact the criminal defense attorney. It is not a breach of confidentiality to contact the defense attorney, who is aware of the commitment. It is usually better practice, however, to consult the client before making contact. The defense attorney may provide more information about the alleged crime and be able to suggest helpful witnesses in the community.

Although the burden of proof is by "preponderance of the evidence," because the burden is on the respondent it may be difficult for the respondent to win release by the court. The criminal defense attorney should have conveyed to the defendant the possibility of a long stay in an inpatient facility. Counsel for the respondent at post-NGRI proceedings may need to reiterate this to the client in discussing possible outcomes.

7.6 Disposition

Respondent prevails. If the court finds by a preponderance of the evidence that the respondent is either no longer mentally ill or is no longer dangerous to others, the respondent must be "discharged and released." G.S. 122C-271(c)(2).

Respondent does not prevail. If the court does not find that the respondent has carried the burden of proof, it must order inpatient treatment for up to ninety days at a 24-hour facility. G.S. 122C-271(c)(1).

7.7 Rehearings

A. Hearing Procedures

Rehearings for NGRI commitments follow the procedures for the initial hearing set forth in G.S. 122C-268.1. G.S. 122C-276.1(b). These procedures are discussed *supra* in § 7.5A through J. As with the initial hearing, the respondent may waive the right to a rehearing. G.S. 122C-276.1(a).

B. Clerk of Court to Calendar and Give Notice

The clerk of court must calendar a rehearing at least fifteen days before the end of any inpatient commitment resulting from an NGRI verdict. Notice is to be given by the clerk according to the same provisions governing the initial hearing. G.S. 122C-276.1(a), (d); *see also supra* § 7.5F.

C. Disposition

As at the initial 122C commitment hearing, the respondent bears the burden of proof at each rehearing. G.S. 122C-276.1(c); *see also supra* § 7.5I. If the respondent carries the burden of proof, the court must order discharge and release. If the burden is not carried, the court may commit the respondent for up to 180 days of inpatient treatment at the first rehearing and for up to one year at each subsequent rehearing. G.S. 122C-276.1(c), (d).

7.8   Discharge or Conditional Release

A. No Discharge or Conditional Release Except Upon Order of Court

A respondent committed as a result of an NGRI verdict may not be discharged except upon order of the court having jurisdiction over the commitment proceedings. G.S. 122C-277(b1). The respondent may not be discharged during the period of automatic commitment ordered by the criminal court. *Id.*

If the attending physician determines that the commitment criteria no longer exist, rather than discharging the respondent, the physician must request a court hearing to present the recommendation to the court. Discharge is not automatic, however, as the burden of proof remains on the respondent.

B. Notice to Clerk of Proposed Discharge or Conditional Release

The attending physician must notify the clerk of superior court fifteen days before the proposed discharge or conditional release. G.S. 122C-277(b1). Notice must be provided so that the clerk may schedule and give notice of the required hearing.

C. Clerk to Calendar Hearing and Give Notice

Upon receiving notice of the proposed discharge or conditional release, the clerk must calendar a hearing before the court with jurisdiction over the commitment. The clerk also must give notice to the same people entitled to notice of the initial hearing and rehearings, within the same time limits. G.S. 122C-277(b1), 122C-264(d1); *see supra* § 7.5F.

D. District Attorney May Represent State's Interests

The district attorney for the criminal trial may represent the state's interests at the commitment hearing regarding discharge or conditional release. G.S. 122C-277(b1); *see supra* § 7.5B.

E. Hearing Procedures

The hearing is conducted according to the same procedures as at the initial hearing and rehearings under Chapter 122C. G.S. 122C-277(b1), 122C-268.1; *see supra* § 7.5.

F. Burden of Proof

The hearing is held according to the same standard of proof as the initial hearing and rehearings under Chapter 122C. G.S. 122C-277(b1). The respondent must prove by a preponderance of the evidence that the respondent no longer has a mental illness *or* no longer is dangerous to others. G.S. 122C-268.1(i); *see supra* § 7.5I.

G. Disposition

There are no dispositional alternatives set out in the statutory section on request for discharge or conditional release. If the respondent prevails, then clearly the court must discharge or conditionally release the respondent. G.S. 122C-271(c)(2), 122C-268.1(:). It is less clear what choices are available to the court if the respondent does not prevail. For example, if the respondent was committed for 180 days at the first rehearing and does not prevail at a hearing on discharge occurring 60 days into the term, may the court commit the respondent for one year? Or does the respondent continue with the remainder of the 180 days and have a rehearing 120 days later? There is a good argument for the latter because the respondent should not be penalized by a longer commitment as a result of the attending physician's request for a discharge hearing.

The trial court on rehearing may order any disposition allowed by Chapter 122C regardless of the specific relief requested by the treating physician. *In re Hayes,* ___ N.C. App. ___, 681 S.E.2d 395 (2009). Therefore, commitment counsel would be well advised to be creative in making recommendations that provide the least restriction on the respondent's liberty as long as the recommendations are within the dispositional alternatives allowed by statute. As always, counsel should advise the respondent of the alternatives available and obtain the respondent's consent before offering dispositional alternatives to the court.

Chapter 8
Commitment of Defendants Found Incapable of Proceeding

8.1 Overview

A defendant in a criminal trial must have the capacity to proceed, that is, to be able to understand the nature of the proceedings and be able to participate in the defense of the case. If the defendant meets the standard for "incapacity to proceed" under Chapter 15A of the North Carolina General Statutes (hereinafter G.S.), the criminal procedure statutes, the trial cannot go forward. The criminal court judge must then determine if the defendant meets the criteria for involuntary commitment under Chapter 122C, the mental health statutes. If so, the defendant is referred by the criminal court for involuntary commitment under the provisions of Chapter 122C. The defendant is sometimes called a "House Bill 95," a reference to the legislative bill number for the original applicable statutes.

The primary provisions of Chapter 15A governing determination of incapacity to proceed and referral for civil commitment proceedings also apply to juveniles alleged to be delinquent under Chapter 7B. A reference to a defendant in this chapter generally applies as well to a juvenile alleged to be delinquent.

This chapter will discuss briefly the criminal court procedures that result in the defendant becoming a respondent in an involuntary commitment proceeding. The focus will be on the Chapter 122C procedures for the involuntary commitment of defendants found incapable of proceeding and the interplay between the relevant provisions of Chapter 122C and Chapter 15A.

8.2 North Carolina Defender Manual: Capacity to Proceed

The North Carolina Defender Manual chapter entitled "Capacity to Proceed" (Chapter 2 in Volume 1, Pretrial) provides a comprehensive explanation of the relevant criminal court procedures from the viewpoint of the defendant's attorney. The Defender Manual is available on the Office of Indigent Defense Services website, www.ncids.org, under reference manuals. A new edition of the Defender Manual, including the "Capacity to Proceed" chapter, is forthcoming in 2011. Counsel is referred to that chapter for additional information concerning the criminal statutes governing capacity to proceed.

8.3   Terminology Used in this Chapter

"Defendant" means, for the purpose of this chapter, an individual charged with a crime in a criminal court proceeding.

"Delinquent juvenile" is "[a]ny juvenile who, while less than 16 years of age but at least 6 years of age, commits a crime or infraction under State law or under an ordinance of local government, including violation of the motor vehicle laws." G.S. 7B-1501(7).

"Incapacity to Proceed" describes the condition of a defendant who "by reason of mental illness or defect . . . is unable to understand the nature and object of the proceedings against him, to comprehend his own situation in reference to the proceedings, or to assist in his defense in a rational or reasonable manner." G.S. 15A-1001(a). The term "incapable of proceeding" is used interchangeably. The term "incompetent" (see definition below) has a separate and distinct legal definition under current North Carolina law and is not interchangeable with "capacity," but is sometimes used as such. Older North Carolina cases, as well as opinions from federal courts and courts of other states, may also use the terms interchangeably.

"Incapacity to Proceed" distinguished from "Insanity Defense." Incapacity to proceed is determined after a defendant has been charged with a crime and prior to or during the trial on those charges. The incapacity refers to the defendant's ability to understand and participate in the criminal trial. An insanity defense relates to the defendant's state of mind at the time the alleged crime was committed. A defendant who is "insane" at the time of trial might be found incapable of proceeding. An insanity defense to the crime charged cannot be raised unless the defendant is capable of proceeding to trial and entering a plea.

"Incompetent" means an individual who has been adjudicated incompetent to make or communicate important decisions concerning one's person, family, or property pursuant to the procedures of Chapter 35A, "Incompetency and Guardianship," of the North Carolina General Statutes and for whom a guardian has been appointed pursuant to that chapter. *See* G.S. 35A-1101(7), (8). For a discussion of proceedings to appoint a guardian, see JOHN L. SAXON, NORTH CAROLINA GUARDIANSHIP MANUAL (UNC School of Government 2008), *available at* www.ncids.org (under reference manuals).

"Respondent" means, for the purpose of this chapter, a defendant in a criminal proceeding who has been referred by the criminal court for involuntary commitment upon a finding of reasonable grounds to believe the individual is mentally ill and dangerous to self or others.

8.4 Applicability to Adults and Juveniles Alleged to Be Delinquent

The provisions of Chapter 15A on incapacity to proceed apply to adult criminal defendants. The primary provisions, G.S. 15A-1001 through 15A-1003, apply as well to juveniles alleged to be delinquent. G.S. 7B-2401. For a discussion of incapacity issues in juvenile delinquency proceedings, see Chapter 7, "Capacity to Proceed," of Lou A. Newman, Alyson Grine, & Eric J. Zogry, North Carolina Juvenile Defender Manual (UNC School of Government 2008), *available at* www.ncids.org (under reference manuals).

8.5 Determination of Incapacity to Proceed

A. Standard for Determination

To be found incapable of proceeding, the defendant must be unable, by reason of mental illness or defect, to do one of the following:

- understand the nature of the criminal proceedings;
- comprehend his or her situation in reference to the criminal proceedings; or
- assist in the defense in a rational or reasonable manner.

G.S. 15A-1001(a).

Case law: Determination of capacity to proceed.

State v. Shytle, 323 N.C. 684 (1989) (stating and applying test); ***State v. Jenkins,*** 300 N.C. 578 (1980) (stating and applying test).

B. Criminal Court Procedure

Defender Manual. For a more extensive discussion of criminal court procedures, see Chapter 2, "Capacity to Proceed," of the North Carolina Defender Manual (Volume 1, Pretrial), *available at* www.ncids.org (under reference manuals).

Flowchart of criminal and civil commitment proceedings. Appendix 8-1 to this chapter, "Capacity and Commitment Flowchart," traces the interplay between criminal and civil commitment proceedings, highlighting the major steps in the process.

Motion. The question of the defendant's capacity may be raised at any time during the criminal court proceedings. A motion may be made by the prosecutor, the defendant, defense counsel, or the court. The motion must set forth the reasons the movant questions the defendant's capacity to proceed. G.S. 15A-1002(a).

Capacity examination. When a motion is made questioning a defendant's capacity, the court may order a local examination by "impartial medical experts, including forensic evaluators," to determine the defendant's current mental condition. The resulting report is admissible at the hearing on capacity. In addition, the examiner may be called to testify by the court at the request of either party. G.S. 15A-1002(b)(1). It is not required by statute that an examination be ordered, but the court typically orders one when the issue of capacity has been raised.

Examination at state facility: misdemeanors. Only after an initial examination by a medical expert may a defendant charged with a misdemeanor be ordered by the court to a state facility for the mentally ill for further evaluation. This might be done because the results of the first examination were not definitive or because the court wants an in-depth evaluation before proceeding. The defendant may be admitted to the state facility for no more than sixty days for observation and treatment necessary to determine capacity to proceed. G.S. 15A-1002(b)(2). As a practical matter, once undertaken, the typical state facility evaluation is far shorter than the sixty-day maximum.

Examination at state facility: felonies. The court may bypass the initial, local examination for a defendant charged with a felony upon finding that an evaluation at a state facility for the mentally ill would be more appropriate. This evaluation may also be ordered following an initial evaluation. In either instance, the evaluation at the state facility may be no more than sixty days for observation and treatment necessary to determine capacity to proceed. G.S. 15A-1002(b)(2). As a practical matter, once undertaken, the typical state facility evaluation is far shorter than the sixty-day maximum.

Report to court. A report of the results of any court-ordered evaluation must be sent to the defense attorney and to the clerk of superior court for delivery to the court. The report is admissible at the hearing on capacity. G.S. 15A-1002(b)(2). It remains a confidential record, however, until introduced into evidence. If the defendant's capacity is questioned following the examination, the full report must be forwarded to the district attorney. G.S. 15A-1002(d). Notwithstanding this limitation, State facilities have been releasing the capacity report to the district attorney when they release the report to the court and the criminal defense attorney, unless the defense attorney has obtained a court order restricting disclosure.

Hearing. If the defendant's capacity to proceed has been questioned, the criminal court must hold a hearing on the issue of the defendant's capacity to proceed. The hearing must occur after any court-ordered examinations.

The statute does not set forth detailed procedures for the hearing. Both the State and the defendant may present evidence and, if an examination was ordered, the examiner may be called to testify. The reports of any examinations are admissible in evidence. G.S. 15A-1002(b).

After hearing the evidence, the court must determine whether the defendant is capable of proceeding upon the criminal charges. If the defendant has the necessary capacity, the trial may proceed on the charges.

Disposition upon finding of incapacity to proceed. If the court finds that the defendant lacks the capacity to proceed, the criminal statute provides several alternative dispositions:

1. The court may enter "appropriate orders to safeguard the defendant and to ensure his return for trial in the event that he subsequently becomes capable of proceeding." Appropriate orders include any of the procedures allowed under Article 26 of the Criminal Procedure Act (Chapter 15A of the North Carolina General Statutes), entitled "Bail." G.S. 15A-1004(a), (b).
2. The court may dismiss the charges:
    i. when it appears that the defendant will not gain the capacity to proceed;
    ii. when the defendant has been confined for a period equal to or in excess of the maximum sentence for the crime charged; or
    iii. five years from the date of the finding of incapacity to proceed for misdemeanor cases or ten years for felony cases. G.S. 15A-1008.
3. The prosecutor may dismiss the charges with leave. G.S. 15A-1009(a).
4. The court may refer the defendant for civil commitment proceedings.

Constitutional principles also may require release of the respondent. *See Jackson v. Indiana*, 406 U.S. 715 (1972), discussed below.

Case law: The indefinite confinement of a defendant found incapable of proceeding, without a civil commitment proceeding required to commit any other person, is unconstitutional.

Jackson v. Indiana, 406 U.S. 715 (1972). The U.S. Supreme Court considered the case of a criminal defendant found unable to proceed to trial and committed to an institution under Indiana law until determined to be "sane." The defendant was deaf and mute with the mental functioning of a preschool child and with limited sign language skills. He was charged with two robberies of money and goods with a total worth of $9.00. *Id.* at 717.

Two psychiatrists were appointed by the court to evaluate the defendant's capacity to proceed to trial, followed by a "competency hearing." The examiners reported that the defendant had almost nonexistent communication skills and lacked the intelligence to develop those skills. Both agreed that the condition of the defendant was unlikely to improve, and a deaf-school interpreter through whom the doctors had tried to communicate with the defendant testified that there were no facilities in the state available to provide treatment designed to improve his condition. *Id.* at 718–19. The trial court found that the defendant "'lack(ed) comprehension sufficient to make his defense'" and committed him to the Indiana Department of Mental Health until such time as the Department certified to the court that the defendant was "sane." *Id.* at 719.

Due Process. The U.S. Supreme Court reviewed the provisions of Indiana law governing involuntary civil commitment for those termed "feeble-minded" and those found to be "mentally ill." The Court noted that in both instances the commitment statutes required an application for commitment with accompanying physician's certificate, examination by two court-appointed physicians, appointment of counsel, notice, and a hearing. Persons committed as feeble-minded may be released at any time the superintendent of the institution determines it is justified by the mental and physical condition of the person. Persons committed as mentally ill had a right to appeal the court's decision and could also be discharged in the discretion of the superintendent of the institution. *Id.* at 721–23. The state did not afford all of these procedures to the defendant. Further, the Court noted that the defendant's commitment rested on proceedings that did not bring into play or even consider any of the articulated bases for indefinite commitment. "At the least, due process requires that the nature and duration of commitment bear some reasonable relation to the purpose for which the individual is committed." *Id.* at 737–38.

Equal Protection. The Court noted that it had previously held in *Baxstrom v. Herold*, 383 U.S. 107 (1966), that persons involuntarily committed upon completion of a prison sentence are entitled to the same protection of the law afforded to others civilly committed. The Court extended the *Baxstrom* ruling to the situation here, stating that the standard for commitment of one charged with a crime should not be more lenient, nor the criteria for release more stringent, than what is generally applicable to one who does not have criminal charges pending. 406 U.S. at 730.

Holding. The court held that the Indiana statute allowing the defendant to be committed indefinitely after being found incompetent to stand trial without the procedural protections afforded those committed under the general statutory provisions for civil commitment violated the defendant's right to equal protection under the law and was a violation of due process. *Id.* at 730, 738. The court also stated:

> "We hold, consequently, that a person charged by a State with a criminal
> offense who is committed solely on account of his incapacity to
> proceed to trial cannot be held more than the reasonable period of time
> necessary to determine whether there is a substantial probability that he
> will attain that capacity in the foreseeable future. If it is determined that
> this is not the case, then the State must either institute the customary
> civil commitment proceeding that would be required to commit

indefinitely any other citizen, or release the defendant."

Id. at 738.

8.6 Referral of Defendant for Civil Commitment Proceedings

A. Determination by Criminal Court

After finding the defendant incapable of proceeding, the court must determine whether the defendant meets the criteria for involuntary commitment under Chapter 122C. The presiding judge has discretion to hold a hearing on the commitment issue but is not required to do so. If "reasonable grounds to believe" that the criteria for involuntary commitment exist, the presiding judge must make findings of fact and issue a custody order. The custody order has the same effect as the custody order issued by the clerk or magistrate after the filing of a petition for involuntary commitment. G.S. 15A-1003(a); *see supra* § 2.3B. The custody order of the criminal court must specify that the clerk shall be notified if the defendant is to be released from the custodial facility. G.S. 15A-1004(c); *see infra* Appendix A, Form AOC-SP-304.

Upon entry of the custody order, the defendant becomes a respondent in the involuntary commitment proceeding, as well as being a defendant in the criminal case until the charges are dismissed.

Defendant charged with violent crime. If the defendant was charged with a violent crime, the custody order issued by the presiding judge must order a law enforcement officer to take the defendant directly to a 24-hour facility. The order must state that the defendant was charged with a violent crime and was found incapable of proceeding. G.S. 15A-1003(a). The order must also provide that the facility may release the defendant only to the custody of a specified law enforcement agency. G.S. 15A-1004(c); *see* Appendix A, Form AOC-SP-304.

Temporary detention of defendant pending involuntary commitment proceedings. The court may enter "appropriate orders for the temporary detention of the defendant" pending the involuntary commitment proceeding. G.S. 15A-1003(b).

B. Law Enforcement Officer to Assume Custody or to Transport

The law enforcement officer designated by the custody order of the court must take the respondent into custody within twenty-four hours of entry of the order. G.S. 122C-261(e).

If the defendant was charged with a violent crime and found incapable of proceeding, the law enforcement officer must take the respondent directly to a 24-

hour facility. G.S. 122C-263(b). Otherwise, the usual procedures of Chapter 122C apply (G.S. 15A-1003(a)), and the respondent is transported for an examination by a physician or eligible psychologist. *See supra* § 2.3D and E.

C. First Examination Requirements

Defendant not charged with a violent crime and found incapable of proceeding.
The procedures and standards applicable to respondents initially taken into custody under Chapter 122C for a first examination apply. G.S. 15A-1003(a); *see supra* § 2.3E, F, and H.

The criminal court judge may enter an order specifying conditions of the defendant's release if outpatient commitment is recommended or if no grounds for commitment are found. The order may include any of the conditions of Article 26 of the Criminal Procedure Act (Chapter 15A of the North Carolina General Statutes), entitled "Bail," including designating an individual or organization to assume custody and supervision of the defendant if released. G.S. 15A-1004(b).

Defendant charged with a violent crime and found incapable of proceeding.
The procedures and standards applicable to respondents initially taken into custody under Chapter 122C apply (G.S. 15A-1003(a)), with the following exceptions:

- The initial examination takes place at the 24-hour facility. G.S. 122C-263(b).
- The examining physician may not release the respondent until ordered to do so by the district court judge presiding over the involuntary commitment proceedings. *Compare* G.S. 122C-266(a) (2), (3) (permitting release by physician in other instances).

See supra § 2.3E.

D. Second Examination by Physician

Defendant not charged with a violent crime and found incapable of proceeding.
If the first examiner finds that the criteria for involuntary commitment exist, the procedures and standards applicable to respondents initially taken into custody under Chapter 122C apply. G.S. 15A-1003(a). A second examination must then be performed. G.S. 122C-266(a); *see supra* § 2.3I.

A physician must perform the second examination. If the physician finds after the second examination that the criteria for involuntary commitment exist, the respondent must be held at the facility pending the district court hearing on involuntary commitment. G.S. 122C-266(a)(1).

If the second examiner does not find that the criteria for involuntary commitment exist, the respondent must be released. G.S. 122C-266(a)(3). The release is subject, however, to conditions that may be imposed by order of the criminal court. These may include bail or placing the defendant in the custody of a designated person or organization. G.S. 15A-1004(b).

Defendant charged with a violent crime and found incapable of proceeding. The statute provides for an examination by a physician of a respondent charged with a violent crime and found incapable of proceeding under the standards and procedures applicable to respondents initially taken into custody under Chapter 122C. G.S. 15A-1003(a), 122C-263(b), 122C-266(a); *see also supra* § 2.3I. However, there is only one examination, at the 24-hour facility, and the examiner may not release the respondent pending the district court hearing, even if the criteria for involuntary commitment no longer exist. G.S. 122C-266(b).

8.7 Attorney Representation

A. Attorney for Respondent

Upon determination by the second examiner that the criteria for involuntary commitment exist, a district court hearing must be held within ten days of the date the respondent was taken into custody. G.S. 122C-268(a). The respondent is then entitled to representation for the involuntary commitment hearing. Special Counsel represents respondents held at a state facility. G.S. 122C-270(a). Counsel is appointed for respondents held at other facilities. For a discussion of the role and responsibilities of counsel, see *infra* Appendix C, "Working with Clients."

The criminal defense attorney does not ordinarily represent the respondent at the involuntary commitment hearing.

B. Attorney for State

Attorney representation for the state's interest is generally the same as for respondents not found incapable of proceeding. *See supra* § 2.5B. The exception is that the district attorney for the county where the respondent was charged with a violent crime and was found incapable of proceeding may elect to represent the state's interest at the commitment hearing. G.S. 122C-268(c). Otherwise, because a defendant found incapable of proceeding is usually sent to one of the state facilities, the staff attorney from the Attorney General's office assigned to the facility will represent the state. G.S. 122C-268(b).

8.8 Preparation for Hearing

Contact with defense attorney. In addition to the usual prehearing preparation, the respondent's attorney should take extra steps when the respondent has been found incapable of proceeding on criminal charges. Because the respondent may be subject to further criminal proceedings, the attorney should contact the respondent's criminal defense attorney, who can shed light on the defense strategy. For example, the defense attorney might be aware of the state's objective, which might be supervised placement in the community rather than a prison sentence.

Note that the defendant's criminal defense attorney is not entitled to notice of the involuntary commitment proceeding under the statutes. Commitment counsel must therefore initiate contact if information is required from the defense attorney.

Because the defense attorney knows of the commitment through the criminal proceedings, counsel is not divulging confidential information by making contact. Still, the better practice is to obtain the client's permission prior to contacting the defense attorney.

Contact with district attorney. After talking with the defense attorney, or if unable to contact the defense attorney, counsel may consider contacting the district attorney. The district attorney is entitled to notice of the involuntary commitment proceedings, so this would not be revealing confidential information. Counsel must take care, however, not to relate any confidential information to the district attorney.

The purpose of this contact is to determine the state's objective in the case, which might affect the strategy in the involuntary commitment case. For example, the district attorney may be planning to dismiss the charges or to dismiss the charges with leave. Supervised placement that would prevent repeated minor crimes related to the mental illness, such as trespass, might be a satisfactory resolution for the state.

Contact with witnesses. Potential witnesses might include individuals connected to the criminal proceeding, including family members. Counsel should check to see if there are orders preventing the defendant from contacting a victim or victims and honor those orders. Consent of the respondent should be obtained before contacting witnesses because of the confidentiality of the proceedings.

Family members might be able to testify as to the respondent's danger to others or lack thereof. A person willing to provide housing or supervision could be valuable to the respondent's case.

8.9   Hearings

A. Time Limit for Hearing

The involuntary commitment hearing in district court must be held within ten days of the date of the custody order issued by the criminal court. G.S. 122C-268(a), 122C-261(e).

B. Venue and Change of Venue

Defendant not charged with a violent crime. The hearing is held in the county where the facility is located. The statute provides further that the respondent may object to venue, and the hearing is then held in the county where the petition was initiated. G.S. 122C-269(a).

Defendant charged with a violent crime. Venue is in the county where the facility is located, unless a motion to change venue is filed. The statute provides that upon motion of "any interested person," the proceeding may be moved to the county where the respondent was found incapable of proceeding "when the convenience of witnesses and the ends of justice would be promoted by the change." G.S. 122C-269(c). It appears that both the State and the respondent could move for change of venue under this provision.

If venue is transferred back to the county where the defendant was found incapable of proceeding, the rules of Chapter 122C regarding place of hearing apply. The hearing is not to be held in a regular courtroom if the respondent objects, "if in the discretion of a judge a more suitable place is available." G.S. 122C-268(g).

C. Continuances

The standards and procedures applicable to routine involuntary commitment proceedings apply. *See supra* § 2.6E.

D. Discharge Pending Hearing

Defendant not charged with a violent crime. A respondent who was not charged with a violent crime may be released at any time pending the district court hearing if the criteria for involuntary commitment no longer exist. G.S. 122C-266(d). The release is subject, however, to conditions that may be imposed by order of the criminal court. These may include bail or placing the defendant in the custody of a designated person or organization. G.S. 15A-1004(b).

Defendant charged with a violent crime. A respondent who was charged with a violent crime may not be released pending the district court hearing. The respondent may be released only if so ordered by the district court following the hearing. G.S. 122C-266(b).

E. Not Contesting/Not Resisting

Although not specifically provided by statute, a respondent may choose to "not contest" or may be "not resisting" because unable to comprehend and participate in the proceedings. For a discussion of the factors involved in making these determinations, see *supra* § 2.6F.

F. Waiver of Appearance

The respondent's presence may be waived by counsel with the permission of the court as in any other involuntary commitment hearing. G.S. 122C-268(e). For a discussion of the issues involved in waiving the respondent's appearance, see *supra* § 2.6G. *See also infra* Appendix B, "Waiver of Appearance and Order Allowing Waiver of Appearance."

G. Criteria for Involuntary Commitment

The criteria for involuntary commitment are the same as for respondents not referred through the criminal justice system. *See supra* § 2.6H.

H. Evidence

The evidentiary standards and burden of proof are the same as for respondents not referred through the criminal justice system. *See supra* § 2.6J.

Note: Chapter 15A provides that "[e]vidence used at the hearing with regard to capacity to proceed is admissible in the involuntary civil commitment proceedings." G.S. 15A-1003(c).

8.10 Dispositional Alternatives

Defendant not charged with a violent crime. The dispositional alternatives for respondents not referred through the criminal justice system are available to the district court at the involuntary commitment hearing. *See supra* § 2.7A.

If the respondent is either released or committed to outpatient treatment, conditions of release imposed by order of the criminal court apply. These may include bail or placing the defendant in the custody of a designated person or organization. G.S. 15A-1004(b).

Defendant charged with a violent crime. The dispositional alternatives for respondents not referred through the criminal justice system are available to the district court for respondents charged with a violent crime, with some additional requirements. *See supra* § 2.7A. If the district court orders either inpatient or outpatient commitment, it must note on the order that the respondent was charged with a violent crime and found incapable of proceeding. G.S. 122C-271(b)(1), (2).

If the respondent is either released or committed to outpatient treatment, conditions of release imposed by order of the criminal court apply. These may include bail or placing the defendant in the custody of a designated person or organization. G.S. 15A-1004(b).

8.11 Rehearings

Involuntary commitment rehearings for respondents initially found incapable of proceeding are generally subject to the same provisions and standards as for respondents initially taken into custody under Chapter 122C. *See supra* § 2.9; *see also* G.S. 122C-276(a) (if the respondent was charged with a violent crime and found incapable of proceeding, the clerk must give notice of the time and place of the rehearing to the district court judge, clerk of superior court, and district attorney in the county in which the respondent was found incapable of proceeding). The proceedings remain subject to any special conditions imposed at the initial involuntary commitment hearing in criminal court following a finding of incapacity to proceed.

8.12 Termination of Commitment

Defendant not charged with a violent crime. A committed respondent who was not charged with a violent crime, who was found incapable of proceeding, and who no longer meets the involuntary commitment criteria may be released without a separate hearing on the issue of release. G.S. 122C-277(a). Any conditions of release imposed by order of the criminal court continue to apply. These may include bail or placing the defendant in the custody of a designated person or organization. G.S. 15A-1004(b). If the criminal court order does not specify to whom the defendant is to be released, the facility may release the defendant "to whomever it thinks appropriate." G.S. 15A-1004(c).

The facility must report "to the clerk if the defendant is to be released from the custody of the hospital or institution." G.S. 15A-1004(c).

Defendant charged with a violent crime and found incapable of proceeding. A committed respondent charged with a violent crime and found incapable of proceeding may not be released without an order of the district court. The attending physician must notify the clerk in the county where the facility is located fifteen days before the proposed discharge or release. The clerk must schedule a district court hearing, which is in effect a rehearing. G.S. 122C-277(b); *see infra* Appendix A, Form DMH 5-76-01.

The dispositional criteria for an initial hearing on involuntary commitment apply. *See supra* § 2.7. At the hearing on release, however, the attending physician would presumably testify that either the respondent is no longer mentally ill or is no longer dangerous to self or others. Counsel for the respondent should subpoena the attending physician if necessary.

Counsel, along with the respondent, will have to decide if the respondent will testify. The court may be less likely to order discharge without the testimony of the respondent. The respondent's testimony and presentation could either jeopardize or enhance the chances for release.

If the respondent is released from involuntary commitment, the respondent may be released only to the custody of the law enforcement agency specified in the criminal court order originally referring the defendant for involuntary commitment. G.S. 15A-1004(c).

8.13 Supplemental Hearings in Criminal Court

The criminal court may hold a supplemental hearing when:

- the defendant has been returned for trial after the facility having custody has determined that the defendant has regained capacity or the court has received a report that the defendant has regained capacity (G.S. 15A-1007(a)); or
- the court determines that a hearing should be held to inquire into the defendant's condition (G.S. 15A-1007(b)); or
- any of the conditions for dismissal of the criminal charges have been met. G.S. 15A-1007(c); *see* G.S. 15A-1008. *See also Jackson v. Indiana,* 406 U.S. 715 (1972), discussed *supra* in § 8.5B.

8.14 Defendant's Return to Stand Trial Upon Regaining Capacity

The defendant must be returned to stand trial if capacity to proceed is regained and the charges have not been dismissed. The criminal court may also order that the defendant be returned to jail or be granted pretrial release pending the criminal court trial. G.S. 15A-1004(e).

If the defendant has been in the custody of a facility, the facility must notify the clerk in the county where the criminal case is pending of the change in the defendant's status. The clerk must then notify the sheriff of that county to transport the defendant back to the county for further criminal proceedings. G.S. 15A-1006.

Prepared by John Rubin, April 2010
© UNC School of Government

Capacity and Commitment Flowchart

Criminal Side: Capacity

From next page

On defendant's release from commitment, criminal court may initiate supplemental hearings on capacity. 15A-1007.*

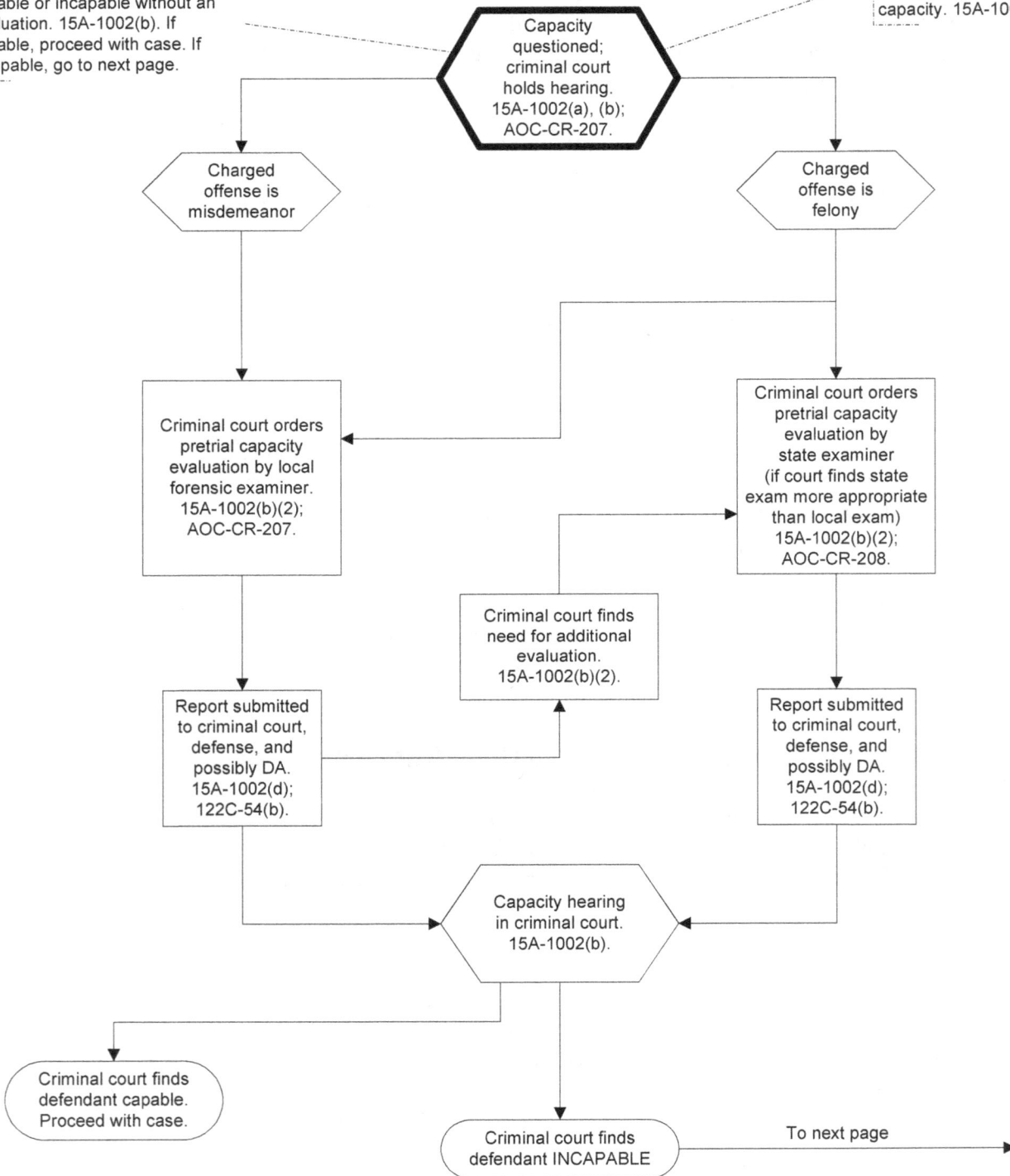

Criminal court may find defendant capable or incapable without an evaluation. 15A-1002(b). If capable, proceed with case. If incapable, go to next page.

Capacity questioned; criminal court holds hearing. 15A-1002(a), (b); AOC-CR-207.

Charged offense is misdemeanor

Charged offense is felony

Criminal court orders pretrial capacity evaluation by local forensic examiner. 15A-1002(b)(2); AOC-CR-207.

Criminal court orders pretrial capacity evaluation by state examiner (if court finds state exam more appropriate than local exam) 15A-1002(b)(2); AOC-CR-208.

Criminal court finds need for additional evaluation. 15A-1002(b)(2).

Report submitted to criminal court, defense, and possibly DA. 15A-1002(d); 122C-54(b).

Report submitted to criminal court, defense, and possibly DA. 15A-1002(d); 122C-54(b).

Capacity hearing in criminal court. 15A-1002(b).

Criminal court finds defendant capable. Proceed with case.

Criminal court finds defendant INCAPABLE

To next page

*At a supplemental hearing, the court may find the defendant capable or incapable of proceeding, modify pretrial release conditions, find that the defendant meets the statutory criteria for dismissal under GS 15A-1008, or find that the defendant is constitutionally entitled to dismissal under *Jackson v. Indiana,* 406 U.S. 715 (1972). If the defendant is incapable and is not entitled to dismissal, the prosecutor still may take a dismissal or, as provided in GS 15A-1009, enter a dismissal with leave (although dismissal with leave may make it difficult for the defendant to obtain treatment because criminal charges remain pending).

Civil Side: Commitment

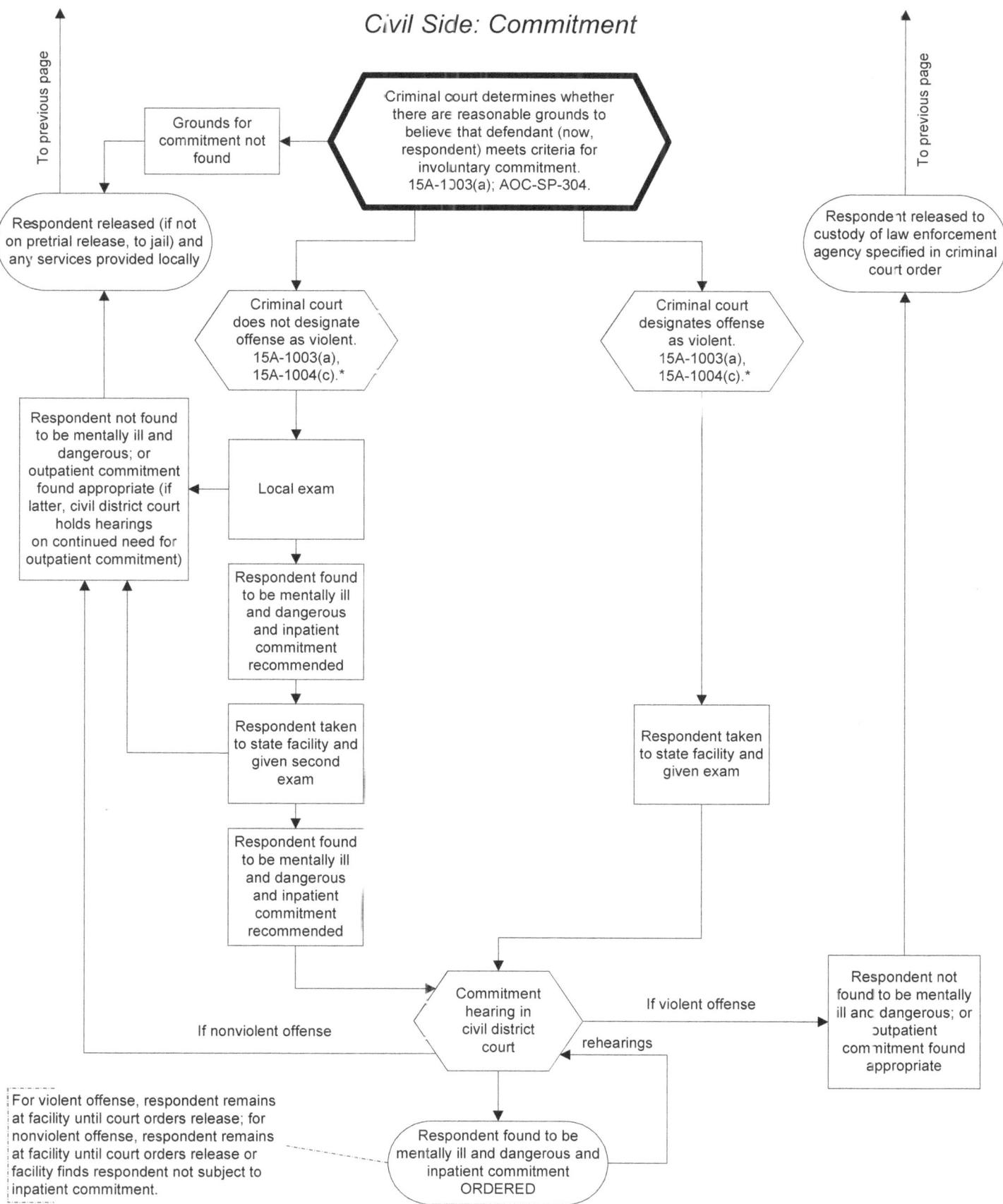

To previous page

To previous page

Criminal court determines whether there are reasonable grounds to believe that defendant (now, respondent) meets criteria for involuntary commitment. 15A-1003(a); AOC-SP-304.

Grounds for commitment not found

Respondent released (if not on pretrial release, to jail) and any services provided locally

Respondent released to custody of law enforcement agency specified in criminal court order

Criminal court does not designate offense as violent. 15A-1003(a), 15A-1004(c).*

Criminal court designates offense as violent. 15A-1003(a), 15A-1004(c).*

Respondent not found to be mentally ill and dangerous; or outpatient commitment found appropriate (if latter, civil district court holds hearings on continued need for outpatient commitment)

Local exam

Respondent found to be mentally ill and dangerous and inpatient commitment recommended

Respondent taken to state facility and given second exam

Respondent taken to state facility and given exam

Respondent found to be mentally ill and dangerous and inpatient commitment recommended

Commitment hearing in civil district court

If violent offense

Respondent not found to be mentally ill and dangerous; or outpatient commitment found appropriate

If nonviolent offense

rehearings

For violent offense, respondent remains at facility until court orders release; for nonviolent offense, respondent remains at facility until court orders release or facility finds respondent not subject to inpatient commitment.

Respondent found to be mentally ill and dangerous and inpatient commitment ORDERED

*Various statutes in GS 122C distinguish between the handling of nonviolent and violent offenses following a finding of incapacity and referral for commitment proceedings. For a more detailed discussion of those requirements, see Chapter 8 of the North Carolina Civil Commitment Manual, available at www.ncids.org under Reference Manuals

Chapter 9
Involuntary Commitment and Voluntary Admission of Inmates

9.1   Overview

Chapter 122C of the North Carolina General Statutes (hereinafter G.S.) contains procedures for the involuntary commitment of inmates of the Department of Correction for treatment of mental illness, as well as for the voluntary admission of inmates for the treatment of mental illness *and* substance abuse. The statutory provisions for commitment of those who are not inmates are generally applicable to inmates as well. This chapter will focus on special provisions and issues concerning inmates only.

9.2   Terminology Used in this Chapter

"Correctional facility" means the facility operated by the North Carolina Department of Correction having physical custody of a person convicted of a criminal offense.

"Inmate" means a person convicted of a crime and placed in the physical custody of the Department of Correction. It does not include a person in jail pending trial.

"State facility" is a facility under the supervision of the Secretary of the Department of Health and Human Services for the provision of "services for the care, treatment, habilitation, or rehabilitation of the mentally ill, the developmentally disabled or substance abusers." G.S. 122C-3(14)f.

9.3 Involuntary Commitment of Inmates

A. Applicability of Chapter 122C Procedures and Exceptions

The procedures of Chapter 122C for involuntary commitment of individuals for mental health treatment apply to inmates unless "manifestly inappropriate" or modified by the statute applicable to inmates, discussed below. G.S. 122C-313(a); *see supra* Chapter 2. The Department of Correction typically petitions for the involuntary commitment of an inmate only at the end of a sentence and not during incarceration.

B. Special Provisions for Inmates

Affidavit by staff psychiatrist or eligible psychologist. Involuntary commitment of an inmate can only be initiated by affidavit of a staff psychiatrist or eligible psychologist of the correctional facility. The affidavit must be transmitted to the clerk of the county where the correctional facility is located. G.S. 122C-313(a), 122C-261(d).

Attorney for inmate-respondent. Upon receipt of the affidavit of the staff psychiatrist or eligible psychologist, the clerk of superior court must give notice of the hearing to the respondent's counsel. G.S. 122C-313(a). If the respondent is confined in a correctional facility located in the same county as a state facility, Special Counsel will represent the respondent. Otherwise, counsel is appointed according to rules adopted by the Office of Indigent Defense Services. G.S. 122C-313(d). Because IDS has not yet adopted statewide rules, the local rules for appointment of counsel of the county where the correctional facility is located will apply.

Inmate remains in correctional facility pending commitment hearing. Unlike the routine proceeding in which the respondent is held at the facility pending hearing, the inmate remains at the correctional facility until the involuntary commitment hearing. If the district court finds that the respondent meets the criteria for inpatient commitment, it then must order a transfer for treatment to a state facility designated by the Secretary of the Department of Health and Human Services. G.S. 122C-313(a).

Hearing. The hearing is held pursuant to Chapter 122C procedures. *See supra* § 2.6.

District court may not order outpatient commitment. The statute specifically provides that outpatient commitment is not a dispositional alternative at the involuntary commitment hearing. G.S. 122C-313(a). If the respondent does not meet the criteria for inpatient commitment, the inmate is returned to the custody of the correctional facility.

Expiration of sentence. If the sentence imposed by the criminal court expires during the term of the involuntary commitment, the respondent is treated as if initially committed under the statutes applicable to those not entering through the corrections system. G.S. 122C-313(b). In other words, the respondent is not released simply because the criminal sentence has expired. As long as the involuntary commitment criteria are met, the respondent may be retained during the term of commitment and may be subject to rehearings.

9.4   Attorney Meeting with Inmate-Respondent

The meeting with the respondent will be at the correctional facility, unless special arrangements can be made with the Department of Correction to transport the inmate elsewhere. Because of security concerns, this may not be possible.

Counsel should call the correctional facility to make arrangements to meet with the client. A private meeting place should be requested and provided, subject to accommodations to ensure counsel's safety. For example, a staff person could be within eyesight, but out of hearing range, during the meeting.

Counsel should make inquiry as to what form of identification is required to be admitted to the correctional facility, as well as what items are not permitted. The correctional facility may allow counsel to bring in only relevant court documents, a legal pad, and a pen. Briefcases and purses are usually prohibited. (Mobile telephone and other wireless communications devices are prohibited on state correctional facility premises except in a motor vehicle in a designated parking area of the premises or as authorized by Department of Correction policy. G.S. 148-23.2.) Prohibited items should be locked in the car trunk to avoid having to leave them in a secure area of the correctional facility. Having these matters in order before attempting to enter the facility will make the meeting go more smoothly and the time expended shorter.

When making an appointment with the client, counsel should also try to arrange meetings with prison staff, such as the social worker and psychiatrist or psychologist. If possible, arrangements to review relevant records should be made. The social worker may be able to obtain the client's consent and have the records available at the time of the appointment with the client.

Counsel should carefully explain that the involuntary commitment is a new proceeding, separate from the prior criminal trial. Counsel should inform the client that representation is for the involuntary commitment only and is not part of the criminal case, but should also explain how the two cases interconnect.

It is important to explain to the client exactly what will happen at the commitment hearing, reiterating that it is not a criminal trial. The dispositional alternatives, including possible confinement in a state facility, should be discussed. The client should be informed that the term of the involuntary commitment might last longer than the criminal sentence.

9.5 Termination of Commitment

Inmate no longer meets involuntary commitment criteria: sentence has not expired. If the attending physician determines that a respondent whose sentence has not expired no longer meets the criteria for involuntary commitment, the Department of Correction must be notified. The Department of Correction must arrange transportation for the inmate back to the correctional facility. G.S. 122C-313(c).

Inmate no longer meets involuntary commitment criteria: sentence expired. If the attending physician determines that a respondent no longer meets the criteria for involuntary commitment and the respondent's sentence has expired, the respondent is treated as if initially committed under the usual involuntary commitment procedures. G.S. 122C-313(b). The respondent must be released unless voluntarily admitted.

9.6 Voluntary Admission and Discharge of Inmates

Chapter 122C contains only one paragraph governing the voluntary admission and discharge of inmates. *See* G.S. 122C-312. In practice, inmates needing psychiatric or substance abuse treatment receive treatment, if any, through the correctional system.

The statute states that the provisions of Chapter 122C for voluntary admission apply, except that the Secretary of the Department of Health and Human Services and the Secretary of the Department of Correction must jointly agree to the voluntary admission. G.S. 122C-312; *see supra* Chapter 4 and *infra* Chapter 10.

Chapter 10
Voluntary Admission of Competent Adults for Treatment of Mental Illness

10.1 Overview

Judicial review is not required for the voluntary admission of a competent adult to a 24-hour facility for the treatment of mental illness, discussed in this chapter, or substance abuse (*see supra* Chapter 4). There is no representation by Special Counsel or an appointed attorney in the process. A voluntary admission may be less restrictive and involve fewer collateral consequences than an involuntary commitment, so the respondent's counsel in involuntary proceedings should assess whether voluntary admission is an option.

10.2 Procedures for Admission and Discharge

A. Application for Admission

Any competent adult may voluntarily seek admission at a 24-hour facility for treatment of a mental illness. The individual must appear at the facility and sign a written application for admission. An evaluation is required prior to admission to "determine whether the individual is in need of care, treatment, habilitation or rehabilitation for mental illness or substance abuse or further evaluation by the facility." N.C. GEN. STAT. § 122C-211(a) (hereinafter G.S.). Note, however, that a private physician or facility is not required to accept a person for treatment or evaluation. G.S. 122C-209.

Voluntary admission to a Veteran's Administration facility generally follows the procedures described above for competent adults. G.S. 122C-331. The Veteran's Administration may impose additional requirements for admission consistent with Chapter 122C of the North Carolina General Statutes. *Id.*

B. Discharge and Notice of Provision for 72-Hour Hold

Persons voluntarily admitted to locked treatment facilities, termed 24-hour facilities by statute, are generally required to be released upon written request. G.S. 122C-212(a). A crucial exception is that the facility is allowed to hold an individual for up to seventy-two hours after a written request for discharge. G.S. 122C-212(b). This information must be included in the written application for voluntary admission. G.S. 122C-211(b).

C. 24-Hour Evaluation

A person voluntarily admitted to a 24-hour facility that provides treatment that includes medical care must be evaluated by a facility physician within twenty-four hours of admission. The evaluation must include a determination of the need for treatment of mental illness and whether the person will benefit from the available treatment. G.S. 122C-211(c). If medical treatment is not a part of the treatment offered, the person is to be medically evaluated within thirty days if treatment is anticipated to continue more than thirty days. This requirement is waived if there is a physical examination report signed by a physician within the preceding twelve months of admission. G.S. 122C-211(d).

D. No Provision for Attorney or Transportation

There is no constitutional or statutory requirement for provision of counsel for a person voluntarily seeking admission to a 24-hour facility. Neither is there a provision for the city or county to provide transportation to the facility for admission or upon discharge.

E. No Hearing Required

There are no court proceedings upon the voluntary admission of a competent adult to a 24-hour facility. Court proceedings are instituted only if a written request for discharge is made and the facility institutes involuntary commitment procedures during a seventy-two-hour hold. *See supra* § 10.2B.

10.3 Collateral Proceedings

A. Voluntary Admission to Have No Effect on Incompetency Proceeding

Voluntary admission, as well as involuntary commitment, to a facility for treatment of mental illness, substance abuse, mental retardation, or developmental disability, is to have no effect on incompetency proceedings. G.S. 122C-203. This presumably means that the fact of admission or commitment alone is not determinative in a guardianship proceeding under Chapter 35A, or former Chapters 33 or 35, of the General Statutes. The underlying facts regarding the respondent's symptoms or behavior may be admissible, however, if relevant to the incompetency proceeding. For an in-depth treatment of incompetency proceedings, see JOHN L. SAXON, NORTH CAROLINA GUARDIANSHIP MANUAL (UNC School of Government 2008), *available at* www.ncids.org (under reference manuals).

B. Voluntary Admission Not Admissible in Involuntary Proceeding

The voluntary admission for treatment of mental illness "shall not be competent evidence in an involuntary commitment proceeding." G.S. 122C-208. There is a statutory exception for use of evidence of "treatment history" in an involuntary *outpatient* proceeding. *Id.* Presumably, the respondent's underlying symptoms and behavior may be admissible if relevant.

Chapter 11
Admission for Mental Health Treatment Pursuant to Advance Instruction or Health Care Power of Attorney

11.1 Overview

The statute provides that an "incapable person" may be admitted to a 24-hour facility for mental health treatment pursuant to advance instruction or by consent of the health care agent appointed pursuant to a health care power of attorney. There is no judicial review of these admissions because they are authorized by the actions of the principal by execution of the documents. The documents must be duly executed pursuant to statute and must authorize the admission.

Special Counsel and other attorneys may receive calls and questions concerning persons so admitted. As the questions often concern the legal propriety of the admission and whether the person's due process rights are being violated, it is important for counsel to be familiar with these procedures.

11.2 Terminology Used in this Chapter

"Advance instruction for mental health treatment" or "advance instruction" is "a written instrument, signed in the presence of two qualified witnesses who believe the principal to be of sound mind at the time of the signing, and acknowledged before a notary public, pursuant to which the principal makes a declaration of instructions, information, and preferences regarding the principal's mental health treatment and states that the principal is aware that the advance instruction authorizes a mental health treatment provider to act according to the instruction. It may also state the principal's instructions regarding, but not limited to, consent to or refusal of mental health treatment when the principal is incapable." N.C. Gen. Stat. § 122C-72(1) (hereinafter G.S.).

"Health care" is "[a]ny care, treatment, service, or procedure to maintain, diagnose, treat, or provide for the principal's physical or mental health or personal care and comfort including life-prolonging measures. 'Health care' includes mental health treatment as defined in [G.S. 32A-16(8)]." G.S. 32A-16(1a).

"Health care agent" is "[t]he person appointed as a health care attorney-in-fact." G.S. 32A-16(2).

"Health care power of attorney" is "[a] written instrument that substantially meets the requirements of this Article, that is signed in the presence of two qualified witnesses, and acknowledged before a notary public, pursuant to which an attorney-in-fact or agent is appointed to act for the principal in matters relating to the health care of the principal." G.S. 32A-16(3).

"Incapable" means that "in the opinion of a physician or eligible psychologist, the person currently lacks sufficient understanding or capacity to make and communicate mental health treatment decisions." G.S. 122C-72(4).

"Mental health treatment" is "the process of providing for the physical, emotional, psychological, and social needs of the principal for the principal's mental illness. 'Mental health treatment' includes, but is not limited to, electroconvulsive treatment . . . , treatment of mental illness with psychotropic medication, and admission to and retention in a facility for care or treatment of mental illness." G.S. 122C-72(5). A nearly identical definition for "mental health treatment" is found in G.S. 32A-16(8).

"Principal" is "[t]he person making the health care power of attorney" (G.S. 32A-16(5)) or "the person making the advance instruction." G.S. 122C-72(6).

11.3 Admission Pursuant to Advance Instruction

A. Public Policy

Statutory provisions govern advance instruction for mental health treatment. G.S. 122C-71 through 122C-77. The statutes codify as public policy a person's right to control decisions concerning mental health care. *See* G.S. 122C-71. Advance instruction could be particularly helpful for a person with a cyclical illness, characterized by periods of remission followed by relapse.

B. Criteria

The individual must be "of sound mind" at the time the advance instruction is signed, witnessed, and notarized. G.S. 122C-72(1). The advance instruction is employed, however, only when a physician or eligible psychologist determines that the person has become "incapable." G.S. 122C-74(d).

C. Revocation and Effectiveness

The advance instruction is revocable at any time that the person is not "incapable," by any manner that communicates the intent to revoke. G.S. 122C-74(j). The statute also directs the treatment provider to continue to obtain informed consent so long as the person is "capable." G.S. 122C-74(e).

It is easily foreseeable that a person who previously consented to treatment by advance instruction, but who now refuses the treatment, may state the intention to revoke the advance instruction. In that case, the treatment provider must determine whether the person has capacity to refuse the treatment or is incapable and must receive the treatment previously consented to by advance instruction.

D. Limitation on Inpatient Admission

An admission to a 24-hour facility pursuant to advance instruction may not exceed ten days, subject to the facility's right to hold the person up to seventy-two hours to pursue involuntary commitment. G.S. 122C-211(f1); *see also* G.S. 122C-77 (statutory form).

E. Statutory Form

Chapter 122C of the North Carolina General Statutes provides a statutory form for advance instruction for mental health treatment. *See* G.S. 122C-77. The statute states that an otherwise valid advance instruction executed prior to January 1, 1999, is not to be construed as invalid. G.S. 122C-77(a). Use of the statutory form is not required as long as the advance instruction conforms with the statutory requirements for an advance instruction.

11.4 Admission Pursuant to Health Care Power of Attorney

A. Public Policy

Chapter 32A, Article 3 of the North Carolina General Statutes contains statutory provisions governing health care powers of attorney. A health care power of attorney is an alternative means for an individual to control decisions regarding medical care, including mental health treatment, through the appointment of an agent to make these decisions during any period of incapacity of the principal. G.S. 32A-15(a), (b), 32A-20(a).

B. Definition of "Legally Responsible Person"

The "legally responsible person" for an "incapable" adult who has not been adjudicated incompetent is the "health care agent named pursuant to a valid health care power of attorney" pursuant to Chapter 32A of the General Statutes. G.S. 122C-3(20). An "incapable" person is one who "in the opinion of a physician or eligible psychologist, . . . currently lacks sufficient understanding or capacity to make and communicate mental health treatment decisions." G.S. 122C-72(4).

C. Criteria for Execution

The principal must sign a written instrument in the presence of two qualified witnesses. G.S. 32A-16(3). A "qualified witness" is a person who observes the signing of the health care power of attorney and "who believes the principal to be of sound mind." G.S. 32A-16(6). The statute contains specific provisions concerning who can and cannot serve as a qualified witness. *Id.*

D. Effectiveness of Power of Attorney

The health care power of attorney contains a provision for the principal to designate a physician or eligible psychologist for mental health treatment, who will "determine in writing that the principal lacks sufficient understanding or capacity to make or communicate decisions relating to the health care of the principal." G.S. 32A-20(a). The statute also provides that if the principal does not designate a physician "based on his religious or moral beliefs as specified in the health care power of attorney," any competent adult designated by the principal may make the capacity decision in writing. *Id.*

E. Revocation

The health care power of attorney is revoked by "any . . . manner by which the principal is able to communicate an intent to revoke" or by the death of the principal. G.S. 32A-20(b). Additionally, the appointment of a health care agent who is a spouse of a principal is automatically revoked upon separation or divorce. A successor agent then serves, if designated; the entire instrument is otherwise considered revoked. G.S. 32A-20(c).

F. Powers Conferred

The statute allows the principal to confer a broad range of powers to the agent in making health care treatment decisions. For mental health treatment, the agent may make decisions, including but not limited to "electroconvulsive treatment, . . . psychotropic medication, and admission to and retention in a facility for care or treatment of mental illness." G.S. 32A-19(a), 32A-16(8). The agent is to make decisions consistent with any advance instruction or in accord with what the agent believes the person would do if able to make and communicate the decision. G.S. 32A-19(a1). This is in contrast with the statutory requirement that a general guardian or guardian of the person substitute the *guardian's* judgment for that of the ward's. G.S. 35A-1241(a)(3).

The statutory form provides space for the principal to designate limitations on the powers conferred. *See* G.S. 32A-25.1. This provision is especially important because, unlike the statutory limitation on days of admission to 24-hour facilities pursuant to advance instruction, there is no limitation on such an admission under a health care power of attorney.

G. Health Care Power of Attorney and Living Will

In the event a person has executed both a health care power of attorney and an "Advance Directive for a Natural Death," commonly called a living will, the provisions of the living will take precedence over the health care power of attorney if an end-of-life issue arises. *See* G.S. 32A-15(c), 90-321.

H. Statutory Form

G.S. 32A-25.1 includes a form complying with the requirements of the statutes for a valid health care power of attorney, although use of the form is not required as long as the health care power of attorney conforms with the statutory requirements.

Chapter 12
Advising Clients on Collateral Matters and Consequences of Commitment

12.1 Overview

Immediate collateral consequences result from an order for involuntary commitment. In addition to the restrictions on personal liberty inherent in the involuntary commitment process, other restrictions on personal rights and freedoms may be experienced during the term of commitment or admission. Some of the most serious and long-lasting consequences may only affect the respondent many months after release or discharge from the facility. This chapter will explore some of the more serious consequences of commitment or admission both during the inpatient stay and after discharge or release.

12.2 Terminology Used in this Chapter

"Client" is "an individual who is admitted to and receiving service from, or who in the past had been admitted to and received services from, a facility." N.C. GEN. STAT. § 122C-3(6) (hereinafter G.S.).

"Client advocate" is "a person whose role is to monitor the protection of client rights or to act as an individual advocate on behalf of a particular client in a facility." G.S. 122C-3(7).

"Human rights committees" are "responsible for protecting the rights of clients . . . at each State facility, for each local management entity, and provider agency." G.S. 122C-64.B.

"Qualified professional" is the "individual with appropriate training or experience as specified by the General Statutes or by rule of the Commission in the fields of mental health or developmental disabilities or substance abuse treatment or habilitation, including physicians, psychologists, psychological associates, educators, social workers, registered nurses, certified fee-based practicing pastoral counselors, and certified counselors." G.S. 122C-3(31).

12.3 Firearm Ownership and Possession

Generally. The right to keep and bear arms is guaranteed by the Second Amendment to the U.S. Constitution. The Federal Gun Control Act contains provisions prohibiting the ownership or possession of a firearm by certain persons because they have been committed or have been adjudicated as a "mental defective." The federal statute provides:

> "It shall be unlawful for any person—
> . . . .
> (4) who has been adjudicated as a mental defective or who has been committed to a mental institution;
> . . . .
> to ship or transport in interstate or foreign commerce, or possess in or affecting commerce, any firearm or ammunition; or to receive any firearm or ammunition which has been shipped or transported in interstate or foreign commerce."

18 U.S.C. § 922(g).

The statute prohibits not only gun ownership but also possession by certain people. Involuntarily committed adults fall under the statutory definition.

Interplay of federal and state law. The National Instant Criminal Background Check System (NICS) is the mechanism by which North Carolina notifies federal authorities of involuntary mental health commitments subject to the Federal Gun Control Act. NICS was established by the Brady Handgun Violence Prevention Act, Public Law 103-159, 107 Stat. 1536 (1993), and it is maintained by the FBI pursuant to 28 C.F.R. § 25.3. Local law enforcement agencies access NICS through their National Crime Information Center (NCIC) terminal to determine an individual's status.

The North Carolina General Assembly created an exception to the confidentiality ordinarily required for involuntary commitment records to allow the clerk of superior court to notify NICS of any individual who is involuntarily committed and found to be a danger to self or others or any individual who is acquitted by reason of insanity or who is found incapable of proceeding to trial on a criminal charge (apparently without regard to whether the crime alleged is violent or nonviolent). G.S. 122C-54(d1). This statute does not require reporting to NICS of a commitment for substance abuse treatment. In North Carolina, individuals who are involuntary committed for mental health reasons and who therefore must be reported to NICS under North Carolina law are prohibited from purchasing, possessing, or transferring a firearm and, pursuant to 18 U.S.C. § 922(g), are subject to federal punishment, including imprisonment, for a violation. *See* 18 U.S.C. § 924. If reported to NICS, an individual who satisfies the conditions in G.S. 122C-54.1 may petition a state court for removal of the firearm bar. *See infra* Appendix A, Form AOC-SP-211.

Under North Carolina statutory and case law, it appears that an adult's Second Amendment Rights become restricted following a mental health commitment and the clerk's submission of a report to NICS. G.S. 122C-54(d1) (describing circumstances in which the state notifies federal authorities of commitment); *see also Waldron v. Batten,* 191 N.C. App. 237 (2008) (holding under G.S. 14-404(c), which prohibits handgun permits to be issued to those who have been "adjudicated mentally incompetent" or "committed to any mental institution," that a petition, custody order, first evaluation, and admission to a 24-hour facility did not constitute commitment to a mental institution and did not disqualify the petitioner from obtaining a handgun permit). Therefore, a respondent who changes his status to voluntary prior to an involuntary commitment, or a respondent who is released before the hearing on involuntary commitment, might not be subject to operation of the federal statute because in those circumstances the clerk is not required to submit a report to NICS.

The dilemma for the respondent's counsel is that NICS reporting does not finally determine whether federal authorities may charge under the federal statute. Counsel cannot assure a respondent that G.S. 122C-54 provides any limitation to federal action. The federal statute restricts the gun rights of an individual "committed" to an institution or adjudicated as a "mental defective." Federal authorities may pursue respondents under either definition.

Thus, respondents may be exposed to criminal liability under the federal statute as a result of ever having been involved in the involuntary commitment process. Many psychiatric "commitments" predate the relatively new North Carolina reporting statute. It is likely that a respondent who has been adjudicated incompetent and in need of a guardian is "mentally defective" under the federal statute. Unlike North Carolina's reporting statute, the federal statute presumably encompasses substance abuse commitments as well. In the federal sense, the term "committed" also has been determined to include outpatient commitments. *See U.S. v. B.H.,* 466 F. Supp. 2d 1139 (N.D. Iowa 2006). Although unlikely, even a magistrate's determination of mental illness and dangerousness might be alleged as an adjudication of mental defect.

Whether there is a restriction on the gun rights of minors who suffer commitment or admission to a psychiatric facility is even more complex. The previous discussion applies. However, a juvenile may petition for the expunction of commitment records once the juvenile reaches eighteen years of age. What is the effect of an expunction on the application of the federal statute? Again, there are no definite answers, although it would appear that expunction is not effective to prevent application of the federal statute. *See* Appendix 12-1, E-mail from David C. Lieberman, Assoc. Chief Counsel (Southeast), Bureau of Alcohol, Tobacco, Firearms & Explosives, U.S. Dep't of Justice, to John Aldridge, Special Deputy Attorney Gen., Law Enforcement Liaison Section, N.C. Dep't of Justice (Sept. 7, 2010). Counsel should therefore inform all of these clients of the federal law and its possible application.

Practical concerns. The ability to own or possess a firearm can be important for a number of reasons. Military service and law enforcement are two of a number of professions that require the ability to legally own and possess a firearm. Many people also enjoy hunting, recreational shooting, and gun collecting, while others desire to keep a firearm for personal safety.

Counsel may advise a client who has not been previously committed of the options to sign in as a voluntary patient if a competent adult or to continue the case pending discharge as ways to lessen the potential for being found to be "committed to a mental institution" under the federal statutes. The lack of clarity and the importance of complying with the federal statutes should be emphasized. Counsel should advise the respondent to consult with an attorney outside the hospital if there is an issue of possessing a firearm, obtaining a permit to own a firearm, or keeping a firearm pursuant to an existing permit. The respondent may want to discuss with outside counsel the possibility of relief under G.S. 122C-54.1 from the federal firearm prohibition under the facts of the respondent's case.

Other resources. A further discussion of relevant federal statutes and regulations and state statutes, as well as a review of case law interpreting 18 U.S.C. § 922(g)(4), is contained in a paper entitled "Involuntary Commitment and the Federal Gun Control Act," presented at the Second Annual Civil Commitment Conference (Jan. 23, 2004). The paper is reprinted *infra* in Appendix D. Counsel is referred to this Appendix for additional information concerning the Federal Gun Control Act, particularly section D, "Advising Your Client." *See also* FIREARMS PROGRAMS DIVISION, BUREAU OF ALCOHOL, TOBACCO, FIREARMS AND EXPLOSIVES, FEDERAL FIREARMS REGULATIONS REFERENCE GUIDE, ATF PUB.

No. 5300.4 (2005), *available at* www.atf.gov/publications/download/p/atf-p-5300-4.pdf.

12.4 Driving Privileges

Report of involuntary substance abuse commitment to DMV. The North Carolina General Statutes provide that the clerk of court of the county of adjudication must report to the Commissioner of the Division of Motor Vehicles (DMV) "[i]f any person shall be adjudicated as incompetent or is involuntarily committed for the treatment of alcoholism or drug addiction." G.S. 20-17.1(b).

Determination by DMV. The statute requires the Commissioner to "make inquiry into the facts for the purpose of determining whether such person is competent to operate a motor vehicle." G.S. 20-17(a). The driving privileges of the person must be revoked unless the Commissioner is "satisfied that such person is competent to operate a motor vehicle with safety to persons and property." *Id.* There are provisions for appeal of the revocation of driving privileges to the Commissioner, with the "right to a review by the review board . . . upon written request filed with the Division." *Id.*

Medical report form. The DMV may require a medical evaluation as part of a review of a person's driving privileges. The DMV has developed a Medical Report Form to be filled out by the physician performing the evaluation. Failure to obtain an evaluation and to return the medical report to the DMV can lead to revocation of driving privileges.

Advising the client. A client facing involuntary commitment for substance abuse treatment should be advised of the possible loss of driving privileges. After involuntary substance abuse commitment, the client may receive a notice of a review by the DMV along with a request to obtain a medical evaluation. In some instances, however, driving privileges have reportedly been revoked by the DMV upon receipt of the notice of substance abuse commitment. The client must then appeal and present evidence of the ability to drive safely. Attorney representation is not required but may be important in prevailing on appeal. Counsel should advise the client that representation on issues related to driving would have to be obtained from a privately-retained attorney.

Because the ability to drive legally can be essential for transportation to work and for independent living, this issue should be stressed to the client. Possible approaches that may avoid the issue are signing in as a voluntary patient, agreeing to an involuntary mental health commitment, and continuing the case from week to week while inpatient treatment is received, followed by either voluntary outpatient treatment or involuntary mental health outpatient commitment, if recommended.

12.5   Restrictions on Patient Rights

Generally. Some statutory rights of patients in an inpatient facility may be limited or restricted under certain prescribed conditions. When discussing an upcoming commitment hearing, counsel may decide not to discuss these rights and the conditions under which they may be limited or restricted unless the client asks about them. The information may be confusing and may divert the client's attention from the issues and decisions to be made in regard to the commitment hearing.

The client more often will contact counsel after a limitation or restriction is imposed. Counsel will need to review the client's patient records, talk with the client, and talk with the appropriate qualified professionals to determine if the limitation or restriction is within the statutory guidelines. If it is not, counsel should talk with the attending physician, the client advocate, or other appropriate persons to address the violation of rights. At state psychiatric hospitals, the violation may be reported to the Human Rights Committee if resolution cannot be reached.

If the restriction or limitation is allowed by statute, counsel should discuss further with the client the circumstances surrounding the limitation or restriction of rights. If the limitation or restriction appears to have been properly imposed, counsel should explain to the client the requirements of the statutes and discuss, perhaps in conjunction with the treatment team, a plan for the client to work toward easing or eliminating the limitation or restriction of a statutory right.

The statutory rights discussed below may be restricted or limited as prescribed by statute. Non-restrictable rights are not included in this discussion.

Forced medication of involuntary patients. Treatment, except for that requiring express written consent, may be given to a person under involuntary commitment in some circumstances despite the refusal of the client, the client's legally responsible person, the health care agent named pursuant to a valid health care power of attorney, or a valid advance instruction. Treatment may be forcibly administered

> "in the event of an emergency or when consideration of side effects related to the specific treatment measure is given and in the professional judgment, as documented in the client's record, of the treating physician and a second physician, who is either the director of clinical services of the facility, or the director's designee, either:
>
> (1)   The client, without the benefit of the specific treatment measure, is incapable of participating in any available treatment plan which will give the client a realistic opportunity of improving the client's condition;

(2) There is, without the benefit of the specific treatment measure, a significant possibility that the client will harm self or others before improvement of the client's condition is realized."

G.S. 122C-57(e).

The following treatment cannot be given without the express written consent of a competent, capable client: electroshock therapy; experimental drugs or procedures; or surgery other than emergency surgery. G.S. 122C-57(f).

Physical restraint or seclusion. A client, however committed or admitted, may be physically restrained or secluded "only when there is imminent danger of abuse or injury to the client or others, when substantial property damage is occurring, or when the restraint or seclusion is necessary as a measure of therapeutic treatment." G.S. 122C-60(a).

Restrictable rights of adults. Certain rights of adult clients enumerated by statute may be limited or restricted by a qualified professional. These are the right to: make and receive confidential telephone calls; receive visitors during times specified by statute; meet by mutual consent with others under appropriate supervision; make visits outside the facility unless committed or admitted in regard to certain criminal proceedings; be outside and have access to exercise facilities several times a week; keep and use personal clothing and possessions legally permitted, unless the person is being held to determine capacity to proceed in criminal court; participate in religious worship; keep and spend a reasonable sum of money; retain a driver's license, unless otherwise prohibited by Chapter 20 of the North Carolina General Statutes (*see supra* § 12.4); and have personal storage space for private use. G.S. 122C-62(b).

The qualified professional responsible for the client's treatment plan must write in the client's record detailed reasons for the restriction or limitation. The restrictions must be reasonable and related to the client's treatment needs. They shall be effective for no more than thirty days and must be reviewed every seven days, but may be renewed by written statement of the qualified professional in the client's record. G.S. 122C-62(e).

Restrictable rights of minors. Certain rights of minors enumerated by statute may be limited or restricted by a qualified professional. These are the right to: make and receive telephone calls; send and receive mail and have access to writing materials, postage, and staff assistance when necessary; receive visitors at times specified by statute under appropriate supervision; receive special education and vocational training in accordance with federal and state law; be outside daily and participate in play, recreation, and physical exercise on a regular basis; keep and use personal clothing and possessions legally permitted, unless the person is being held to determine capacity to proceed in criminal court; participate in religious worship; have individual storage space; keep and spend a reasonable sum of money; and retain a driver's license, unless otherwise prohibited by Chapter 20 of the North Carolina General Statutes (*see supra* § 12.4). G.S. 122C-62(d).

The qualified professional responsible for the client's treatment plan must write in the client's record the detailed reasons for the restriction or limitation. The restrictions must be reasonable and related to the client's treatment needs. They shall be effective for no more than thirty days and must be reviewed every seven days, but may be renewed by written statement of the qualified professional in the client's record. G.S. 122C-62(e).

12.6 Expunction of Minors' Records of Admission and Commitment

Court records regarding an admission or commitment of a minor may be expunged after the minor has "both been released and reached adulthood." G.S. 122C-54(e). The request may be made by the individual admitted or committed or by the individual's legally responsible person. *Id.* The records of the admission and commitment of minors are confidential special proceedings records maintained by the clerk of court. Records may be maintained in separate counties if petitions were filed or treatment was received in more than one county.

The statute provides that the minor and the legally responsible person "shall be informed in writing by the court of the right provided by this subsection at the time that the application for admission is filed with the court." *Id.* Because application for voluntary admission may be made at the facility or a petition for involuntary commitment may be filed by someone other than the legally responsible person without the minor being present, it is uncertain whether this notice is being accomplished. Counsel should advise minor clients of the right to have the court records expunged (erased), and to seek assistance of the clerk of court to do so after being released and reaching the age of eighteen.

12.7 Civil Rights and Remedies

The statute states that, unless otherwise provided,

> "each adult client of a facility keeps the same right as any other citizen of North Carolina to exercise all civil rights, including the right to dispose of property, execute instruments, make purchases, enter into contractual relationships, register and vote, bring civil actions, and marry and get a divorce, unless the exercise of a civil right has been precluded by an unrevoked adjudication of incompetency. This section shall not be construed as validating the act of any client who was in fact incompetent at the time he performed the act."

G.S. 122C-58.

Clients often have legal issues that are beyond the scope of counsel's representation for the admission or commitment. Counsel should advise the client of the need to seek separate counsel for these issues. Special Counsel is not allowed to engage in the private practice of law. G.S. 122C-270(a). Representation by appointed counsel on other legal issues could lead to confusion concerning the attorney's role with both the client and the treatment provider.

Appendix 12-1
Involuntary Commitments and Federal Firearms Disabilities[*]

From: Lieberman, David C.
Sent: Tuesday, September 07, 2010 3:53 PM
To: Aldridge, John
Subject: RE: involuntary commitments

John, per our phone call and e-mails, I have finished my review of this issue. For your information, I have also run my response by an attorney in ATF HQ who has dealt with similar issues in the past and am advised that HQ concurs with this response. I apologize for the length of this e-mail, but I decided to make it fairly detailed in case you are questioned about this issue in the future.

The question you presented is whether a person who has the record of his or her juvenile involuntary commitment expunged under N.C. Gen. Stat. § 122C-54(e) is subject to Federal firearms disabilities under the Gun Control Act of 1968 (GCA), as amended, 18 U.S.C. Chapter 44. The brief answer is that such an expungement does not remove the disability.

As you know, the GCA makes it "unlawful for any person - who has been adjudicated as a mental defective or who has been committed to a mental institution . . . to ship or transport in interstate or foreign commerce, or possess in or affecting commerce, any firearm or ammunition; or to receive any firearm or ammunition which has been shipped or transported in interstate or foreign commerce." 18 U.S.C. § 922(g)(4).

While the GCA does not define the term "committed to a mental institution," the implementing regulations define the term to mean a "formal commitment of a person to a mental institution by a court, board, commission or other lawful authority. The term includes a commitment to a mental institution involuntarily. The term includes commitment for mental defectiveness or mental illness. It also includes commitments for other reasons, such as drug use. The term does not include a person in a mental institution for observation or a voluntary admission to a mental institution." 27 C.F.R. § 478.11.

As an initial matter, it is clear that a person who has been involuntarily committed as a juvenile under North Carolina law falls within the definition of someone who has been "committed to a mental institution," as the commitment comes after a hearing in front of a State district court judge. As a result, the person would be subject to the Federal firearms disabilities imposed by 18 U.S.C. § 922(g)(4).

---

[*] David C. Lieberman is Associate Chief Counsel (Southeast), Bureau of Alcohol, Tobacco, Firearms and Explosives, U.S. Department of Justice. John Aldridge is Special Deputy Attorney General, Law Enforcement Liaison Section, N.C. Department of Justice.

In determining whether a subsequent expungement under section 122C-54(e) serves to remove that disability, I reviewed both the GCA and the NICS Improvement Amendments Act of 2007 (NIAA), Pub. L. No. 110-108. For your information, the NIAA provides that a State may set up relief from disabilities programs for persons previously committed to a mental institution as described in the GCA. As set forth below, my opinion is that such an expungement does not remove the firearms disability.

In this regard, while the GCA provides that what constitutes a conviction of a "crime punishable by imprisonment for a term exceeding one year" does not include any conviction "which has been expunged, or set aside, or for which a person has been pardoned or has had civil rights restored," 18 U.S.C. § 921(a)(20), there is no similar language in the definition of the term "committed to a mental institution." Similarly, while the language of the NIAA refers to "relief from disabilities" it does not include language about "expunged" commitments. So, under strict construction principles, it does not appear that a subsequently expunged involuntary commitment such as one addressed in N.C. Gen. Stat. § 122C-54(e) relieves a person of the Federal firearms disabilities contained in 18 U.S.C. § 922(g)(4). Had Congress intended to exclude "expunged" commitments, it would have done so in the NIAA, since it was aware that a person with an expunged conviction was no longer subject to the firearms prohibitions contained in the GCA. Finally, I note that section 122C-54 does not set forth a legal standard for issuance of the expungement. While it is arguable that existence of a statutory standard for granting expungement would make the process more like the relief process envisioned in the NIAA, the lack of such a standard at the present time makes such analysis impossible. Thus, a person who has his or her juvenile commitment expunged under N.C. Gen. Stat. § 122C-54(e) is still subject to Federal firearms disabilities.

Appendix A
Forms

Administrative Office of the Courts (AOC) Forms[*]

AOC-SP-203   Involuntary Commitment Order Mentally Ill

AOC-SP-205   Order to Appear at Supplemental Hearing for Involuntary Commitment

AOC-SP-206   Order Supplemental Hearing on Involuntary Commitment

AOC-SP-210   Petition and Appointment of Defense Counsel for Committed Respondent Charged with Violent Crime

AOC-SP-211   Petition and Order for Removal of a Mental Commitment Bar to Purchase, Possess or Transfer a Firearm

AOC-SP-220   Request for Transportation Order and Order (Outpatient Fails but Does Not Clearly Refuse to Comply with Treatment)

AOC-SP-221   Request for Supplemental Hearing (Outpatient Clearly Refuses to Comply with Treatment)

AOC-SP-222   Notice of Need for Transportation Order and Order (From One 24-Hour Facility to Another)

AOC-SP-223   Request for Transportation Order and Order (Committed Substance Abuser Fails to Comply with Treatment or Is Discharged from 24-Hour Facility)

AOC-SP-224   Request for Transportation Order and Order (Outpatient Fails to Appear for Prehearing Examination)

AOC-SP-300   Affidavit and Petition for Involuntary Commitment

AOC-SP-301   Notice of Hearing/Rehearing for Involuntary Commitment

AOC-SP-302   Findings and Custody Order Involuntary Commitment

---

[*] AOC forms are available on the North Carolina Judicial Department website, www.nccourts.org, under "Forms."

AOC-SP-304	Involuntary Commitment Custody Order Defendant Found Incapable to Proceed
AOC-SP-305	Findings and Order Involuntary Commitment Physician-Petitioner Recommends Outpatient Commitment
AOC-SP-306	Order Involuntary Commitment Proceedings Substance Abuser
AOC-SP-350	Appellate Entries Involuntary Commitment
AOC-SP-902M	Request and Authorization to Deliver Respondent
AOC-SP-904M	Outpatient Commitment Order of Assignment or Denial of Counsel
AOC-SP-909M	Petition and Custody Order for Special Emergency Substance Abuse Involuntary Commitment
AOC-SP-910M	Automatic Involuntary Commitment of Defendant Found Not Guilty by Reason of Insanity
AOC-SP-912M	Appointment of Counsel and Notice of Hearing/Rehearing Voluntary Admission of Minor
AOC-SP-913M	Order Voluntary Admission of Minor
AOC-SP-914M	Release of Physical and Mental Health, Substance Abuse and Confidential Court Records for Concealed Handgun Permit

Department of Health and Human Services, Division of Mental Health, Developmental Disabilities, and Substance Abuse Services (DMH) Forms[*]

DMH 5-72-01	Examination and Recommendation to Determine Necessity for Involuntary Commitment (under link for DMH 5-72-09 on Department of Health and Human Services website)
DMH 5-72-01-A	Supplement to Examination and Recommendation for Involuntary Commitment: Certificate to Support Immediate Hospitalization
DMH 5-72-01-B	Supplement to Examination and Recommendation for Involuntary Commitment: Certificate to Support Immediate Hospitalization

---

[*] DMH forms are available on the Department of Health and Human Services website, www.ncdhhs.gov/mhddsas/statspublications/manualsforms/#forms, under "Legal Forms for Hospitals."

DMH 5-73-01   Evaluation for Admission/Continued Stay (Restrictive 24-hour
                Facilities) Voluntary Minors and Incompetent Adults

DMH 5-76-01   Request for Hearing

DMH 5-79-01   Notice of Commitment Change

DMH 5-82-02   Request to Return Escapee or Conditional Release

DMH 5-83-01   Notice of Return of Escapee or Conditional Release

	File No.
STATE OF NORTH CAROLINA	
_____ County	In The General Court Of Justice District Court Division

IN THE MATTER OF:	
Name Of Respondent	**INVOLUNTARY COMMITMENT ORDER** **MENTALLY ILL** G.S. 122C-267, 122C-268, 122C-271

FINDINGS

The Court finds that:

1. The petitioner ☐ was ☐ was not represented by counsel. The respondent ☐ was ☐ was not represented by counsel.

Based on the evidence presented, the Court

☐ 2. by clear, cogent and convincing evidence finds as facts all matters set out in the physician's/eligible psychologist's report, specified below, and the report is incorporated by reference as findings.

Date Of Last Examiner's Report	Name Of Physician/Eligible Psychologist

☐ 3. by clear, cogent and convincing evidence finds these other facts:

☐ 4. finds that the respondent does not meet the criteria for commitment.

☐ 5. finds that this proceeding was begun after the respondent was charged with a violent crime and was found incapable of proceeding.

CONCLUSIONS

Based on the above findings, the Court concludes that the respondent:

☐ 1. is mentally ill.

☐ 2. is not mentally ill.

☐ 3. in addition to being mentally ill, is mentally retarded.

☐ 4. is dangerous ☐ to self ☐ others.

☐ 5. is not dangerous to self or others.

☐ 6. _(only for nondangerous mentally ill)_ is capable of surviving safely in the community with available supervision from family, friends or others; and based on respondent's psychiatric history, the respondent is in need of treatment in order to prevent further disability and deterioration which would predictably result in dangerousness to self or others. And, that the respondent's inability to make an informed decision to voluntarily seek and comply with recommended treatment is caused by:
   ☐ the respondent's current mental status.
   ☐ the nature of the respondent's mental illness.

NOTE: _Use AOC-SP-911M for involuntary commitment of defendant found not guilty by reason of insanity._

AOC-SP-203, Rev. 1/97
© 1997 Administrative Office of the Courts   See ORDER on reverse

ORDER

It is ORDERED that:

☐ 1. the respondent be committed/recommitted to the inpatient 24-hour facility named below for the period specified.

☐ 2. the respondent be committed/recommitted to outpatient commitment under the supervision and management of the center/physician named below for the period specified.

    ☐ the respondent may be held at the 24-hour facility where he/she is now being held, for up to 72 hours in order for the facility to notify the designated outpatient center of respondent's treatment needs.

☐ 3. the respondent be committed/recommitted to an inpatient 24-hour facility named below not to exceed the specified period. Following discharge from the 24-hour facility, the respondent shall be committed to outpatient commitment under the supervision of the center/physician named below for the specified period.

☐ 4. the respondent be discharged and this matter dismissed.

☐ 5. the respondent be discharged. Since the respondent was charged with a violent crime and found incapable of proceeding, it is further ordered that the respondent be released to the custody of the law enforcement agency named below.

Name Of Law Enforcement Agency

☐ 6. this matter be transferred to the county named below for further proceedings.

County

INPATIENT COMMITMENT	OUTPATIENT COMMITMENT
Committed/recommitted to inpatient facility for a period not to exceed	Committed/recommitted to outpatient facility for a period not to exceed

INPATIENT COMMITMENT

☐ _____ days.   ☐ 90 days.

☐ 180 days.   ☐ 1 year.

Name And Address Of 24-Hour Facility

OUTPATIENT COMMITMENT

☐ _____ days.   ☐ 90 days.   ☐ 180 days.

Name And Address Of Treatment Center/Physician

Date

Signature Of District Court Judge

Name Of District Judge (Type Or Print)

STATE OF NORTH CAROLINA

_____ County

File No. _____

In The General Court Of Justice
District Court Division

IN THE MATTER OF:

Name And Address Of Respondent

ORDER TO APPEAR
AT SUPPLEMENTAL HEARING
FOR INVOLUNTARY COMMITMENT

G.S. 122C-274, -277, -290, -291

ORDER TO RESPONDENT NAMED ABOVE

You are now under a commitment order.

☐ 1. It has been alleged that you have clearly refused to comply with the treatment prescribed for you under an outpatient commitment order.

☐ 2. It has been alleged that you intend to move to another county within the State of North Carolina and are in need of further treatment at your new residence.

☐ 3. You have been committed as a substance abuser, and it has been alleged that you need to be held in a 24-hour facility for longer than forty-five (45) consecutive days.

☐ 4. You have been committed after being charged with a violent crime and were found not guilty by reason of insanity or incapable of proceeding. The physician now treating you has determined that you do not need further treatment, but you may not be released without a hearing.

☐ 5. The physician now treating you at the inpatient facility where you are being held has determined that you meet the criteria for outpatient commitment.

☐ 6. You have requested a hearing to determine whether you should be discharged.

You are ORDERED to appear before a district court judge at the date, time and location indicated below. At that hearing, it will be determined whether your commitment will be continued or modified, or whether you will be discharged.

At the hearing you will be allowed to present evidence. You may hire an attorney to represent you. If you cannot afford to hire an attorney and have been committed as a substance abuser, an attorney will be appointed for you. If you have been committed to outpatient commitment, you may ask the judge to appoint an attorney for you. Based on the facts in the particular case, the judge may appoint one for you.

Date Of Hearing	Time Of Hearing ☐ AM ☐ PM	Date	Signature
Location of Hearing		☐ Assistant CSC	☐ Clerk Of Superior Court

NOTE TO CLERK: *In addition to service on the respondent, this ORDER must be mailed to the petitioner (unless the petitioner waived his/her right to notice), the designated treatment center or physician and the respondent's counsel, if any, by first-class mail at least seventy-two (72) hours before the hearing. (If respondent was committed as a substance abuser, counsel appointed at the initial hearing remains responsible for representation.)*

TO PETITIONER-ATTORNEY-TREATMENT CENTER

This ORDER to the respondent is sent to you to give you notice of the hearing described above.

Name And Address Of Attorney For Respondent

Name And Address Of Petitioner

Name And Address Of Treatment Center Or Physician

NOTICE TO SHERIFF

This Notice must be served on the respondent personally at least seventy-two (72) hours before the hearing.

RETURN OF SERVICE

I certify that this Order was received and served on the respondent as follows:

Date Served	Time Served ☐ AM ☐ PM	Name Of Respondent

☐ By delivering to the respondent named above a copy of this Order.

☐ Respondent WAS NOT served for the following reason:

Date Received	Date Returned	Signature Of Deputy Sheriff Making Return
		Name Of Deputy Sheriff Making Return (Type Or Print)
		County Of Sheriff

CLERK'S CERTIFICATION OF SERVICE

I certify that I have mailed a copy of this Order to the following, whose names and addresses are shown on the front of this form:

☐ petitioner
☐ treatment center/physician
☐ respondent's attorney

Date	Signature	☐ Deputy CSC ☐ Assistant CSC ☐ Clerk Of Superior Court

STATE OF NORTH CAROLINA

_____ County

File No. _____

In The General Court Of Justice
District Court Division

IN THE MATTER OF:

Name And Address Of Respondent

**ORDER
SUPPLEMENTAL HEARING ON
INVOLUNTARY COMMITMENT**

G.S. 122C-274, -291

FINDINGS

Based on the evidence presented, the Court finds by clear, cogent and convincing evidence that the respondent is currently under an involuntary commitment order issued by the Court, on the date and for the period listed below, and that: _(check appropriate blocks)_

☐ 1. The respondent ☐ has ☐ has not complied with the prescribed treatment.

☐ 2. The respondent ☐ does ☐ does not meet the criteria for ☐ outpatient ☐ substance abuse commitment.

☐ 3. The respondent has been committed as a substance abuser and will be held in a 24-hour facility for longer than forty-five (45) consecutive days. Further treatment in a 24-hour facility ☐ is ☐ is not necessary.

☐ 4. The respondent intends to move to _____ County.

☐ 5. Other: _(Give specific findings of fact supporting each statement checked above.)_

Court Of Commitment	Date Of Commitment	Length Of Commitment In Days

AOC-SP-206, Rev. 3/02
© 2002 Administrative Office of the Courts

(See ORDER on reverse)

ORDER

It is ORDERED that:

☐ 1. respondent's commitment order be continued.

☐ 2. respondent's commitment order be modified as follows:

    ☐ a. respondent's treatment in a 24-hour facility be continued for not more than
       ☐ _____ days.   ☐ 90 days.

    ☐ b. respondent's substance abuse commitment order be continued, but respondent is ordered released from the 24-hour facility.

☐ 3. respondent be discharged and the case dismissed.

☐ 4. Other:

☐ 5. treatment center/physician named below is designated to be the new supervisor of the respondent and this matter is transferred to the county named below.

☐ 6. respondent appear at the treatment center or physician's office named below on or before the date designated.

Designated Treatment Center/Physician	Date By Which Respondent To Appear
Address	County To Which Matter Transferred
City, State, Zip	Signature Of District Court Judge
Telephone No.	Name Of District Court Judge (Type Or Print)

STATE OF NORTH CAROLINA

_____ County

Special Proceeding File No.

Criminal File No.

Additional File Nos.

In The General Court Of Justice
☐ District   ☐ Superior Court Division

STATE VERSUS

Name Of Defendant/Respondent

Social Security No.
[ ][ ] - [ ][ ] - [ ][ ][ ][ ]   ☐ Has No Social Security No.

State Mental Health Facility Where Defendant/Respondent Is Committed

PETITION AND APPOINTMENT OF DEFENSE COUNSEL FOR COMMITTED RESPONDENT CHARGED WITH VIOLENT CRIME

G.S. 7A-451; 15A-1008, -1009; 122C-261(c), -268, -268.1, -270(a)

INSTRUCTIONS: _Special Counsel at a state mental health facility completes Part I of this form to petition the Court for appointment of criminal defense counsel for a respondent who has been involuntarily committed after a finding of incapacity to proceed in a criminal case, and may be entitled to dismissal of the criminal charges pursuant to G.S. 15A-1008. The Court completes Part II of this form to assign or deny appointed counsel for the criminal case and completes AOC-CR-224. The Clerk records the criminal case appointment in the Automated Criminal Information System and provides a copy of the form to the appointed criminal defense attorney._

I. SPECIAL COUNSEL PETITION FOR APPOINTMENT OF DEFENSE COUNSEL

The above named defendant/respondent is charged in the above named county with the violent crime of _(specify offense)_
_____ , and was previously found by the Court to be incapable of proceeding to trial pursuant to G.S. 15A-1002 and involuntarily committed pursuant to G.S. 122C-268.

Upon information and belief, the defendant/respondent was previously found to be indigent and entitled to appointed counsel in the criminal case pursuant to G.S. 7A-450(a); was again found to be indigent pursuant to G.S. 122C-261(c) and -270(a), or refused to retain counsel in the commitment proceedings as provided in G.S. 122C-268(d) or -268.1(d); and has been committed since that time.

The criminal charge(s) identified above is still pending or has been dismissed with leave pursuant to G.S. 15A-1009.

The undersigned Special Counsel believes that _(check all that apply):_

☐ 1. The defendant/respondent will not gain capacity to proceed and the court may dismiss the criminal charge(s) pursuant to G.S. 15A-1008(1).

☐ 2. The defendant/respondent has been substantially deprived of his liberty for a period of time equal to or in excess of the maximum permissible period of confinement for the crime(s) charged and the court may dismiss the criminal charge(s) pursuant to G.S. 15A-1008(2).

☐ 3. The charge(s) identified above is a misdemeanor, 5 years have passed from the date of determination of incapacity to proceed in the case, and the court may dismiss the criminal charge(s) pursuant to G.S. 15A-1008(3).

☐ 4. The charge(s) identified above is a felony, 10 years have passed from the date of determination of incapacity to proceed in the case, and the court may dismiss the criminal charge(s) pursuant to G.S. 15A-1008(3).

I, the undersigned, am employed as Special Counsel at the above named state mental health facility and make application for appointment of a criminal defense attorney in the above named county to take appropriate action in the criminal case(s) pursuant to G.S. 15A-1008 and any other applicable provision of law.

Date	Signature Of Special Counsel	Name Of Special Counsel (Type Or Print)

II. ASSIGNMENT OR DENIAL OF COUNSEL

It appears to the Court that the above named defendant/respondent is charged in the above named county with a violent crime, which is a proceeding listed in G.S. 7A-451(a); and, after consideration of the prior indigency findings and involuntary commitment in this case, it is determined that the defendant/respondent:

☐ 1. is financially able to provide the necessary expenses of legal representation in the criminal case; it is ORDERED that the defendant/respondent is not an indigent and the petition is denied.

☐ 2. is **not** financially able to provide the necessary expenses of legal representation in the criminal case; it is ORDERED that the defendant/respondent is an indigent and is entitled to the services of counsel as contemplated by law, and that he/she shall be represented by: ☐ the attorney named below.   ☐ the public defender in this judicial district.

It is further ORDERED that the Clerk of Superior Court shall record this appointment of counsel in the Automated Criminal Information System.

Name Of Appointed Criminal Defense Attorney (If Applicable)	Next Court Date

Date	Signature Of Judge	Name Of Judge (Type Or Print)

STATE OF NORTH CAROLINA

_____ County

File No. _____

Originating Co. File No. _____

In The General Court Of Justice
District Court Division

IN THE MATTER OF:

Name And Current Mailing Address Of Petitioner

Race	Sex	Date Of Birth

PETITION AND ORDER FOR REMOVAL OF A MENTAL COMMITMENT BAR TO PURCHASE, POSSESS OR TRANSFER A FIREARM
G.S. 122C-54.1

Name And Address Of Attorney For Petitioner

NOTE TO PETITIONER:

1. _This petition must be filed in the district court of the county where you were the subject of the most recent judicial determination that either inpatient or outpatient treatment was appropriate or in the district of the county of your residence. If you were disqualified from firearm possession due to a comparable out-of-state mental commitment you must file your petition in the district court of your county of residence._
2. _Upon request, you must sign a release for the district attorney to receive your mental health records._
3. _You must serve a copy of this petition on the director of the inpatient and outpatient treatment facility, in-State or out-of-State, and the district attorney in your current county of residence._

I. PETITION

The petitioner named above hereby moves, pursuant to G.S. 122C-54.1, for the removal of the petitioner's mental commitment bar to purchase, possess, or transfer a firearm from the National Instant Criminal Background Check System, and in support of this petition states the following:

1. I am over the age of 18.
2. I am a resident of _____ County.
3. The most recent judicial determination that I needed ☐ inpatient ☐ outpatient treatment was made in _____ County, _(name of state)_ _____ .
4. I no longer suffer from the condition that resulted in my involuntary commitment for ☐ inpatient ☐ outpatient mental health treatment and no longer pose a danger to myself or others for purposes of the purchase, possession, or transfer of firearms pursuant to 18 U.S.C. § 922, G.S. 14-404, and G.S. 14-415.12.
5. My most recent ☐ inpatient ☐ outpatient mental commitment expired on _(date)_ _____ .
6. I was not committed for mental health treatment based on a finding of not guilty by reason of insanity.
☐ 7. _If applicable_, previously, I filed a petition in district court for the removal of the mental commitment bar under G.S. 122C-54.1, which was denied on _(date)_ _____ , in _(name of county)_ _____ .
☐ 8. _If applicable_, previously, I appealed the district court decision to the superior court on _(date)_ _____ , and my petition was denied. One year or more has passed since the date of the denial.

Date	Name Of Petitioner (Type Or Print)	Signature Of Petitioner

NOTE TO CLERK:

1. _Calendar the hearing for a session of district court when the court regularly hears commitment matters. (G.S. 122C-54.1(b)). If your county does not have a regular commitment hearing calendar, schedule the hearing before a district court judge at a time when the petition can be heard in a closed session of court._ **HEARING IS CONFIDENTIAL. DO NOT PLACE ON A REGULAR DISTRICT COURT CALENDAR.**
2. _Complete AOC-G-180 (Notice Of Hearing), attach a copy of this petition and send to the Petitioner and your District Attorney._

II. CERTIFICATE OF SERVICE: SERVICE ON DIRECTOR OF THE INPATIENT/OUTPATIENT TREATMENT FACILITY

I certify that a copy of this petition was served by:

☐ delivering a copy personally to the director of the inpatient/outpatient treatment facility that provided mental health treatment to me based on a judicial determination that I needed mental health treatment.
☐ depositing a copy of the enclosed in a postpaid properly addressed envelope in a post office or official depository under the exclusive care and custody of the U.S. Postal Service directed to the director of the inpatient/outpatient treatment facility that provided mental health treatment to me based on a judicial determination that I needed mental health treatment.
☐ leaving a copy with an employee at the office of the director of the inpatient/outpatient treatment facility that provided mental health treatment to me based on a judicial determination that I needed mental health treatment.

Name Of Person With Whom Copy Left (Type Or Print)

Date	Name (Type Or Print)	Signature

AOC-SP-211, Rev. 4/09
© 2009 Administrative Office of the Courts

III. CERTIFICATE OF SERVICE: SERVICE ON DISTRICT ATTORNEY

I certify that a copy of this petition was served by:

☐ delivering a copy personally to the district attorney of my county of residence.

☐ depositing a copy of the enclosed in a postpaid properly addressed envelope in a post office or official depository under the exclusive care and custody of the U.S. Postal Service directed to the district attorney of my county of residence.

☐ leaving a copy at the office of the district attorney of my county of residence.

Name Of Person With Whom Copy Left (Type Or Print)

Date	Name (Type Or Print)	Signature

IV. FINDINGS OF FACT

This matter was heard before the undersigned judge upon the petition of the person named on the reverse. Having considered the petition, and after hearing the evidence, the Court finds by a preponderance of the evidence that:

☐ 1. The petitioner is over the age of 18.

☐ 2. The petitioner is a resident of _____ County.

☐ 3. The petitioner's most recent judicial determination that the petitioner needed ☐ inpatient ☐ outpatient treatment was made in _____ County, *(name of state)* _____ .

☐ 4. The petitioner ☐ does ☐ does not continue to suffer from the condition that resulted in the petitioner's involuntary commitment for ☐ inpatient ☐ outpatient mental health treatment pursuant to Article 5 of Chapter 122C. *(State reasons; G.S. 122C-54.1(c) requires the court to make "specific findings of fact on which it bases its decision.")*

☐ 5. The petitioner ☐ does ☐ does not continue to pose a danger to himself/herself or others. *(State reasons; G.S. 122C-54.1(c) requires the court to make "specific findings of fact on which it bases its decision.")*

☐ 6. The petitioner's most recent ☐ inpatient ☐ outpatient mental commitment expired on *(date)* _____ .

☐ 7. If the petitioner has filed a previous petition under G.S. 122C-54 that was denied, one year or more has passed since the date of the denial.

☐ 8. The petitioner ☐ was ☐ was not committed for mental health treatment based on a finding of not guilty by reason of insanity.

V. CONCLUSIONS OF LAW

After a hearing on this petition, and based on the foregoing findings, the Court concludes as follows: *(check one)*

☐ 1. The petitioner does not continue to suffer from the condition that resulted in the commitment and does not continue to pose a danger to self or others for the purposes of the purchase, possession, or transfer of firearms pursuant to 18 U.S.C. § 922, G.S. 14-404, and G.S. 14-415.12.; and therefore is entitled to the relief requested.

☐ 2. The petitioner continues to suffer from the condition that resulted in the commitment and therefore is **NOT** entitled to the relief requested.

☐ 3. The petitioner continues to pose a danger to self or others and therefore is **NOT** entitled to the relief requested.

☐ 4. The petitioner was found not guilty by reason of insanity and is **NOT** entitled to the relief requested.

VI. ORDER

NOTE: *If Conclusion of Law 2 or 3 is checked, check number 2 below.*

It is hereby ordered that: *(check one)*

☐ 1. The relief requested by the petitioner is granted. The petitioner no longer suffers from the condition that resulted in the commitment and no longer poses a danger to self or others. The record of the petitioner's involuntary commitment transmitted to the National Instant Criminal Background Check System (NICS) shall be removed. The clerk will transmit a copy of this Order to NICS.

☐ 2. The relief requested by the petitioner is **NOT** granted. The petitioner continues to suffer from the condition that resulted in the commitment or continues to pose a danger to self or others. The record of the petitioner's involuntary commitment shall remain in NICS.

☐ 3. The relief requested by the petitioner is **NOT** granted. The petitioner was found not guilty by reason of insanity.

Date	Name Of Judge (Type Or Print)	Signature Of Judge

STATE OF NORTH CAROLINA

_____ County

File No. _____

In The General Court Of Justice
District Court Division

IN THE MATTER OF:

Name And Current Address Of Respondent

REQUEST FOR TRANSPORTATION ORDER
AND ORDER
(OUTPATIENT FAILS BUT DOES NOT CLEARLY REFUSE TO COMPLY WITH TREATMENT)

G.S. 122C-273(a)(2)

Date Of Outpatient Commitment Order

Transport To (Name And Address Of Physician Or Center)

Date Period Of Commitment Expires

NOTE: *Use this form only when (1) an Outpatient Commitment Order has been entered after a hearing in district court; (2) the respondent has failed, but has not clearly refused, to comply with all or part of the prescribed treatment, and (3) the respondent is to be taken to a physician or outpatient treatment center for examination.* **DO NOT** *use this form when the respondent has clearly refused to comply; instead use "Request For Supplemental Hearing (Outpatient Fails Or Clearly Refuses To Comply With Treatment)," AOC-SP-221. Other transportation orders are: "Notice Of Need For Transportation Order (From One 24-Hour Facility To Another)," AOC-SP-222; "Request For Transportation Order And Order (Committed Substance Abuser Fails To Comply Or Is Discharged From 24-Hour Facility)," AOC-SP-223; Request For Transportation Order And Order (Outpatient Fails To Appear For Prehearing Examination), AOC-SP-224.*

REQUEST

The outpatient physician, physician's designee or outpatient treatment center named below requests that the Clerk of Superior Court enter an order pursuant to G.S. 122C-273(a)(2) to take the Respondent named above into custody and to take the Respondent immediately to the outpatient treatment physician or center specified above for examination. In support of this request the undersigned states:

1. An Outpatient Commitment Order was entered in this proceeding on the date shown above and the Respondent was ordered to comply with prescribed treatment. The period of outpatient commitment has not expired.

2. The Respondent has failed to comply, but does not clearly refuse to comply, with all or part of the prescribed treatment after reasonable efforts to solicit compliance, in that *(Summarize facts showing failure to comply and reasonable efforts to solicit compliance):*

Date	Signature Of Physician, Physician's Designee Or Representative Of Center	
	Name Of Physician Or Center (Type Or Print)	☐ Physician
		☐ Physician's Designee
	Name Of Person Signing Request (Type Or Print)	☐ Representative Of Center (Title)
		_____

ORDER

TO ANY LAW ENFORCEMENT OFFICER:

You are ORDERED to take the Respondent into custody, take the Respondent immediately to the specified outpatient treatment physician or center and turn the Respondent over to the custody of that physician or center.

Date	Signature	
		☐ Clerk Of Superior Court
		☐ Assistant Clerk Of Superior Court

NOTE: *See Side Two for Officer's Return.*

AOC-SP-220, New 7/04
© 2004 Administrative Office of the Courts

OFFICER'S RETURN

Respondent Taken Into Custody			Respondent Turned Over To Physician Or Center	
Date	Time	☐ AM ☐ PM	Date	Time ☐ AM ☐ PM

☐ On the date and time shown above, I took the Respondent into custody. I took the Respondent immediately to the specified outpatient treatment physician or center and turned the Respondent over to the custody of that physician or center.

☐ I DID NOT take the Respondent named above into custody because:

Date Of Return	Signature Of Deputy Sheriff Or Law Enforcement Officer Making Return
	Name Of Deputy Sheriff Or Law Enforcement Officer Making Return (Type Or Print)
	County Of Sheriff Or City Of Law Enforcement Officer

STATE OF NORTH CAROLINA

_____ County

File No.

In The General Court Of Justice
District Court Division

IN THE MATTER OF:

Name And Current Address Of Respondent

Date Of Outpatient Commitment Order	Date Period Of Commitment Expires

REQUEST FOR
SUPPLEMENTAL HEARING
(OUTPATIENT CLEARLY REFUSES TO COMPLY WITH TREATMENT)

G.S. 122C-273(a)(1)

NOTE: *Use this form only when (1) an Outpatient Commitment Order has been entered after a hearing in district court; (2) the Respondent has clearly refused to comply with all or part of the prescribed treatment, and (3) a supplemental hearing is requested.* **DO NOT** *use this form when the Respondent has failed, but has* **not** *clearly refused to comply; instead use "Physician's Request For Transportation Order And Order (Outpatient Fails But Does Not Clearly Refuse To Comply With Treatment), AOC-SP-220.* **NO TRANSPORTATION ORDER SHOULD BE ISSUED ON THIS REQUEST.**

REQUEST

The outpatient physician, physician's designee or outpatient treatment center named below requests that the Clerk of Superior Court enter an order, pursuant to G.S. 122C-273(a)(1), for a supplemental hearing in this matter. In support of this request, the undersigned states:

1. An Outpatient Commitment Order was entered in this proceeding on the date shown above, and the Respondent was ordered to comply with prescribed treatment. The period of commitment has not expired.

2. The Respondent clearly refuses to comply with all or part of the prescribed treatment after reasonable efforts to secure compliance, in that (Summarize facts showing clear refusal to comply with treatment and reasonable efforts to solicit compliance.):

Date Of Request	Signature Of Outpatient Treatment Physician, Physician's Designee Or Representative Of Center	
	Name Of Outpatient Treatment Physician Or Center (Type Or Print)	☐ Physician
		☐ Physician's Designee
	Name Of Person Signing Request (Type Or Print)	☐ Representative Of Center (Title)

NOTE: *To order a supplemental hearing, the Clerk should use Order To Appear At Supplemental Hearing For Involuntary Commitment, AOC-SP-205, and check Finding #1 on that form.*

AOC-SP-221, New 7/04
© 2004 Administrative Office of the Courts

STATE OF NORTH CAROLINA

_____ County

File No. _____

In The General Court Of Justice
District Court Division

IN THE MATTER OF:

Name And Address Of Respondent

NOTICE OF NEED FOR TRANSPORTATION ORDER AND ORDER

(FROM ONE 24-HOUR FACILITY TO ANOTHER)

G.S. 122C-206

Transport From (Name And Address Of Current 24-Hour Facility)

Transport To (Name And Address Of Receiving 24-Hour Facility)

NOTE: _Use this form only to transport the Respondent from one 24-hour facility to another when the Respondent is in the current 24-hour facility either (1) pending district court hearing or upon commitment in an involuntary commitment proceeding or (2) under a voluntary admission effected by a minor or by a responsible person for a minor or incompetent adult. Other transportation orders are: Request For Transportation Order And Order (Outpatient Fails But Does Not Clearly Refuse To Comply With Treatment)," AOC-SP-220; "Request For Transportation Order And Order (Committed Substance Abuser Fails To Comply With Treatment Or Is Discharged From 24-Hour Facility)," AOC-SP-223; Request For Transportation Order And Order (Outpatient Fails To Appear For Prehearing Examination), AOC-SP-224._

NOTICE OF PROPOSED TRANSFER

The responsible professional named below gives notice pursuant to G.S. 122C-206(c1) that the Respondent named above is to be transferred from the current 24-hour facility named above to the receiving 24-hour facility named above, and that transportation is needed for this purpose. The undersigned requests that the Clerk of Superior Court or Magistrate issue an order to take the Respondent into custody for that purpose, and in support of this request states:

☐ **Respondent In Involuntary Commitment Proceeding**

1. ☐ a. The Respondent is being held at the current 24-hour facility for a district court hearing.

   ☐ b. An Inpatient Commitment Order has been entered in this proceeding and the Respondent is being held at the current 24-hour facility pursuant to that Order.

2. I have obtained authorization from the receiving facility that the facility will admit the Respondent, have provided reasonable notification to the Respondent, or legally responsible person, of the reason for the transfer, and have documented the notice in the client's record.

☐ **Respondent Minor Or Incompetent Adult Who Was Voluntarily Admitted**

1. The Respondent is a minor or incompetent adult who was admitted to the 24-hour facility pursuant to Part 3 or Part 4 of Chapter 122C of the General Statutes.

2. I have obtained authorization from the receiving facility that the facility will admit the Respondent, have provided reasonable notification to the Respondent, or legally responsible person, of the reason for the transfer, have documented the notice in the client's record, and have consulted with the legally responsible person.

Date

Signature Of Responsible Professional

Name Of Responsible Professional (Type Or Print)

ORDER

TO ANY LAW ENFORCEMENT OFFICER:

You are ORDERED to take the Respondent into custody at the current 24-hour facility specified above and to transport the Respondent to the receiving 24-hour facility specified above.

Date

Signature

☐ Clerk Of Superior Court ☐ Magistrate
☐ Assistant CSC

NOTE: _See Side Two for Officer's Return._

AOC-SP-222, New 7/04
© 2004 Administrative Office of the Courts

(Over)

OFFICER'S RETURN

Respondent Taken Into Custody At Current 24-Hour Facility		Respondent Turned Over To 24-Hour Facility	
Date	Time ☐ AM ☐ PM	Date	Time ☐ AM ☐ PM

☐ On the date and time shown above, I took the Respondent into custody at the specified current 24-hour facility. I took the Respondent immediately to the specified receiving 24-hour facility and turned the Respondent over to the custody of that facility.

☐ I DID NOT take the Respondent named above into custody because:

Date Of Return	Signature Of Deputy Sheriff Or Law Enforcement Officer Making Return
	Name Of Deputy Sheriff Or Law Enforcement Officer Making Return (Type Or Print)
	County Of Sheriff Or City Of Law Enforcement Officer

STATE OF NORTH CAROLINA

_____ County

File No. _____

In The General Court Of Justice
District Court Division

IN THE MATTER OF:

Name And Current Address Of Respondent

**REQUEST FOR TRANSPORTATION ORDER
AND ORDER
(COMMITTED SUBSTANCE ABUSER
FAILS TO COMPLY WITH TREATMENT
OR IS DISCHARGED FROM 24-HOUR FACILITY)**

G.S. 122C-290(b), -205.1(b)

Date Of Substance Abuse Commitment Order

Transport To (Name And Address Of Area Facility Or Physician)

Date Period Of Commitment Expires

NOTE: _Use this form only when (1) the respondent has been committed as a substance abuser after a hearing in district court; (2) the respondent has either (a) failed to comply with all or part of prescribed outpatient treatment or (b) has been discharged from a 24-hour facility after escaping or breaching a condition of his/her release from the 24-hour facility, and 3) the respondent is to be taken to an area facility or physician for examination. **DO NOT** use this form in mental health cases. Mental health transportation orders are: Request For Transportation Order And Order (Outpatient Fails But Does Not Clearly Refuse To Comply With Treatment)," AOC-SP-220; "Notice Of Need For Transportation Order And Order (From One 24-Hour Facility To Another)," AOC-SP-222; "Request For Transportation Order And Order (Outpatient Fails To Appear For Prehearing Examination)," AOC-SP-224._

REQUEST

The area facility or physician named below requests that the Clerk of Superior Court or Magistrate enter an order, pursuant to G.S. 122C-290(b), to take the Respondent named above into custody and to take the Respondent to the area facility or physician designated above for examination. In support of this request, the undersigned states:

☐ 1. A Substance Abuse Commitment Order was entered in this proceeding on the date shown above. The period of substance abuse commitment has not expired.

2. ☐ a. The area facility or physician responsible for management and supervision of the Respondent's commitment prescribed treatment on an outpatient basis; the Respondent failed to comply with all or part of the prescribed treatment after reasonable efforts to solicit the Respondent's compliance, in that _(Summarize facts showing failure to comply and reasonable efforts to solicit compliance):_

☐ b. The Respondent was discharged from a 24-hour facility in accordance with G.S. 122C-205.1(b).

Date	Signature Of Physician Or Representative Of Area Facility	☐ Physician
	Name Of Physician Or Representative Of Area Facility	☐ Representative Of Area Facility (Title)

ORDER

TO ANY LAW ENFORCEMENT OFFICER:

You are ORDERED to take the Respondent named above into custody, take the Respondent immediately to the area facility or physician designated above for examination, and to turn the Respondent over to the custody of that area facility or physician.

Date	Signature	☐ Clerk Of Superior Court ☐ Magistrate
		☐ Assistant Clerk Of Superior Court

NOTE: _See Side Two for Officer's Return(s)._

AOC-SP-223, New 7/04
© 2004 Administrative Office of the Courts

NOTE: *The officer who first takes the Respondent into custody shall turn the Respondent over to the custody of the specified area facility or physician. The area facility of physician may release the Respondent or "have the Respondent taken" to a 24-hour facility. If the officer who took the Respondent into custody is also officer by whom the Respondent is taken to the 24 hour facility, that officer should complete the "Officer's Return" below by checking both Option #1 and Option #3. If a different officer takes the Respondent to the 24-hour facility, the first officer should complete the "Officer's Return" below by checking only Option #1. The second officer should complete the portion headed "F⊃ Use When A Different Officer Takes Respondent To 24-Hour Facility."*

OFFICER'S RETURN

Respondent Taken Into Custody		Respondent Turned Over To Custody Of Area Facility Or Physician	
Date	Time ☐ AM ☐ PM	Date	Time ☐ AM ☐ PM

☐ 1. On the date and time shown above, I took the Respondent into custody. I took the Respondent to the specified area facility or physician and, on the date and time shown above, turned the Respondent over to the custody of that area facility or physician.

☐ 2. I DID NOT take the Respondent named above into custody because:

☐ 3. In addition to turning the Respondent over to the custody of the specified area facility or physician, I then, at the examiner's request, took the Respondent to the 24-hour facility named below and turned the Respondent over to the custody of that 24-hour facility.

Respondent Taken From Area Facility Or Physician		Respondent Turned Over To 24-Hour Facility	
Date	Time ☐ AM ☐ PM	Date	Time ☐ AM ☐ PM
Date Of Return		Signature Of Deputy Sheriff Or Law Enforcement Officer Making Return	
Name And Address Of 24-Hour Facility		Name Of Deputy Sheriff Or Law Enforcement Officer Making Return (Type Or Print)	
		County Of Sheriff Or City Of Law Enforcement Officer	

FOR USE WHEN A DIFFERENT OFFICER TAKES RESPONDENT TO 24-HOUR FACILITY

At the examiner's request, I took the Respondent into custody at the specified area facility or physician and took the Respondent to the 24-hour facility named below and turned the Respondent over to the custody of that 24-hour facility.

Respondent Taken From Area Facility Or Physician		Respondent Turned Over To 24-Hour Facility	
Date	Time ☐ AM ☐ PM	Date	Time ☐ AM ☐ PM
Date Of Return		Signature Of Deputy Sheriff Or Law Enforcement Officer Making Return	
Name And Address Of 24-Hour Facility		Name Of Deputy Sheriff Or Law Enforcement Officer Making Return (Type Or Print)	
		County Of Sheriff Or City Of Law Enforcement Officer	

STATE OF NORTH CAROLINA

_____ County

File No. _____

In The General Court Of Justice
District Court Division

IN THE MATTER OF:

Name And Current Address Of Respondent

REQUEST FOR TRANSPORTATION ORDER AND ORDER
(OUTPATIENT FAILS TO APPEAR FOR PREHEARING EXAMINATION)

G.S. 122C-265(a); 122C-263(f)

Date Of First Examination	Name Of Examining Physician Or Eligible Psychologist
Date Of Missed Appointment	Name And Address Of Proposed Outpatient Treatment Physician Or Center
Time Of Missed Appointment ☐ AM ☐ PM	

NOTE: _Use this form only when (1) a physician or eligible psychologist has conducted a first examination at the initiation of an involuntary commitment proceeding and has recommended outpatient treatment, (2) no hearing has yet held in district court, (3) the physician or eligible psychologist has scheduled an appointment for the Respondent with a proposed outpatient treatment physician or center and has provided the Respondent with written notice of the appointment, and (4) the Respondent has failed to keep the appointment. Other transportation orders are: Request For Transportation Order And Order (Outpatient Fails But Does Not Clearly Refuse To Comply With Treatment)," AOC-SP-220; "Notice Of Need For Transportation Order And Order (Outpatient Fails To Appear For Prehearing Examination)," AOC-SP-221; "Request For Transportation Order And Order (Committed Substance Abuser Fails To Comply With Treatment Or Is Discharged From 24-Hour Facility)," AOC-SP-223._

REQUEST

The proposed outpatient treatment physician or center named below requests that the Clerk of Superior Court enter an order, pursuant to G.S. 122C-265(a), to take the Respondent named above into custody and to take the Respondent to the outpatient treatment physician or center specified above for examination. In support of this request, the undersigned notifies the Clerk that:

1. The physician or eligible psychologist named above has conducted the first examination provided for in G.S. 122C-263 and has recommended outpatient treatment; no hearing has yet been held in district court.

2. The physician or eligible psychologist scheduled an appointment for the Respondent with the proposed outpatient treatment physician or center named above for the date and time shown above, and provided the Respondent with written notice of the appointment and of the name, address and phone number of that physician or center.

3. The examining physician or eligible psychologist is different from the proposed outpatient treatment physician or center.

4. The Respondent failed to appear for examination at the scheduled date and time.

Date	Signature Of Proposed Outpatient Treatment Physician Or Representative Of Center	☐ Physician
	Name Of Proposed Outpatient Treatment Physician Or Center (Type Or Print)	☐ Representative Of Center (Title) _____

ORDER

TO ANY LAW ENFORCEMENT OFFICER:

You are ORDERED to take the Respondent named above into custody, take the Respondent immediately to the proposed outpatient treatment physician or center specified above and turn the Respondent over to the custody of that physician or center.

Date	Signature	☐ Clerk Of Superior Court ☐ Assistant Clerk Of Superior Court

NOTE: _See Side Two for Officer's Return._

AOC-SP-224, New 7/04
© 2004 Administrative Office of the Courts

OFFICER'S RETURN

Respondent Taken Into Custody				Respondent Turned Over To Physician Or Center		
Date	Time	☐ AM ☐ PM		Date	Time	☐ AM ☐ PM

☐ On the date and time shown above, I took the Respondent into custody. I took the Respondent immediately to the specified outpatient treatment physician or center and turned the Respondent over to the custody of that physician or center.

☐ I DID NOT take the Respondent named above into custody because:

Date Of Return	Signature Of Deputy Sheriff Or Law Enforcement Officer Making Return
	Name Of Deputy Sheriff Or Law Enforcement Officer Making Return (Type Or Print)
	County Of Sheriff Or City Of Law Enforcement Officer

STATE OF NORTH CAROLINA

_____ County

File No. _____

In The General Court Of Justice
District Court Division

IN THE MATTER OF:

Name, Address And Zip Code Of Respondent

AFFIDAVIT AND PETITION FOR INVOLUNTARY COMMITMENT

G.S. 122C-261, 122C-281

Social Security No. Of Respondent	*Date Of Birth*	*Drivers License No. Of Respondent*	*State*

I, the undersigned affiant, being first duly sworn, and having sufficient knowledge to believe that the respondent is a proper subject for involuntary commitment, allege that the respondent is a resident of, or can be found in the above named county, and is:

(Check all that apply)

☐ 1. mentally ill and dangerous to self or others or mentally ill and in need of treatment in order to prevent further disability or deterioration that would predictably result in dangerousness.

  ☐ in addition to being mentally ill, respondent is also mentally retarded.

☐ 2. a substance abuser and dangerous to self or others.

The facts upon which this opinion is based are as follows: *(State facts, not conclusions, to support ALL blocks checked.)*

Name, Address And Zip Code Of Nearest Relative Or Guardian	*Name, Address And Zip Code Of Other Person Who May Testify To Facts*

Home Telephone No.	*Business Telephone No.*	*Home Telephone No.*	*Business Telephone No.*

Petitioner requests the court to issue an order to a law enforcement officer to take the respondent into custody for examination by a person authorized by law to conduct the examination for the purpose of determining if the respondent should be involuntarily committed.

SWORN AND SUBSCRIBED TO BEFORE ME

Signature Of Petitioner

Date

Name, Address And Zip Code Of Petitioner (Type Or Print)

Signature

☐ Deputy CSC ☐ Assistant CSC ☐ Clerk Of Superior Court ☐ Magistrate
☐ Notary (use only with physician or psychologist petitioner)

Relationship To Respondent

Date Notary Commission Expires

SEAL

Home Telephone No. | *Business Telephone No.*

AOC-SP-300, Rev. 9/03
© 2003 Administrative Office of the Courts

PETITIONER'S WAIVER OF NOTICE OF HEARING

I voluntarily waive my right to notice of all hearings and rehearings in which the Court may commit the respondent or extend the respondent's commitment period, or discharge the respondent from the treatment facility.

Signature Of Witness	Date
	Signature Of Petitioner

STATE OF NORTH CAROLINA

_____ County

File No.

In The General Court Of Justice
District Court Division

IN THE MATTER OF:

Name And Address Of Respondent

Date Of Birth

NOTICE OF HEARING/REHEARING
FOR INVOLUNTARY COMMITMENT

G.S. 122C-264, -274, -276, -284, -292

NOTICE TO THE RESPONDENT NAMED ABOVE

(Check only one)

☐ 1. It has been alleged that you are mentally ill and a proper subject for involuntary ☐ inpatient ☐ outpatient commitment.

☐ 2. It has been alleged that you are a substance abuser and a proper subject for involuntary commitment.

☐ 3. The physician now treating you has determined that you are in need of further care and treatment beyond your present period of commitment.

☐ 4. You have been committed after (a) being charged with a violent crime and being found incapable of proceeding or (b) being found not guilty by reason of insanity. The physician now treating you has determined that further treatment is not necessary. However, you may not be released without the hearing referred to below.

A hearing will be held before a district court judge at the date, time and place indicated below. At that hearing it will be determined if you should be committed, released, or recommitted for treatment.

At this hearing you will be allowed to present evidence. If the hearing is for inpatient commitment or for commitment as a substance abuser, you have a right to be represented by an attorney. If you cannot afford an attorney, one will be appointed for you.

If the hearing is for an outpatient commitment, you may hire an attorney to represent you. If you cannot afford an attorney, you may ask the court to appoint one for you. However, the court may or may not appoint an attorney based upon the facts in your particular case.

Date Of Hearing	Place Of Hearing
Time Of Hearing ☐ AM ☐ PM	

NOTICE TO SHERIFF

This Notice must be served on the respondent at least seventy-two (72) hours before the hearing.

Date	Signature	☐ Deputy CSC ☐ Assistant CSC ☐ Clerk Of Superior Court

Original-File Copy-Petitioner Copy-Respondent Copy-Attorney
(Over)

AOC-SP-301, Rev. 3/02
© 2002 Administrative Office of the Courts

RETURN OF SERVICE

I certify that this Notice was received and served on the respondent as follows:

Date Served	Time Served ☐ AM ☐ PM	Name Of Respondent

☐ 1. By delivering to the respondent named above a copy of this Notice.

☐ 2. By leaving a copy of this Notice at the respondent's dwelling house or usual place of abode with a person of suitable age and discretion then residing therein.

Name Of Person With Whom Copies Left

Address Where Copies Delivered Or Left

☐ Service Accepted By Attorney For Respondent

Signature	Date Accepted

☐ Respondent WAS NOT served for the following reason:

Date Received	Date Returned	Name Of Sheriff
County		Deputy Sheriff Making Return

NOTE TO CLERK: (In Addition To Service On Respondent)

For cases in which the examiner recommends inpatient commitment for a person who is mentally ill:
The clerk in the county where the 24-hour facility is located must deposit in the mail a copy of this Notice by first-class mail at least 72 hours before the hearing to the respondent's counsel and the petitioner, unless the petitioner has waived his/her right to notice on form AOC-SP-300. If the respondent has been found not guilty by reason of insanity or has been charged with a violent crime and been found incapable of proceeding, the clerk must also mail a copy of the notice to the chief district court judge and the district attorney in the county in which the defendant was found not guilty by reason of insanity or incapable of proceeding.

For cases in which the examiner recommends outpatient commitment for a person who is mentally ill:
The clerk in the county where the petition was initiated must deposit in the mail a copy of this Notice by first-class mail at least 72 hours before the hearing to the proposed outpatient treatment center or physician and the petitioner, unless the petitioner has waived his/her right to notice. If the respondent was charged with a violent crime and found incapable of proceeding, see instructions immediately above for additional persons to be served.

For cases in which the examiner finds that the respondent is a substance abuser:
The clerk in the county where the facility is located if respondent is held in a 24-hour facility or the clerk in the county where the petition was initiated if not held in a 24-hour facility must deposit in the mail a copy of this Notice by first-class mail at least 72 hours before the hearing to the respondent's counsel and the petitioner, unless the petitioner has waived his/her right to notice. Notice should also be sent to the area authority or physician that will be responsible for the commitment.

CLERK'S CERTIFICATION OF SERVICE

I certify that I have mailed copies of this Notice by first class mail at least 72 hours before the hearing to the persons whose name and address are listed below (fill in only those appropriate):

Name And Address Of Petitioner	Name And Address Of Counsel For Respondent
Name And Address Of Proposed Outpatient Treatment Center/Physician	Name And Address Of Area Authority/Physician

Date	Signature	☐ Deputy CSC ☐ Assistant CSC ☐ Clerk Of Superior Court

AOC-SP-301, Side Two, Rev. 3/02
© 2002 Administrative Office of the Courts

STATE OF NORTH CAROLINA

_____ County

File No. _____

In The General Court Of Justice
District Court Division

IN THE MATTER OF:

Name And Address Of Respondent

FINDINGS AND CUSTODY ORDER
INVOLUNTARY COMMITMENT

G.S. 122C-261, -263, -281, -283

Social Security No. Of Respondent	Date Of Birth	Drivers License No. Of Respondent	State

I. FINDINGS

The Court finds from the petition in the above matter that there are reasonable grounds to believe that the facts alleged in the petition are true and that the respondent is probably:

(Check all that apply)

☐ 1. mentally ill and dangerous to self or others or mentally ill and in need of treatment in order to prevent further disability or deterioration that would predictably result in dangerousness.
　　☐ In addition to being mentally ill, the respondent probably is also mentally retarded.

☐ 2. a substance abuser and dangerous to self or others.

CUSTODY ORDER

TO ANY LAW ENFORCEMENT OFFICER:

The Court ORDERS you to take the above named respondent into custody

☐ 1. and take the respondent for examination by a person authorized by law to conduct the examination. (A COPY OF THE EXAMINER'S FINDINGS SHALL BE TRANSMITTED TO THE CLERK OF SUPERIOR COURT IMMEDIATELY.)

➡ IF the examiner finds that the respondent IS NOT a proper subject for involuntary commitment, then you shall take the respondent home or to a consenting person's home in the originating county and release him/her.

➡ IF the examiner finds that the respondent IS mentally ill and a proper subject for outpatient commitment, then you shall take the respondent home or to a consenting person's home in the originating county and release him/her.

➡ IF the examiner finds that the respondent IS mentally ill and a proper subject for inpatient commitment, then you shall transport the respondent to the 24-hour facility named below for temporary custody, examination and treatment pending a district court hearing.

➡ IF the examiner finds that the respondent IS a substance abuser and subject to involuntary commitment, the examiner must recommend whether the respondent be taken to a 24-hour facility or released, and then you shall either release him/her or transport the respondent to the 24-hour facility named below for temporary custody, examination and treatment pending a district court hearing.

☐ 2. and transport the respondent directly to the 24-hour facility named below, for temporary custody, examination and treatment pending a district court hearing. (FOR PHYSICIAN/PSYCHOLOGIST PETITIONERS ONLY.)

Name Of 24-Hour Facility For Mentally Ill	Date
Or following facility designated by area authority:	Time ☐ AM ☐ PM
Name Of 24-Hour Facility For Substance Abuser	Signature
Or following facility designated by area authority:	☐ Deputy CSC ☐ Assistant CSC ☐ Clerk Of Superior Court ☐ Magistrate

NOTE TO MAGISTRATE OR CLERK:

If the respondent is mentally retarded in addition to being mentally ill, you must contact the area authority before issuing a custody order to determine the facility to which the respondent will be taken. If the area mental health authority where the respondent resides has a single portal plan, you must call the area authority to determine the appropriate 24-hour facility or other treatment before issuing any custody order.

NOTE TO ANY LAW ENFORCEMENT OFFICER:

You shall take the respondent into custody within 24 hours after the date this Order is signed. Without unnecessary delay after assuming custody, you shall take the respondent to an area facility for examination by a person authorized by law to conduct the examination; if an authorized examiner is not immediately available in the area facility, you shall take the respondent to any authorized examiner locally available. If an authorized examiner is not available, you may temporarily detain the respondent in an area facility if one is available; if an area facility is not available, you may detain the respondent under appropriate supervision, in the respondent's home, in a private hospital or clinic, or in a general hospital, but not in a jail or other penal facility.
Complete the Return Of Service on the reverse and return to the Clerk of Superior Court immediately.

II. RETURN OF SERVICE

☐ Respondent WAS NOT taken into custody for the following reason:

☐ I certify that this Order was received and served as follows:

Date Respondent Taken Into Custody	Time	☐ AM ☐ PM
Name Of Law Enforcement Officer	Signature Of Law Enforcement Officer	

A. PATIENT DELIVERY TO LOCAL EVALUATION SITE

☐ 1. The respondent was presented to an authorized examiner locally available as shown below.
☐ 2. The respondent was temporarily detained at the facility named below until the respondent could be examined by an authorized examiner locally available.

Date Presented	Time ☐ AM ☐ PM	Name Of Examiner
Name Of Local Facility	Name Of Law Enforcement Officer	Signature Of Law Enforcement Officer

B. FOR USE AFTER PRELIMINARY EXAMINATION

☐ 1. Upon examination, the examiner named above found that the respondent is mentally ill and meets the criteria for outpatient commitment, or is a substance abuser and meets the criteria for commitment and the examiner recommends release pending a hearing. I returned the respondent to his/her regular residence or the home of a consenting person.

☐ 2. Upon examination, the examiner named above found that the respondent is mentally ill and meets the criteria for inpatient commitment, or is a substance abuser and meets the criteria for commitment and the examiner recommends that the respondent be held pending the district court hearing.

 ☐ I transported the respondent and placed the respondent in the temporary custody of the facility named below for observation and treatment.
 ☐ I placed the respondent in the custody of the agency named below for transportation to the 24-hour facility.

☐ 3. Upon examination, the examiner named above found that the respondent did not meet the criteria for inpatient or outpatient commitment. I returned the respondent to his/her regular residence or the home of a consenting person.

The examiner's written statement ☐ is attached. ☐ will be forwarded.

Name Of 24-Hour Facility	Date Delivered	Time Delivered ☐ AM ☐ PM	Date Of Return
Name Of Transporting Agency	Signature Of Law Enforcement Official		

C. FOR USE WHEN PETITIONER IS PHYSICIAN/PSYCHOLOGIST

(**NOTE:** Section II above **MUST** be completed. Sections A and B should **NOT** be completed.)
☐ I transported the respondent directly to and placed him/her in the temporary custody of the facility named below.

Name Of 24-Hour Facility	Date Delivered	Time Delivered ☐ AM ☐ PM	Date Of Return
Name Of Transporting Agency	Signature Of Law Enforcement Official		

D. FOR USE WHEN ANOTHER AGENCY TRANSPORTS THE RESPONDENT

☐ I took custody of the respondent from the officer named above, transported the respondent and placed him/her in the temporary custody of the facility named below for observation and treatment.

Name Of 24-Hour Facility	Date Delivered	Time Delivered ☐ AM ☐ PM	Date Of Return
Name Of Person Taking Custody of Respondent	Signature Of Person Taking Custody Of Respondent		

E. FOR USE WHEN STATE FACILITY TRANSFERS WITHOUT ADMISSION

☐ Pursuant to G.S. 122C-261(f), I took custody of the respondent from the state 24-hour facility named above, where he/she was not admitted, and transported the respondent and placed him/her in the temporary custody of the facility named below for observation and treatment.

Name Of Facility To Which Transferred	Date Delivered	Time Delivered ☐ AM ☐ PM	Date Of Return
Name Of Transporting Agency	Signature Of Law Enforcement Or State Facility Official		

STATE OF NORTH CAROLINA

_____ County

File No. _____

In The General Court Of Justice
District Court Division

IN THE MATTER OF:

Name And Address Of Respondent

INVOLUNTARY COMMITMENT CUSTODY ORDER DEFENDANT FOUND INCAPABLE TO PROCEED

G.S. 15A-1003, -1004; 122C-261, -262, -263

I. FINDINGS

The respondent has been charged in File No. _____ with a criminal offense in the above named county has been found incapable of proceeding to trial under G.S. 15A-1002.

Based on the evidence presented, the Court finds that there are reasonable grounds to believe that the respondent is probably mentally ill and either dangerous to self or others or in need of treatment in order to prevent further disability or deterioration that would predictably result in dangerousness in that (insert appropriate findings)

In addition, the Court finds that the respondent

☐ 1. is probably mentally retarded, in that (insert appropriate findings)

☐ 2. is charged with a violent crime in violation of G.S. _____ , in that (insert appropriate findings)

Notice To 24-hour Facility:

Criminal charges are still pending against the respondent. You must report to the Clerk in the above named county the condition of the defendant-respondent and the likelihood of the defendant's gaining capacity to proceed at the time of each commitment rehearing. You must also report if the defendant-respondent regains capacity to proceed or if the defendant-respondent is released. If the defendant-respondent is released, he/she must be released to the law enforcement agency named below. _Name Of Law Enforcement Agency_

CUSTODY ORDER

To The Sheriff Of _____ **County:**

The Court ORDERS you to take the above named respondent into custody and transport the respondent:

☐ 1. to a local person authorized by law to conduct an examination, for examination. (Use when not charged with a violent crime.)

☐ 2. directly to the 24-hour facility named below for temporary custody, examination and treatment pending a district court hearing. (Use when charged with a violent crime.)

Name And Address Of 24-Hour Facility

Date

Signature Of Judge

Or following facility designated by area authority:

Name Of Judge (Type Or Print)

NOTE: _Use AOC-SP-910M for involuntary commitment if defendant found not guilty by reason of insanity._

AOC-SP-304, Rev. 9/03
© 2003 Administrative Office of the Courts

(Over)

II. RETURN OF SERVICE

☐ I certify that this Order was received and served as follows:

Date Respondent Taken Into Custody	Time	☐ AM ☐ PM

A. FOR USE WHEN RESPONDENT NOT CHARGED WITH VIOLENT CRIME

☐ 1. The respondent was presented to an authorized examiner locally available as shown below.

☐ 2. The respondent was temporarily detained at the facility named below until the respondent could be examined by an authorized examiner locally available.

Date Presented	Time	☐ AM ☐ PM	Name Of Examiner

Name Of Local Facility

☐ 1. Upon examination, the examiner named above found that the respondent did meet the criteria for outpatient commitment. I returned the respondent to his/her regular residence or to the home of a consenting person.

☐ 2. Upon examination, the examiner named above found that the respondent did meet the criteria for inpatient commitment.

    ☐ I transported the respondent and placed the respondent in the temporary custody of the 24-hour facility named below for observation and treatment.

    ☐ I placed the respondent in the custody of the agency named below for transportation to the 24-hour facility.

☐ 3. Upon examination, the examiner named above found that the respondent did not meet the criteria for inpatient or outpatient commitment. I returned the respondent to his/her regular residence or the home of a consenting person.

The examiner's written statement   ☐ is attached.   ☐ will be forwarded.

Name Of 24-Hour Facility	Date Delivered	Time Delivered	☐ AM ☐ PM	Date Of Return
Name Of Transporting Agency	Signature Of Law Enforcement Official			

B. FOR USE WHEN RESPONDENT CHARGED WITH VIOLENT CRIME

☐ I transported the respondent directly to and placed him/her in the temporary custody of the facility named below.

Name Of 24-Hour Facility	Date Delivered	Time Delivered	☐ AM ☐ PM	Date Of Return
Name Of Transporting Agency	Signature Of Law Enforcement Official			

C. FOR USE WHEN ANOTHER AGENCY TRANSPORTS THE RESPONDENT

☐ I took custody of the respondent from the officer named above, transported the respondent and placed him/her in the temporary custody of the facility named below for observation and treatment.

Name Of 24-Hour Facility	Date Delivered	Time Delivered	☐ AM ☐ PM	Date Of Return
Name Of Transporting Agency	Signature And Rank Of Law Enforcement Official			

D. FOR USE WHEN STATE FACILITY TRANSFERS WITHOUT ADMISSION

☐ Pursuant to G.S. 122C-261(f), I took custody of the respondent from the state 24-hour facility named above, where he/she was not admitted, and transported the respondent and placed him/her in the temporary custody of the facility named below for observation and treatment.

Name Of Facility To Which Transferred	Date Delivered	Time Delivered	☐ AM ☐ PM	Date Of Return
Name Of Transporting Agency	Signature Of Law Enforcement Or State Facility Official			

STATE OF NORTH CAROLINA

File No. _____

_____ County

In The General Court Of Justice
Superior Court Division

IN THE MATTER OF:

Name And Address Of Respondent

FINDINGS AND ORDER
INVOLUNTARY COMMITMENT
PHYSICIAN-PETITIONER
RECOMMENDS OUTPATIENT COMMITMENT

G.S. 122C-261

NOTICE: *This form is to be used instead of the Findings And Custody Order (AOC-SP-302) only when the petitioner is a physician or psychologist who recommends outpatient commitment or release pending hearing for a substance abuser.*

FINDINGS

The petitioner in this case is a physician/eligible psychologist who has recommended outpatient commitment/substance abuse commitment with the respondent being released pending hearing.

The Court finds from the petition in the above matter that there are reasonable grounds to believe that the facts alleged in the petition are true and that the respondent is probably:

☐ mentally ill and in need of treatment in order to prevent further disability or deterioration that would predictably result in dangerousness.

☐ a substance abuser and dangerous to himself/herself or others.

ORDER

It is ORDERED that a hearing before the district court judge be held to determine whether the respondent will be involuntarily committed.

Date	Signature

☐ Deputy CSC   ☐ Assistant CSC
☐ Clerk Of Superior Court   ☐ Magistrate

NOTE TO CLERK: *Schedule an initial hearing for the respondent pursuant to G.S. 122C-264 or G.S. 122C-284 and give notice of the hearing as required by those statutes.*

AOC-SP-305, Rev. 1/98
© 1998 Administrative Office of the Courts

STATE OF NORTH CAROLINA

_____ County

File No.

In The General Court Of Justice
District Court Division

IN THE MATTER OF:

Respondent

ORDER INVOLUNTARY
COMMITMENT PROCEEDINGS
SUBSTANCE ABUSER

G.S. 122C-287

FINDINGS

The Court finds that:

1. The petitioner ☐ was ☐ was not represented by counsel.

2. The respondent ☐ was ☐ was not represented by counsel.

Based on the evidence presented

☐ 3. by clear, cogent and convincing evidence finds as facts all matters set out in the physician's/eligible psychologist's/qualified professional's report, specified below, and the report is incorporated by reference as findings.

Date	Name Of Examiner

☐ 4. by clear, cogent and convincing evidence finds these other facts:

☐ 5. finds that the respondent does not meet the criteria for commitment.

CONCLUSIONS

Based on the above findings, the Court concludes that the respondent:

☐ 1. is a substance abuser.

☐ 2. is not a substance abuser.

☐ 3. is dangerous to ☐ himself. ☐ others.

☐ 4. is not dangerous to himself or others.

AOC-SP-306, Rev. 12/94
© 2007 Administrative Office of the Courts

(See ORDER on reverse)

ORDER

It is ORDERED that:

☐ 1. the respondent be committed/recommitted to the area authority/physician named below for the period specified.

    ☐ The respondent is now being held at the 24-hour facility listed below and the respondent is ordered returned to that facility to be held until the area authority/physician to whom the respondent is committed authorizes release.

    ☐ and that venue be transferred to _____ County.

☐ 2. the respondent be discharged and this matter dismissed.

Committed/recommitted to the area authority/physician for a period not to exceed ☐ _____ days. ☐ 180 days. ☐ 1 year.	Name And Address Of 24-Hour Facility
Name And Address Of Area Authority/Physician	*Date*
	Signature Of District Court Judge
	Name Of District Court Judge (Type Or Print)

AOC-SP-306, Side Two, Rev. 12/94
© 2007 Administrative Office of the Courts

STATE OF NORTH CAROLINA

_____ County

File No. _____

In The General Court Of Justice
District Court Division

IN THE MATTER OF:

**APPELLATE ENTRIES
INVOLUNTARY COMMITMENT**

G.S. 122C-272, -288

Name And Address Of Appealing Respondent

Name And Address Of Appealing Respondent's Attorney in District Court (if respondent did not have an attorney, indicate that fact in this box, e.g. "Respondent Represented Self")

Name And Address Of Petitioner's Attorney

Telephone No.

Respondent 1's Attorney's Email Address (if available)

Petitioner's Attorney's Email Address (if available)

Respondent's Initial Appellate Counsel

☐ The Appellate Defender, 123 W. Main Street, Suite 500
Durham, NC 27701   (919) 560-3334
email: appellatedefender@nccourts.org
(The Appellate Defender is appointed when the respondent is indigent.)

Telephone No.

☐ Name, address, and telephone number of retained appellate counsel

Date(s) Of Hearings(s) On Which Appealed Order(s) Is Based

INITIAL APPEAL ENTRIES

1. Pursuant to G.S. 122C-272 or G.S. 122C-288, the respondent has given Notice of Appeal to the N.C. Court of Appeals from the District Court's Order entered (signed by the judge and filed) on (specify date) _____.

2. The respondent does not read or speak the English language, but reads and/or speaks his or her native language of _____ . The Court therefore authorizes the services of a language translator or interpreter during the pendency of the appeal for the purposes of (1) written translation of attorney-client correspondence, list of proposed issues on appeal, appellate briefs filed by the defendant and the State, and appellate opinion(s), and/or (2) verbal interpretation of attorney-client communication at each critical stage of the appellate proceedings.

   The Court further Orders that a language translator or interpreter with the necessary knowledge, skill, experience, training and education to perform the above services shall be selected and paid by the Administrative Office of the Courts.

3. Based on the respondent-appellant's affidavit of indigency, the Court finds that
   ☐ The respondent is not indigent.
   ☐ The respondent is indigent. Therefore, it is ORDERED that the respondent is allowed to appeal as an indigent and:

   a. The Office of Indigent Defense Services shall pay the costs of producing a transcript for the respondent and of reproducing the record and the respondent's brief and other pleadings.

   b. The Appellate Defender is appointed to perfect the respondent's appeal.

   c. The Clerk shall furnish to the respondent's appellate counsel a copy of the complete trial division file in the involuntary commitment proceeding and, upon request, any documentary exhibits, unless the clerk has furnished a copy to trial counsel for use in the appeal.

   d. The Clerk shall duplicate the audio recording of the hearing(s), date(s) listed above, and shall deliver the duplicate recording and two copies of these Appellate Entries to the person designated by the AOC Court Reporter Coordinator to produce a transcript of the hearing(s). No fee shall be charged for the cost of the duplicate recording.

   e. The Clerk shall deliver to the Office of the Appellate Defender a copy of these Appellate Entries and a copy of the order(s) from which the respondent appeals.

   f. The Clerk also shall deliver a copy of these Appellate Entries to counsel for all other parties, or to the parties themselves if not represented by counsel.

Date	Name Of Presiding Judge (Type or Print)	Signature Of Presiding Judge Or Chief District Court Judge

ORDER OF TRANSCRIPT

The Clerk of Court hereby designates the person named below to receive a duplicate recording of the hearing(s) in this action. The designated person is authorized to listen to the duplicate recording and to transcribe the proceedings verbatim

Name, Address And Telephone No. Of Authorized Person (Type Or Print)

The Court orders that the authorized person maintain strict confidentiality of the record(s) in accordance with the statutes. This person shall return the duplicate recording of this proceeding to the custody of the Clerk of Superior Court immediatel upon the completion of the transcription of this matter. The Clerk, upon receipt of the duplicate recording of this confidentia proceeding, shall erase it.

The Court orders that the authorized person named above shall transmit a copy of the transcript to each of the parties who have made arrangements to pay for the copy.

TRACKING AND RECEIPT

I have transmitted to the authorized person named above the duplicate recording and two copies of these Appellate Entrie by ☐ personally delivering it to that person. ☐ mailing it via the U.S. Postal Service to that person.

Date Transmitted	*Signature*	☐ *Deputy CSC* ☐ *Assistant CSC* ☐ *Clerk Of Superior Court*

I have received the duplicate recording from the Clerk of Superior Court and have acknowledged receipt by promptly returning to the Clerk this signed copy of the Court's Appellate Entries.

Date Received	*Signature Of Person Authorized To Transcribe*

The duplicate of the recording has been returned to the Clerk Of Superior Court by the authorized person.

Date Returned	*Signature*	☐ *Deputy CSC* ☐ *Assistant CSC* ☐ *Clerk Of Superior Court*

THIRTY DAY EXTENSION OF TIME TO PREPARE TRANSCRIPT

Pursuant to Rules 7 and 27 of the N.C. Rules of Appellate Procedure, upon motion of the respondent, and for good cause shown,

It is ORDERED that the time for preparation of the transcript is extended 30 days to and including _____

NOTE: *The trial court may grant only one extension of time for a maximum of thirty days to prepare the transcript. A motion for any further extension of time must be made in the Appellate Division. Rules 7(b)(1) and 27(c)(2), N.C. Rules of Appellate Procedure.*

Date	*Name Of Presiding Judge (Type or Print)*	*Signature Of Presiding Judge*

THIRTY DAY EXTENSION OF TIME TO SERVE PROPOSED RECORD ON APPEAL

Pursuant to Rules 7 and 27, N.C. Rules of Appellate Procedure, upon motion of the respondent, and for good cause shown,

It is ORDERED that the time for service of the proposed record on appeal is extended for 30 days to and including

_____ .

NOTE: *The trial court may grant only one extension of time for a maximum of thirty days to serve the proposed record on appeal. A motion for any further extension of time must be made in the Appellate Division. Rules 7(b)(1) and 27(c)(2), N.C. Rules of Appellate Procedure.*

Date	*Name Of Presiding Judge (Type or Print)*	*Signature Of Presiding Judge*

CERTIFICATION

I certify that this Appellate Entries form is a true and complete copy of the original on file in this case.

Date	*Signature And Seal*	☐ *Deputy CSC* ☐ *Assistant CSC* ☐ *Clerk Of Superior Court*

STATE OF NORTH CAROLINA

_____ County

File No. _____

In The General Court Of Justice
District Court Division

IN THE MATTER OF:

Name Of Respondent

REQUEST AND AUTHORIZATION
TO DELIVER RESPONDENT

G.S. 122C-251(f)

REQUEST

I request that I be authorized to transport the above named respondent to the mental health facility named below, and agree to bear the cost of such transportation. I believe the respondent is not substantially dangerous to himself/herself or others.

Date

Signature Of Person Making Request

AUTHORIZATION

Under North Carolina law, and upon request, the individual named below is authorized and directed to immediately transport and deliver the respondent to the facility named below.

Name And Address Of Person Authorized To Transport And Deliver Respondent

Name And Address Of Mental Health Facility

You are also directed to deliver the court records pertaining to respondent's admission to the admitting official of the facility, and obtain an acknowledgment of your delivery of the respondent and the court records from the admitting official of the facility. The acknowledgment of delivery shall be immediately returned to the Clerk.

Date

Signature

☐ Magistrate   ☐ Deputy CSC   ☐ Assistant CSC   ☐ CSC

ACKNOWLEDGMENT BY MENTAL HEALTH FACILITY

I acknowledge receipt of respondent and copies of the court records relating to admission of the respondent at this facility. I understand that under North Carolina law the findings of the physician must be returned to the Clerk within forty-eight (48) hours.

Name Of Facility

Date

Signature

Title

STATE OF NORTH CAROLINA

_____ County

File No. _____

In The General Court Of Justice
District Court Division

IN THE MATTER OF:

Name And Address Of Respondent

OUTPATIENT COMMITMENT
ORDER OF ASSIGNMENT OR
DENIAL OF COUNSEL

G.S. 122C-267(d)

FINDINGS

From the petition heard in this matter, it appears to the Court that the respondent named above is party to a proceeding listed in G.S. 122C-267.

And from the affirmation of the applicant, his/her guardian or family member, and from inquiry made by the Court, which is documented in the record, it is determined that the respondent is not represented by counsel and:

☐ is not financially able to provide the necessary expenses of legal counsel.

☐ is financially able to provide the necessary expenses of legal counsel.

Further, the Court determines that:

☐ legal or factual issues to be raised in this matter are of such complexity that the assistance of counsel is necessary for adequate presentation of the merits.

☐ respondent is unable to speak for himself/herself and needs counsel appointed to represent him/her

☐ respondent is not required to be represented by counsel under G.S. 122C-267(d).

ORDER

It is ORDERED that:

☐ the respondent is entitled to the services of court appointed counsel, and that he/she shall be represented by
    ☐ the attorney named below.   ☐ the public defender in this judicial district.

☐ the hearing in this matter is continued until the date, time and location set out below. _(Hearing must be held within 5 days of this Order.)_

☐ the respondent is not entitled to the services of court appointed counsel and this petition is denied.

Date Of Hearing	Time ☐ AM ☐ PM	Location Of Hearing
Name And Address Of Attorney (if applicable)		Date
		Signature
Telephone No.		☐ Judge ☐ Assistant CSC ☐ Clerk Of Superior Court

AOC-SP-904M, Rev. 7/95
® 1997 Administrative Office of the Courts

STATE OF NORTH CAROLINA

File No. _____

_____ County

In The General Court Of Justice
District Court Division

IN THE MATTER OF:

Name And Address Of Respondent

Drivers License No., If Known	State

Date Of Birth Of Respondent

PETITION AND CUSTODY ORDER FOR SPECIAL EMERGENCY SUBSTANCE ABUSE INVOLUNTARY COMMITMENT

G.S. 122C-282

I, the undersigned affiant, being first duly sworn, and having sufficient knowledge to believe that the respondent is a proper subject for involuntary commitment, allege that the respondent is a resident of, or can be found in the above named county, and is a substance abuser who is dangerous to himself or others. I have taken the respondent into custody and brought the respondent immediately before the Court because he/she is violent and requires restraint and the delay which would result from obtaining a medical examination would endanger life or property.

Name And Address Of Nearest Relative Or Guardian (Including Zip Code)	Name And Address Of Other Person Who May Testify To Facts (Including Zip Code)

Home Telephone No.	Business Telephone No.	Home Telephone No.	Business Telephone No.

I request the Court to authorize the transportation of the respondent to a 24-hour facility for temporary custody, observation and treatment pending a district court hearing.

SWORN AND SUBSCRIBED TO BEFORE ME	Signature Of Petitioner-Officer
Date	Name And Address Of Petitioner-Officer (Including Zip Code) (Type Or Print)
Signature	

☐ Deputy CSC   ☐ Assistant CSC   ☐ Clerk Of Superior Court
☐ Magistrate

Original-File   Copy-hospital   Copy-Special Counsel   Copy-Attorney General
(Over)

AOC-SP-909M, Rev. 9/03
© 2003 Administrative Office of the Courts

FINDINGS

The Court finds that there ☐ are ☐ are not reasonable grounds to believe that the facts alleged in the petition are true and that the respondent is probably a substance abuser and dangerous to himself or others.

The Court further finds by clear, cogent, and convincing evidence that the respondent ☐ is ☐ is not in fact violent and requires restraint, and delay in taking the respondent to a person authorized by law to conduct an examination, for examination would endanger life or property.

CUSTODY ORDER

TO ANY LAW ENFORCEMENT OFFICER

The Court orders you to take the named respondent into custody and transport the respondent directly to the 24-hour facility named below, for temporary custody, examination and treatment pending a district court hearing.

Name And Address of 24-Hour Facility For Substance Abuser	Date	Time ☐ AM ☐ PM
	Signature	
	☐ Deputy CSC ☐ Assistant CSC ☐ Clerk Of Superior Court ☐ Magistrate	

RETURN OF SERVICE

☐ The respondent WAS NOT taken into custody for the following reason:

☐ I certify that this Order was received and served as follows:

Date Respondent Taken Into Custody	Time ☐ AM ☐ PM

☐ I transported the respondent directly to and placed him in the temporary custody of the facility named below.

Name Of 24-Hour Facility For Substance Abuser	Date Order Received	Date Of Return
Date Delivered	Signature Of Law Enforcement Officer	
Time ☐ AM ☐ PM	Name Of Transporting Agency	

PETITIONER'S WAIVER OF NOTICE OF HEARING

I voluntarily waive my right to notice of all hearings and rehearings in which the Court may commit the respondent or extend the respondent's commitment period, or discharge the respondent from the treatment facility.

Signature Of Witness	Date
	Signature Of Petitioner-Officer

STATE OF NORTH CAROLINA

_____ County

File No. _____

In The General Court Of Justice
District Court Division

IN THE MATTER OF:
Name And Address Of Respondent (Including Zip Code)

AUTOMATIC
INVOLUNTARY COMMITMENT OF
DEFENDANT FOUND NOT GUILTY
BY REASON OF INSANITY

G.S. 15A-1321; 122C-268.1

FINDINGS AND COMMITMENT

The respondent has been charged in File No. _____ with a criminal offense in the above named county and has been found not guilty by reason of insanity.

Therefore, the Court ORDERS the respondent committed to the State 24-hour facility named below.

The Court also ORDERS the law enforcement agency named below to take the respondent into custody and transport the respondent directly to the State 24-hour facility named below for commitment.

Name Of State 24-Hour Facility	Date
	Signature Of Judge
Name Of Law Enforcement Agency To Transport	Name Of Judge (Type Or Print)

RETURN OF SERVICE

I certify that this Order was received and served as follows:

☐ I took respondent into custody and transported respondent directly to and placed respondent in the custody of the facility named below.

Date Respondent Taken Into Custody	Date Delivered
Name Of State 24-Hour Facility	

☐ I did not carry out the order for the following reason:

Date Order Received	Signature Of Law Enforcement Officer
Date Of Return	Name Of Transporting Agency

AOC-SP-910M, Rev. 7/98
© 1998 Administrative Office of the Courts

STATE OF NORTH CAROLINA

_____ County

File No.

In The General Court Of Justice
District Court Division

IN THE MATTER OF:

Name And Address Of Respondent

Name And Address Of Attorney For Respondent

APPOINTMENT OF COUNSEL AND
NOTICE OF HEARING/REHEARING
VOLUNTARY ADMISSION OF MINOR

G.S. 122C-224.1

To The Attorney For Respondent Named Above:

The respondent named above has been admitted to a 24-hour facility as a minor who is mentally ill or a substance abuser and is in need of treatment and is entitled to the appointment of counsel.

You are appointed as the attorney to represent the respondent in this matter.

A hearing will be held before a district court judge at the date, time and place indicated below. At that hearing it will be determined whether the Court concurs in the admission/readmission and whether the respondent's admission will be continued.

Date Of Hearing	Time	☐ AM ☐ PM	Place Of Hearing

I certify that I have mailed copies of this Notice by first class mail at least 72 hours before the hearing to the persons whose name and address are listed below:

Name And Address Of Respondent's Legally Responsible Person	Name And Address Of Responsible Professional At 24-hour Facility

Date	Signature	☐ Assistant CSC ☐ Clerk Of Superior Court

RETURN OF SERVICE

NOTE TO SHERIFF: _This Notice must be served on the respondent's attorney at least seventy-two (72) hours before the hearing._

I certify this Notice was received and served on the respondent as follows:

Date Served	Name Of Respondent's Attorney

☐ By delivering to the respondent's attorney a copy of this Notice.
☐ By leaving a copy of this Notice at the dwelling house or usual place of abode of the respondent's attorney with a person of suitable age and discretion residing therein.

Name And Address Of Person With Whom Copy Left

☐ Respondent's Attorney WAS NOT served for the following reason:

Date Received	Date Returned	Name Of Sheriff
County		Deputy Sheriff Making Return

AOC-SP-912M, Rev. 4/97
© 1997 Administrative Office of the Courts

STATE OF NORTH CAROLINA

_____ County

File No.

In The General Court Of Justice
District Court Division

IN THE MATTER OF:

Name And Address Of Respondent

ORDER
VOLUNTARY ADMISSION
OF MINOR

G.S. 122C-224, -224.3

FINDINGS

The Court finds that:

1. The respondent is a minor.
2. The respondent is represented by the attorney named below:

   Name Of Attorney

- [ ] 3. The respondent is present at the hearing.
- [ ] 4. The respondent appears before the Court to provide testimony and to answer the Court's questions; otherwise, respondent's appearance is waived.
- [ ] 5. The respondent's appearance is waived.
- 6. The respondent was voluntarily admitted to the 24-hour facility named below on the date specified.

   Name Of Facility

   Date Of Admission

- [ ] 7. The Court previously concurred in the admission, and the matter before the Court is the readmission of the respondent.

Based on the evidence presented, the Court

- [ ] 8. by clear, cogent and convincing evidence finds as facts all matters set out in the evaluation for admission/continued stay of the physician or other professional specified below, and the report is incorporated by reference as findings.

   Date Of Report

   Name Of Physician/Professional

- [ ] 9. by clear, cogent and convincing evidence finds these other facts:

CONCLUSIONS

Based on the above findings, the Court concludes that

- [ ] 1. the respondent
  - [ ] is [ ] is not mentally ill.
  - [ ] is [ ] is not a substance abuser.
  - [ ] is [ ] is not in need of continued treatment at the 24-hour facility to which the respondent has been admitted.
- [ ] 2. less restrictive measures would not be sufficient.
- [ ] 3. reasonable grounds exist to believe that the respondent is [ ] mentally ill [ ] a substance abuser and is in need of treatment at the 24-hour facility to which the respondent has been admitted but additional diagnosis and evaluation is needed before the court can concur in the admission.
- [ ] 4. the respondent does not meet the criteria for admission.

ORDER

- [ ] 1. The Court concurs with the voluntary admission and authorizes the continued admission of the respondent for the length of time specified below.

Length Of Admission	
	days

- [ ] 2. The Court authorizes an additional stay for the length of time specified below for further diagnosis and evaluation and ORDERS this matter rescheduled for further hearing at the date, time and place specified below:

Length Of Additional Stay	
	days (cannot exceed 15)

Date Of Hearing	Place Of Hearing
Time Of Hearing [ ] AM [ ] PM	

- [ ] 3. The Court does not concur in the voluntary admission and the respondent is ordered released.
- [ ] 4. Other:

Date	Name Of District Court Judge (Type Or Print)	Signature Of District Court Judge

AOC-SP-913M, Side Two, New 12/94
© 1997 Administrative Office of the Courts

STATE OF NORTH CAROLINA

_____ County

RELEASE OF PHYSICAL AND MENTAL HEALTH, SUBSTANCE ABUSE AND CONFIDENTIAL COURT RECORDS FOR CONCEALED HANDGUN PERMIT

Name And Address Of Applicant	Date Of Birth
	Social Security No.

State Drivers License No. (State Identification No. If No Drivers License)	State

I hereby authorize and require any and all doctors, hospitals or other providers who have ever provided physical or mental health or substance abuse treatment or care to me, including without limitation the providers named below, to release to the sheriff of the above named county any and all records concerning my physical capacity, mental health, mental capacity or substance abuse that the sheriff may reasonably request in connection with my application for a concealed handgun permit. The purpose of the release is to enable the sheriff to determine my qualification and competence to handle a handgun. I understand that alcohol and substance abuse information is protected by federal regulations and that other confidential records such as psychiatric information may be protected by North Carolina statute. Accordingly, I specifically authorize the release of any and all alcohol, substance abuse and psychiatric information that may be documented in my records.

I understand that further disclosure or redisclosure by the sheriff of any information disclosed to the sheriff pursuant to this Release is prohibited without my further written consent unless otherwise provided for by state of federal law. I understand that I may revoke this authorization at any time except to the extent that action has already been taken in reliance on this Release. Even without my express revocation, this Release will expire upon the satisfaction of the request or one year from the date below, whichever occurs first.

Name Of Provider	Address Of Provider

I also request and authorize any and all clerks of superior court of North Carolina to inform the sheriff of this County whether or not the clerk's records contain the record of any involuntary commitment proceeding under Article 5 of Chapter 122C of the General Statutes in which I have been named as a respondent and, if so, to reveal to the sheriff any confidential information in the court files or records of each such proceeding that the sheriff may reasonably require in order to determine whether or not to issue a concealed handgun permit to me. This Release may be treated as a motion in the cause within the meaning of G.S. 122C-54(d) and a clerk may reveal information to the sheriff pursuant to any specific or standing order entered in response to or anticipation of this motion.

Any expenses relating to the search, production, copying and certification of a medical or court record pursuant to this Release shall be my responsibility. I authorize the sheriff to photocopy this Release after I sign it, and I authorize any provider to whom a photocopy of this Release is presented to rely on the photocopy as being as effective as the original.

SWORN AND SUBSCRIBED TO BEFORE ME		Date
Date	Signature Of Person Authorized To Administer Oaths	Signature Of Applicant
Title		
Date Commission Expires		**SEAL**

AOC-SP-914M, New 12/95,
© 1997 Administrative Office of the Courts

STATE OF NORTH CAROLINA Department of Health and Human Services

Division of Mental Health, Developmental Disabilities, and Substance Abuse Services

County_____   File #_____

EXAMINATION AND RECOMMENDATION TO DETERMINE
NECESSITY FOR INVOLUNTARY COMMITMENT

Patient Record #_____   Film # _____

Name of Respondent:	Age	DOB	Sex	Race	M.S.

Address (Street, Box Number, City, State, Zip (use facility address after 1 year in facility):	County:
	Phone:

Legally Responsible Person ☐Next of Kin (Name and Address)	Relationship:
	Phone:

Petitioner (Name and address)	Relationship:
	Phone

The above-named respondent was examined on _____, 20___ at _____ o'clock ____.M. at _____ _____. OR, I examined the respondent via telemedicine technology on _____ 20___ at _____o'clock ___M. Included in the examination was an assessment of the respondent's: ☐ (1) current and previous mental illness or mental retardation including, if available, previous treatment history; (2) dangerousness to self or others as defined in G.S. 122C-3 (11*); (3) ability to survive safely without inpatient commitment, including the availability of supervision from family, friends, or others; and (4) capacity to make an informed decision concerning treatment. ☐ (1) current and previous substance abuse including, if available, previous treatment history; and (2) dangerousness to himself or others as defined in G.S. 122C-3 (11*). The following findings and recommendations are made based on this examination. For telemedicine evaluations only: ☐ I certify to a reasonable degree of medical certainty that the results of the examination via telemedicine were the same as if I had been personally present with the respondent OR ☐The respondent needs to be taken to a facility for face to face evaluation. (*Statutory Definitions are on reverse side)

SECTION I - CRITERIA FOR COMMITMENT

Inpatient. It is my opinion that the respondent is: ☐ mentally ill; ☐ dangerous to self; ☐ dangerous to others
(1st Exam – Physician or Psychologist)   ☐ in addition to being mentally ill is also mentally retarded
(2nd Exam – Physician only)   ☐   none of the above

Outpatient. It is my opinion that:
(Physician or Psychologist)
- ☐   the respondent is mentally ill
- ☐   the respondent is capable of surviving safely in the community with available supervision
- ☐   based upon the respondent's treatment history, the respondent is in need of treatment in order to prevent further disability or deterioration which would predictably result in dangerousness as defined by G.S. 122C-3 (11*)
- ☐   the respondent's current mental status or the nature of his illness limits or negates his/her ability to make an informed decision to seek treatment voluntarily or comply with recommended treatment
- ☐   none of above

Substance Abuse. It is my opinion that the respondent is:
(1st Exam – Physician or Psychologist; 2nd Exam – If 1st
Exam done by Physician, 2nd exam may be done by Qual. Prof.)
- ☐   a substance abuser
- ☐   dangerous to himself or others
- ☐   none of the above

SECTION II – DESCRIPTION OF FINDINGS

Clear description of findings (findings for each criterion checked above in Section I must be described):

over

Notable Physical Conditions: Current Medications (medical and psychiatric)

Impression/Diagnosis:

SECTION III - RECOMMENDATION FOR DISPOSITION

❑ Inpatient Commitment for _____ days (respondent must be mentally ill **and** dangerous to self or others)
❑ Outpatient Commitment (respondent must meet **ALL** of the first four criteria outlined in Section I, **Outpatient**)
Proposed Outpatient Treatment Center or Physician: (Name)_____
(Address and Phone Number)_____
_____
LME notified of appointment: (Name of LME and date)_____
❑ Substance Abuse Commitment (respondent must meet both criteria outlined in Section I, **Substance Abuse**)
    ❑ Release respondent pending hearing - Referred to:_____
    ❑ Hold respondent at 24-hour facility pending hearing – Facility: _____
❑ Respondent does not meet the criteria for commitment but custody order states that the respondent was charged with a
violent crime, including a crime involving assault with a deadly weapon, and that he was found not guilty by reason of insanity or
incapable of proceeding: therefore, the respondent will not be released until so ordered following the court hearing.
❑ Respondent or Legally Responsible Person Consented to Voluntary Treatment
❑ Release Respondent and Terminate Proceedings (insufficient findings to indicate that respondent meets commitment criteria)
❑ Respondent was held 7 days from issuance of custody order but continues to meet commitment criteria. A new petition will be filed.

❑ Other (*Specify*) _____

_____M.D. Physician Signature	This is to certify that this is a true and exact copy of the Examination and Recommendation for Involuntary Commitment
_____ Signature/Title – Eligible Psychologist/Qualified Professional	
_____ Print Name of Examiner	_____ Original Signature – Record Custodian
_____ Address or Facility	_____ Title
_____ City and State	_____ Address or Facility
_____ Telephone Number	_____ Date **NOTE:** Only copies to be introduced as evidence need to be certified

CC: Clerk of Superior Court where petition was initiated (initial hearing only)
Clerk of Superior Court where 24-hour facility is located or where outpatient treatment is supervised
Respondent or Respondent's Attorney and State's Attorneys, when applicable
Proposed Outpatient Treatment Center or Physician (Outpatient Commitment); Area Program / Physician (Substance Abuse Commitment)
NOTE: If it cannot be reasonably anticipated that the clerk will receive the copies within 48 hours of the time that it was signed, the physician
or eligible psychologist/qualified professional shall communicate his findings to the clerk by telephone.
*STATUTORY DEFINITIONS
"Dangerous to self". Within the relevant past: (a) the individual has acted in such a way as to show: (1) that he would be unable without car
supervision, and the continued assistance of others not otherwise available, to exercise self-control, judgment, and discretion in the conduct
his daily responsibilities and social relations or to satisfy his need for nourishment, personal or medical care, shelter, or self-protection a
safety; and (2) that there is a reasonable probability of his suffering serious physical debilitation within the near future unless adequate treatme
is given. A showing of behavior that is grossly irrational, of actions that the individual is unable to control, of behavior that is grossly inappropria
to the situation, or of other evidence of severely impaired insight and judgment shall create a **prima facie** inference that the individual is unab
to care for himself; or (b) the individual has attempted suicide or threatened suicide and that there is a reasonable probability of suicide unle
adequate treatment is given; or (c) the individual has mutilated himself or attempted to mutilate himself and that there is a reasonable probabil
of serious self-mutilation unless adequate treatment is given. NOTE: Previous episodes of dangerousness to self, when applicable, may
considered when determining reasonable probability of physical debilitation, suicide, or self-mutilation.
"Dangerous to others". Within the relevant past, the individual has inflicted or attempted to inflict or threatened to inflict serious bodily harm
another, or has acted in such a way as to create a substantial risk of serious bodily harm to another, or has engaged in extreme destruction
property; and that there is a reasonable probability that this conduct will be repeated. Previous episodes of dangerousness to others, wh
applicable, may be considered when determining reasonable probability of future dangerous conduct.
"Mental illness:. (a) when applied to an adult, an illness which so lessens the capacity of the individual to use self-control, judgment, a
discretion in the conduct of his affairs and social relations as to make it necessary or advisable for him to be under treatment, care, supervisio
guidance or control; and (b) when applied to a minor, a mental condition, other than mental retardation alone, that so lessens or impairs th
youth's capacity to exercise age adequate self-control and judgment in
the conduct of his activities and social relationships so that he is in need of treatment.
"Substance abuser". An individual who engages in the pathological use or abuse of alcohol or other drugs in a way or to a degree th
produces an impairment in personal, social, or occupational functioning. Substance abuse may include a pattern of tolerance and withdrawal.

STATE OF NORTH CAROLINA
Department of Health and Human Services
Division of Mental Health, Developmental Disabilities, and Substance Abuse Services

SUPPLEMENT TO EXAMINATION AND RECOMMENDATION FOR
INVOLUNTARY COMMITMENT

SUPPLEMENT TO SUPPORT IMMEDIATE HOSPITALIZATION
(To be used in addition to "Examination and Recommendation for Involuntary Commitment, Form 572-01)

CERTIFICATE

The Respondent, _____
requires immediate hospitalization to prevent harm to self or others because:

I certify that based upon my examination of the Respondent, which is attached hereto,
the Respondent is (check all that apply):

☐ Mentally ill and dangerous to self
☐ Mentally ill and dangerous to others
☐ In addition to being mentally ill, is also mentally retarded

_____
Signature of Physician or Eligible Psychologist

Address: _____
City State Zip: _____
Telephone: _____
Date/Time: _____

Name of 24-hour facility: _____
Address of 24-hour facility: _____

NORTH CAROLINA

_____ County
Sworn to and subscribed before me this
_____ day of _____, 20___

(seal)

_____
Notary Public

My commission expires:_____

CC: 24-hour facility
Clerk of Court in county of 24-hour facility

Note: If it cannot be reasonably anticipated that
the clerk will receive the copy within 24 hours
(excluding Saturday, Sunday and holidays) of the
time that it was signed, the physician or eligible
psychologist shall also communicate the findings
to the clerk by telephone.

Pursuant to G.S. 122C-262 (d), this certificate *shall serve as
the Custody Order* and the law enforcement officer or other
person *shall* provide transportation to a 24-hr. facility n
accordance with G.S. 122C-251.

TO LAW ENFORCEMENT: See back side for Return of Service

STATE OF NORTH CAROLINA
Department of Health and Human Services
Division of Mental Health, Developmental Disabilities, and Substance Abuse Services

SUPPLEMENT TO EXAMINATION AND RECOMMENDATION FOR
INVOLUNTARY COMMITMENT

RETURN OF SERVICE

☐ Respondent **WAS NOT** taken into custody for the following reason:

☐ I certify that this Order was received and served as follows:

Date Respondent Taken into Custody	Time	☐ AM ☐ PM
Name of 24-Hour Facility	*Date Delivered*	*Time Delivered* AM ☐ PM ☐ — *Date of Return*
Name of Transporting Agency	*Signature of Law Enforcement Official*	

STATE OF NORTH CAROLINA
Department of Health and Human Services
Division of Mental Health, Developmental Disabilities, and Substance Abuse Services

SUPPLEMENT TO EXAMINATION AND RECOMMENDATION FOR
INVOLUNTARY COMMITMENT

SUPPLEMENT TO SUPPORT IMMEDIATE HOSPITALIZATION
(To be used in addition to "Examination and Recommendation for Involuntary Commitment, Form 572-01)

CERTIFICATE

The Respondent, _____
requires immediate hospitalization to prevent harm to self or others because:

I certify that based upon my examination of the Respondent, which is attached hereto,
the Respondent is (check all that apply):

☐ Mentally ill and dangerous to self
☐ Mentally ill and dangerous to others
☐ In addition to being mentally ill, is also mentally retarded

_____
Signature of Physician or Eligible Psychologist

Address: _____
City State Zip: _____
Telephone: _____
Date/Time: _____

NORTH CAROLINA

_____ County
Sworn to and subscribed before me this
_____ day of _____, 20___

(seal)

| CC: 24-hour facility |
| Clerk of Court in county of 24-hour facility |

_____
Notary Public

My commission expires:_____

STATE OF NORTH CAROLINA   **EVALUATION FOR ADMISSION / CONTINUED STAY**
Department of Health and Human Services
Division of Mental Health, Developmental Disabilities, and Substance Abuse Services

County _____   **(Restrictive 24-hour Facilities)**   File # _____
Client Record # _____   **Voluntary Minors and Incompetent Adults**   File # _____

NAME OF MINOR OR INCOMPETENT ADULT	AGE	BIRTHDATE	SEX	RACE	M.S.
ADDRESS (Street, Apt., Route, Box Number, City, State, Zip - Use facility address after 1 year in facility)				County	
				Phone	
LEGALLY RESPONSIBLE PERSON (Name and Address)				Relationship	
				Phone	

The above-named ☐ minor ☐ incompetent adult was examined on _____, 20____, at _____ o'clock _____.m.
in _____. The results of the examination are as
follows:

DESCRIPTION OF FINDINGS   (Include indications for mental illness or substance abuse and need for further treatment or evaluation. Also include information provided by family members regarding the individual's need for further treatment).

(OVER)

DESCRIPTION OF FINDINGS (continued): _____

Form No. DMH 5-73-01   EVALUATION FOR ADMISSION / CONTINUED STAY
Revised September 2001   (Restrictive 24-hour facilities)
                                 Voluntary Minors and Incompetent Adults

NOTABLE PHYSICAL CONDITIONS:

CURRENT MEDICATIONS (Medical and Psychiatric):

IMPRESSION / DIAGNOSIS:

As a result of my examination, it is my opinion that the above-named individual:

☐ IS ☐ IS NOT mentally ill or a substance abuser
☐ IS ☐ IS NOT in need of further evaluation by the facility
☐ DOES NEED OR CAN BENEFIT ☐ DOES NOT NEED OR CANNOT BENEFIT from the care, treatment, habilitation or rehabilitation available at the facility

RECOMMENDATION FOR DISPOSITION:

☐ Admit for treatment / rehabilitation (applies to initial hearings only)
☐ Admit for further diagnosis and evaluation not to exceed an additional 15 days following the initial hearing
☐ Continue treatment for _____ days (applies to rehearings only)
☐ Other (Specify) _____
_____

_____ Signature / Title - Responsible Professional	This is to certify that this is a true and exact copy of the Evaluation For Admission / Continued Stay. _____ Original Signature - Record Custodian
_____ Print Name of Responsible Professional	_____ Title
_____ Facility Name and Address	_____ Facility Name and Address
_____ City, State, Zip	_____ Date
_____ Telephone Number	NOTE: Only copies to be introduced as evidence need to be certified.

Original: Medical Record
cc: Clerk of Superior Court
 Where facility is located
 Respondent's Attorney
 State's Attorney

STATE OF NORTH CAROLINA
Department of Health and Human Services
Division of Mental Health, Developmental Disabilities, and Substance Abuse Services

REQUEST FOR HEARING

House Bill 95   ☐ Yes   ☐ No   If "Yes", Clerk of Court notified by phone on Date: _____   File #_____ Film #_____

Facility Name: _____

Facility Address: _____
                                                                                    COUNTY

IN THE MATTER OF:

Respondent's name: _____ Client Record Number: _____

Unit/ Building/ Ward (when applicable): _____

TO: Clerk of Superior Court of _____ County

This serves as official notice that an ☐ initial hearing,☐ supplemental hearing, ☐first rehearing, or
☐ **subsequent rehearing needs to be scheduled for the above named respondent for the following reason:**

☐   ☐ Inpatient   ☐ Outpatient   ☐ Combination Inpatient-Outpatient
      ☐ Substance Abuse treatment will be necessary beyond _____(Commitment Expiration Date)
      Attached is the Examination and Recommendation to Determine Necessity for Involuntary Commitment (DMH 572-01).

☐   A hearing is required to determine the appropriateness of the respondent's:
      ☐ Continued inpatient treatment   ☐ Outpatient treatment   ☐ Discharge
      ☐ Conditional release and the respondent was committed as a result of conduct resulting in his being charged with a
      violent crime including a crime involving an assault with a deadly weapon, and the respondent was found not guilty by
      reason of insanity or incapable of proceeding to trial.

☐   The respondent has failed to comply or clearly refuses to comply with all or part of the prescribed Outpatient treatment.
      A report of reasonable efforts made to solicit the respondent's compliance is attached.

☐   The respondent is an ☐ outpatient ☐ substance abuse commitment and intends to move or has moved to another
      county within the state. Attached is the Examination and Recommendation to Determine Necessity for Involuntary
      Commitment (DMH 572-01).

☐   The respondent is currently under inpatient commitment but now meets the criteria for outpatient commitment. Attached
      is the Examination and Recommendation to Determine Necessity for Involuntary Commitment (DMH 572-01).

☐   The respondent is a ☐ minor ☐ incompetent adult in a restrictive 24-hour facility as a hearing needs to be scheduled to
      determine whether the court concurs with the voluntary admission/continued stay. Treatment will be necessary beyond
      _____ (Expiration date). Attached is the Evaluation for Admission/Continued Stay (DMH 573-01). If
      initial hearing, please attach copy of Application for Admission.

☐   The respondent was transferred to the above named facility on _____(date) from
      _____ (transferring facility) in _____ County prior to the
      ☐ initial judicial commitment hearing ☐ initial judicial determination (involuntary minors and voluntary incompetent
      adults).

☐   The respondent, who is under substance abuse commitment, will require treatment in a 24-hour facility beyond 45
      consecutive days. The 45 days will expire on _____ (date). Attached is the Examination and
      Recommendation to Determine Necessity for Involuntary Commitment.

☐
      Clerk: Please issue Subpoena To Testify to respondent for hearing requested above. .

DISTRIBUTION WHEN REQUEST TO RETURN IS ISSUED:
Original: Clerk of Superior Court where facility is located   _____
          Outpatient or Substance Abuse – Clerk of Superior Court   Signature & Title
          Where commitment is supervised
CC: Medical Records   NOTE: If current status is:
        Respondent's Attorney, when applicable   - Inpatient Commitment – must be signed by Attending Physician
        State's Attorney, when applicable   - Outpatient or Substance Abuse Commitment -- must be signed by
        * Respondant   ** Petitioner   Responsible Professional

DMH 5-76-01   REQUEST FOR HEARING
Revised September 2001

STATE OF NORTH CAROLINA
Department of Health and Human Services
Division of Mental Health, Developmental Disabilities, and Substance Abuse Services

NOTICE OF COMMITMENT CHANGE

Facility Name: _____ File #:_____

Film #:_____

Facility Address: _____ (Physical location) _____

IN THE MATTER OF: Respondent's Name:_____

Client Record Number: _____

Unit/Building/Ward (When Applicable): _____
Date of ☐ Inpatient   ☐ Outpatient   ☐ Substance Abuse Commitment_____

TO: Clerk of Superior Court, _____ County

This is to certify that the commitment status of the above-named respondent has changed due to the following:

☐ The respondent is no longer in need of inpatient hospitalization and is unconditionally discharged on _____(date).

☐ The respondent no longer meets the criteria for ☐ outpatient ☐ substance abuse commitment and is discharged on _____.
(Date)

☐ The respondent is no longer in need of inpatient treatment and is conditionally released on _____(date) to be followed by unconditional discharge on _____(date).

Conditions of release are: _____

☐ The respondent ☐ escaped ☐ breached conditions of release on _____(date); and is discharged from unauthorized absence on _____ (date).

☐ The respondent or legally responsible person signed a consent for voluntary treatment on _____(date).

☐ The respondent was admitted as a voluntary minor and has turned 18 years of age. The respondent signed a consent for voluntary treatment on _____ (date).

☐ The respondent was admitted to a 24-hour facility on an involuntary basis on _____ (date). Therefore, outpatient commitment is terminated.

☐ The respondent has moved to another state or location of respondent is unknown so commitment is terminated on _____(date).

☐ The respondent is no longer in need of inpatient treatment. The respondent is released from inpatient commitment and is committed by the court to outpatient treatment for _____ days on _____(date). The respondent was discharged from the 24-hour facility on _____(date).

☐ The respondent is on a split commitment and is no longer in need of inpatient treatment. The respondent is released from inpatient hospitalization and is committed to outpatient treatment for _____ days on _____ (date).

☐ The respondent was transferred to _____ in _____ County on _____(date).

☐ The respondent expired on _____ (date).

☐ Other (Specify):_____

_____   _____
Signature/Title   **Date**

NOTE: If current status is Inpatient Commitment signature must be that of Attending Physician.
If current status is Outpatient or Substance Abuse Commitment, signature must be that of Responsible Professional.

Original: Clerk of Superior Court where petition initiated _____ (date). (Specify: _____)
Copy: Clerk of Superior Court where facility located _____(date).
          Clerk of Superior Court where outpatient or substance abuse commitment supervised _____ (date).
          (Specify: _____).
          Medical Record
          Respondent and State's Attorney _____ (date).
          Designated outpatient treatment center or physician _____ (Date).(Specify_____)

Form No. DMH 5-79-01   NOTICE OF COMMITMENT CHANGE
Revised September 2001

STATE OF NORTH CAROLINA
Department of Health and Human Services
Division of Mental Health, Developmental Disabilities, and Substance Abuse Services

REQUEST TO RETURN ESCAPEE OR CONDITIONAL RELEASEE

DATE: _____ TO: _____ FROM: _____
(Sheriff/Law Enforcement Officer)   (Facility)   (Where Facility is Located)

Patient's name: _____ Also known as_____

Hospital Number: _____ SS#: _____

Last known home address: _____ Admit date: _____

Hospital Unit/Bldg/Ward_____

This is to notify you that the above named patient from _____County ❏ ESCAPED on _____
                                                    (home county)

❏ BREACHED THE CONDITION OF
HIS/HER RELEASE ON _____

The patient is: ❏ Under involuntary commitment
❏ following being charged with a violent crime and found not guilty by reason of insanity (**NGRI**) or incapable of proceeding (**HB 95**)

❏ A competent adult voluntarily admitted and in my opinion is reasonable foreseeable that:
  1) he/she may cause physical harm to others or himself;
  2) he/she may cause damage to property
  3) he/she may commit a felony or a violent misdemeanor; or
  4) the health or safety of the client may be endangered unless he/she is immediately returned to the facility

❏ A minor or incompetent adult voluntarily admitted
❏ Admitted pending a judicial hearing
❏ Under conditional release from the facility
❏ Involuntarily committed or voluntarily admitted and under a **DETAINER** issued by _____

Patient was last seen: Date: _____ Time: _____ Wearing: _____

Location:
❏ Activity Area	❏ Clinic	❏ Dining room	❏ Gym	❏ Work Activity
❏ Activity Trip	❏ Courtroom	❏ Elevator	❏ Hallway	❏ Unknown
❏ Bathroom	❏ Courtyard	❏ Grill/Canteen	❏ Medical Transport	❏ Other _____
❏ Bedroom	❏ Dayroom	❏ Grounds	❏ Stairway	

The above named patient is to be taken into custody and returned to the above named facility pursuant to G.S. 122C-205.

PATIENT IDENTIFYING INFORMATION

Race _____ Sex ___ Place of birth (state)_____ Date of birth _____ Age ____ Height _____ Weight _____

Eye color _____ Hair color _____ Hair style _____ Skin tone _____

Scars/Marks/Tattoos _____Facial features _____

Build _____ Gait _____ Other distinguishing features _____

Patient has vehicle at hospital ❏ yes ❏ no If yes, vehicle license number: _____ Vehicle lic state: _____

Type of vehicle: _____ Vehicle year: _____ Vehicle make: _____

Vehicle style:_____ Vehicle color:_____

Dangerous to self ❏ no ❏ yes (specify) _____

Dangerous to others: ❏ no ❏ yes (specify)_____

Avoids people ❏ no ❏ yes **Medical Conditions/Impairments:**_____ **Needs further treatment:** ❏ yes ❏ no

ADDITIONAL INFORMATION

Additional information that is reasonably necessary to assure the expeditious return of the client and protect the patient and/or the general public (including possible locations and contacts): _____
_____

Signature of Authorizing Physician	**Printed name**	**Date**

DISTRIBUTION WHEN REQUEST TO RETURN IS ISSUED:
Nursing Staff: HIM (original copy)   Official placing patient on detainer
                Initial examiner if involuntarily committed   Area program (if appropriate)   Next of kin/legally responsible party
                Any law enforcement office notified   Clerk of Superior Court in county of commitment

DMH 5-82-02   REQUEST TO RETURN ESCAPEE OR CONDITIONAL RELEASEE
Revised September 2001

NOT CE OF RETURN OF ESCAPEE OR CONDITIONAL RELEASE

Date: _____ Date of UA: _____   Facility:_____

Re: _____   Address:_____
                (Patient)   _____

Last known address: _____

Medical Record Number: _____   Unit/Bldg: _____

This is to notify you that the above named patient was returned to the above named facility
on _____ at _____ **following his/her** ❏ ESCAPE ❏ BREACH OF CONDITIONAL RELEASE.
   (date)   (time)

Patient returned via: ❏ self   ❏ police _____ ❏ family   ❏ other _____
                           (specify agency)   (specify)

Location of patient when found: _____

Incident(s) that occurred to patient during elopement

❏ None/unknown   ❏ Assault   ❏ Drug/Alcohol use   ❏ Rape   ❏ Self-injurious behavior   ❏ Suicide

❏ Suicide attempt   ❏ Other _____

Severity of injury/damage to patient

❏ No treatment/injury   ❏ Medica intervention required   ❏ No property damage

❏ Unknown   ❏ Hospitalization required   ❏ Minimal property damage

❏ Minor first aide   ❏ Death   ❏ Substantial property damage

Incident(s) committed by patient during elopement

❏ Assault   ❏ Homicide   ❏ Rape   ❏ Theft   ❏ Breaking & Entering   ❏ None/Unknown

❏ Other _____

Severity of injury/damage to victim (other than patient)

❏ No treatment/injury   ❏ Medica intervention required   ❏ No property damage

❏ Unknown   ❏ Hospitalization required   ❏ Minimal property damage

❏ Minor first aide   ❏ Death   ❏ Substantial property damage

_____
Signature and Title of Responsible Professional

DISTRIBUTION: Any law enforcement office notified   Risk management coordinator
                 HIM   Official placing patient on detainer
                 Initial examiner if involuntarily committed   Next of kin/legally responsible party
                 Area program (if appropriate)   Clerk of Superior Court in county of commitment

Appendix B
Motions

Motion for Continuance and Order Allowing Continuance

Waiver of Appearance and Order Allowing Waiver of Appearance
(Adults and Involuntary Minors)

Motion to Waive Appearance and Order Allowing Waiver of Appearance
(Voluntary Minor)

Motion to Waive Right to Testify and Order Allowing Waiver of Right to Testify
(Voluntary Minor)

Notice of Objection to Venue and Order Transferring Venue
(Involuntary Adults and Minors)

STATE OF NORTH CAROLINA

COUNTY OF WAKE

IN THE GENERAL COURT OF JUSTICE
DISTRICT COURT DIVISION
FILE NO. _____

IN THE MATTER OF   )
)
)
_____)
           Respondent   )

MOTION FOR CONTINUANCE

Now comes the undersigned (Special Counsel)(attorney) for the above-named Respondent whose involuntary commitment hearing or voluntary admission hearing is calendared for this date _____, and requests that the Court continue the case (for the reasons stated) (for the following reasons: _____), until the date _____, pursuant to G.S. 122C-268(a)(2) or G. S. 122C-232(a)(2) or G.S. 122C-224(a).

This the ____ day of _____, 2006.

_____
Jane Doe
(Special Counsel) (Attorney at Law)
(Hospital)(Business address)
Raleigh, NC 27---

ORDER ALLOWING CONTINUANCE

Based upon the reasons stated, the Court finds good cause for continuance of this matter; it is therefore ORDERED that this matter be continued until the ____ day of _____, 2006.

This the ____ day of _____, 2006.

_____
Judge Presiding

STATE OF NORTH CAROLINA

COUNTY OF WAKE

IN THE GENERAL COURT OF JUSTICE
DISTRICT COURT DIVISION
FILE NO. _____

IN THE MATTER OF)
)
_____)
_____)
Respondent)

WAIVER OF APPEARANCE
(Adults and Involuntary Minors)

      Now comes the undersigned (Special Counsel)(attorney) for the above-named Respondent whose involuntary commitment hearing or voluntary admission hearing is scheduled for the ____ day of _____, 2006, and requests that the presence of the Respondent at this hearing be waived as provided by G.S. 122C-268(e).

      This the ____ day of _____, 2006.

_____
Jane Doe
(Special Counsel)(Attorney at Law)
(Hospital)(Business address)
Raleigh, NC 27---

ORDER ALLOWING WAIVER OF APPEARANCE

      Based upon the written request of the counsel for Respondent in the above-captioned matter, the Court consents to the waiver of the personal appearance of Respondent at the hearing of this matter.

      IT IS ORDERED that the hearing on involuntary commitment or voluntary admission of the above-named Respondent shall proceed without the personal presence of the Respondent and the Respondent's right to be present at the proceeding is hereby waived.

      This the ____ day of _____, 2006.

_____
Judge Presiding

STATE OF NORTH CAROLINA   IN THE GENERAL COURT OF JUSTICE
                                       DISTRICT COURT DIVISION
COUNTY OF WAKE   FILE NO. _____

IN THE MATTER OF   )
)   MOTION TO WAIVE
)   APPEARANCE
_____   )   (Voluntary Minor)
          Minor   )

       Now comes the undersigned (Special Counsel)(attorney) for the above-named minor whose hearing on voluntary admission is scheduled for the ____ day of _____, 2006, and moves that the presence of the minor at this hearing be waived as provided by G.S. 122C-224.2(b).

       This the ____ day of _____, 2006.

                                   _____
                                   Jane Doe
                                   (Special Counsel)(Attorney at Law)
                                   (Hospital)(Business address)
                                   Raleigh, NC 27---

ORDER ALLOWING WAIVER OF APPEARANCE

       Based upon motion of counsel for the minor in the above-captioned matter, the Court consents to the waiver of the personal appearance of the minor at the hearing of this matter.

       IT IS ORDERED that the hearing on voluntary admission of the above-named minor shall proceed without the personal presence of the minor and minor's right to be present at the proceeding is hereby waived.

       This the _____ day of _____, 2006.

                                   _____
                                   Judge Presiding

STATE OF NORTH CAROLINA

COUNTY OF WAKE

IN THE GENERAL COURT OF JUSTICE
DISTRICT COURT DIVISION
FILE NO. _____

IN THE MATTER OF)
)
)
_____)
          Minor   )

MOTION TO WAIVE
RIGHT TO TESTIFY
(Voluntary Minor)

      Now comes the undersigned (Special Counsel)(attorney) for the above-named minor whose hearing on voluntary admission is scheduled for the ____ day of _____, 2006, and moves that the right of the minor to testify at this hearing be waived as provided by G.S. 122C-224.2(b).

      This the ____ day of _____, 2006.

                                _____
                                  Jane Doe
                                  (Special Counsel)(Attorney at Law)
                                  (Hospital)(Business address)
                                  Raleigh, NC 27---

ORDER ALLOWING WAIVER OF RIGHT TO TESTIFY

      Based upon motion of counsel for the minor in the above-captioned matter, the Court consents to the waiver of the right of the minor to testify at the hearing of this matter.

      IT IS ORDERED that the hearing on voluntary admission of the above-named minor shall proceed without the testimony of the minor and minor's right to testify at the proceeding is hereby waived.

      This the _____ day of _____, 2006.

                                  _____
                                  Judge Presiding

STATE OF NORTH CAROLINA   IN THE GENERAL COURT OF JUSTICE
                                            DISTRICT COURT DIVISION
COUNTY OF WAKE   FILE NO. _____

IN THE MATTER OF   )
)   NOTICE OF OBJECTION
)   TO VENUE
_____)   (Involuntary Adults and Minors)
              Respondent   )

        Now comes the undersigned (Special Counsel)(attorney) for the above-named
Respondent and gives notice of objection to venue in the District Court, _____
Judicial District, _____ County, North Carolina and requests pursuant to G.S. 122C-
269 (a) that the hearing in this matter be held in the county where the petition was
initiated.

        This the ____ day of _____, 2006.

                                            _____
                                            Jane Doe
                                            (Special Counsel) (Attorney at Law)
                                            (Hospital)(Business address)
                                            Raleigh, NC 27---

                        ORDER TRANSFERRING VENUE

        The attorney for the Respondent in the above-captioned matter having objected to
venue in _____, it is ORDERED that venue is transferred to _____
County.

        This the ____ day of _____, 2006.

                                            _____
                                            Judge Presiding

Appendix C
Working with Clients

Judith L. Kornegay, "Working with Clients," *from* Training in Civil Commitment Law: Representing People Facing Commitment (Feb. 21–22, 2003) (training program co-sponsored by UNC School of Government and Office of Indigent Defense Services)

WORKING WITH CLIENTS
INVOLUNTARY COMMITMENT CLE
DURHAM, NORTH CAROLINA
Friday, February 21, 2003

INTRODUCTION

The 3 most important things I have to share:

1) The main difference between our clients and the rest of us is that we know their diagnoses.

2) You do not have to listen to everything a bi-polar client in a manic phase has to say.

3) We work for the client.

In our society, there is an almost inherent paternalistic, human quality of wanting to take care of/protect those whom we perceive to be disadvantaged and a tendency to believe that we know better than they do what is best for them. Even though we are trained to zealously advocate for our clients, we are only human and can fall prey to this tendency. If a person is perceived to be mentally ill or a substance abuser, this human quality and tendency encourages many lay people--including attorneys, and judges--to want to do what is in the best interest of mental patients--often deferring completely to the doctor's recommendations or giving the doctor's opinion undue weight.

If we want to represent respondents in involuntary commitment hearings, then we have to disabuse ourselves of this notion and the related tendency. We must remember that we work for our clients and let them determine their own position. This is true even if the client has been declared incompetent. The incompetent client already has a guardian to act in his best interest, and our job is to protect the client's rights. If the client is unable to determine his/her own position, we cannot assume that the client consents to commitment or that this inability to do so invites or requires us to substitute our judgment of what is best for our client. The involuntary commitment procedure, like other legal procedures, is designed to require that the prosecuting attorney must make the case for commitment and the court must make the ultimate decision. If we substitute our judgment for our client's, we thwart the process and the system, as well as violate our client's right to a zealous advocate.

I. HOW WE DO OUR JOB MAY DETERMINE IF WE MAKE THINGS BETTER OR WORSE FOR OUR CLIENTS

A. There is an underlying conflict between legal rights and right to treatment

1. Medical point of view

Treatment staff may focus on the patient's medical need for treatment as being paramount to other legal rights. They may see legal process as intruding on their

1

work and client's treatment rights and interfering with treatment. Specifically, they may express:

(a) Concerns that patient access to medical evidence may prematurely reveal information that the patient is not ready to know.

(b) Concerns that legal process undermines the patient/therapist relationship.

(c) Concerns that the patient treatment time, energy, and focus is diverted to fighting commitment rather than participating in and benefiting from treatment.

(d) Concerns that their finite treatment resources are being depleted by court related demands.

(e) Concerns that may become pressure on the patient's attorney to do or refrain from doing certain things for treatment purposes (e.g., not reveal certain information to the client, not engage with family members because they fear this may undermine other treatment goals, etc.)

And may be is a legitimate basis for all of these concerns.

2. Legal point of view

The constitutional rights to liberty, freedom of speech, and freedom of association demand that due process requirements be strictly followed in order to force psychiatric hospitalization and treatment on anyone involuntarily.

B. How we approach client may influence/direct their position regarding IVC

1. It is our job to be sure that our clients understand:

a. Their legal rights regarding involuntary commitment

b. The legal process

c. Their options

2. Not our job to:

a. Direct/influence the client's decision regarding whether or not to contest IVC

b. Direct the client's decision regarding treatment or to interfere in treatment

C. How we approach client may influence their treatment

1. We may upset the client-

IVC clients may already feel criminalized due to their treatment by law enforcement and outpatient experience prior to admission and may fear imprisonment.

The client may have directly or tangentially related criminal charges, domestic violence protective orders, or DSS child protection proceedings and the client may have concerns that IVC will adversely affect these matters or their ability to participate in them due to their confinement.

The client may have irrational fears or response to having an attorney.

The client may learn from the attorney for the first time that he or she is hospitalized on involunary commitment status or what that status means. The client may have sought treatment and believe that he or she is a voluntary patient; have been coerced into IVC; been told that the hospitalization would only be for 3 days; or given other erroneous information.

If the client becomes preoccupied with the court hearing, s/he may disengage from treatment or behave in ways that may be used to provide more evidence for IVC or may act out in ways that lead to more intrusive treatment.

2. We may calm or relieve the client-

The client may believe for the first time since hospitalization that someone is really supporting him or her, is willing to consider his or her point of view, or that s/he has a voice in the decision making regarding treatment and hospitalization. The client may find it easier to make treatment decisions knowing that s/he has a legal advocate.

If the client's rights were violated in the process or if s/he feels treated badly, the client may appreciate an advocate who recognizes and validates that.

II. GENERAL CONSIDERATIONS IN DECIDING HOW TO APPROACH A CLIENT

A. WHEN TO SEE THE CLIENT

It is important to see the client as soon as possible. The timing of the first contact may be determined by a number of factors, including how far in advance of the hearing the attorney is appointed/notified of the appointment; when the attorney is notified of the doctor's recommendations regarding commitment (it may be difficult to interview the client without knowing what the doctor is recommending because the client usually wants to know the recommendation and the uncertainty of not knowing can cause additional problems for the client); and whether the attorney will have more than one opportunity to meet with the client prior to the hearing.

N.C.G.S. 122C-224.2 requires that the attorney for a minor must meet with the minor client within 10 days of appointment but not later than 48 hours before the hearing.

B. WHETHER OR NOT TO REVIEW THE RECORD IN ADVANCE (OR DISCUSS CLIENT WITH HOSPITAL STAFF)

There are differing points of view about how much information the attorney should obtain prior to initially interviewing the client. Those who advise against reviewing records prior to the initial client contact base their objection on the possibility that the attorney will be influenced to believe the validity of allegations and medical evidence and conclusions regarding mental illness and danger, thereby undermining their objectivity. It is obviously necessary for the attorney not to have preconceived notions regarding the client's mental illness, substance abuse, or dangerousness.

As with other types of representation, many find it ill advised not to obtain information in advance of the initial client interview for a number of reasons, including assessing personal safety; and to identify issues and matters necessary to discuss with the client.

It is appropriate for the attorney to carefully review the allegations of petitioner and referral sources upon which petition is based and medical conclusions may be based.

In addition to a thorough review of the legal documents attendant to the IVC proceeding, it is helpful to review the following information which is found in the client's hospital chart:

> Referral information
> Triage information
> Admission summary
> Admission physical exam
> Toxicology screens
> 2nd QPE
> Medications (checking for compliance/noncompliance, effects, side effects)
> Restraints/take downs
> Progress reports

Recorded observations of treatment team members of client behavior in the hospital may or may not tend to support the factual allegations and medical conclusions and recommendations.

It may also be helpful to ask staff about medical/medication issues you don't understand, safety concerns, and details or the basis of chart notes.

C. SAFETY CONSIDERATIONS-The attorney should have healthy concern for his or her own physical safety from dangerous or unpredictable clients and should take care to try to avoid placing clients in situations in which they may threaten, harm or attempt to harm the attorney or behave in a manner that provides additional evidence of commitability. Note allegations of dangerousness in the petition and the 1st and 2nd QPEs and follow up in the chart or with hospital staff to determine if evidence of danger to others, or threats of danger, have occurred or continued during hospitalization. Sometimes behavior or threats of danger to others occurs during hospitalization even if it is not alleged in the petition or required exams.

D. INTERVIEW SPACE-The hospital is required to provide space for the attorney/client interview. Be sure that the space is suitable for the needs of the particular client and interview, and request an alternative space if it is not suitable; or suggest how the space might be modified to be suitable. Sometimes simply arranging the furniture so that the attorney will sit near the door and the client will sit across a desk or table from the attorney and providing for a hospital staff member to escort the client into and out of the room provides sufficient protection.

E. CONFIDENTIALITY-The client has the right to confidential communication with his/her attorney. If the client understands that s/he is entitled to a confidential interview but wants to have someone else present during the interview anyway, those wishes should be accommodated, if possible. Otherwise, unless safety concerns require the presence of a third person, the interview space should allow for a confidential exchange. There are a number of ways that might provide enough safety without actually having another person present, such as interviewing in an observation room without the sound system on or leaving the room door open with a third party outside able to see in, but not within hearing distance.

F. DISCLOSURE OF ALLEGATIONS AND EVIDENCE TO THE CLIENT-
A client is entitled to know the allegations and evidence against him or her. G.S. 122C-53 governs disclosure of confidential mental health records to patients, allowing the attending physician (or in the absence of an attending physician, the facility director of his designee) to determine if the information "would be injurious to a client's physical or mental well being" and if so, to refuse patient requests to see the information. There is no case law construing this provision, and good legal reasoning can determine that all QPEs, medical records upon which they are based, and any other relevant evidentiary information contained in the medical record is evidence against the client and he or she is entitled to be informed of the contents of those records or to see them. It is difficult, if not impossible, to adequately represent a client without candid discussion of the evidence supporting the petition and the doctor's recommendations.

It is important to be mindful that these records may contain information unknown to or withheld from the client and from sources who wish not to be identified. The information may be sensitive and could cause additional problems for the client. Utmost care should be exercised in discussing information contained in the medical record with the client. Also bear in mind any safety considerations that may apply.

III. CLIENT SPECIFIC CONSIDERATIONS IN INTERVIEWS

A. PHYSICAL CONSIDERATIONS-Usually the client's significant physical conditions are identified by medical history, during intake, or during the course of hospitalization, and this information is available to counsel. However, sometimes a client may have an unidentified physical or medical problem that impacts communication, participation in treatment, cooperation with counsel, or participation in the client's defense. Be alert to your own observations of the client and follow up on indications of an unidentified problem. Also be sure to ask the client if they can hear and understand you, see you, etc. If you are unsure if they understand or of the reliability of their response, try a common sense check of your own.

1. MOBILITY-Does the client have the physical ability to get comfortably to, from, in, and out of the interview space? If the client is bedridden, try to arrange the interview when the client's roommate is out of the room. If the client is in a wheelchair or has difficulty ambulating, is the interview space conveniently located? Is it appropriate for the attorney to wheel a patient to and from the interview? Is the attorney comfortable doing so, or is there hospital policy concerning non employees doing this? Is there someone available who can push the wheelchair? Is there some other seating arrangement that meets the physical needs of the client?

2. HEARING IMPAIRMENT-Determine in advance if the client has an identified hearing impairment, what accommodations are needed to communicate with the client, and if they are available. Do not assume the client can hear and understand you. Ask or otherwise determine to your own satisfaction if the client is able to hear and understand you.

Does the client have a hearing aid and, if so, is it at the hospital? Involuntary clients do not usually get to pack their things before being transported and often do not have eye glasses, false teeth, hearing aids, prosthetic limbs, and other necessary appliances. If the client's hearing aid is not at the hospital, can anything be done to get it for him or her?

Is it necessary to speak very loudly? If so, does the interview space provided allow the attorney and client to talk loud enough without being overheard by others?

Will writing or typing assist the client in communicating and understanding and, if so, are writing implements or a keyboard available?

Does the client read lips? If so, take care to be sure that the space (and the court room) is set up so that the attorney and client can be positioned appropriately and with enough light for the client to lip read. Also be sure that during the hearing, everyone in the process is positioned and speaks so that the client can see/hear what is being said. This may require reminders from counsel during the course of the hearing.

Is an interpreter needed and, if so, is one available? Is there a qualified court interpreter available? If the client has a hearing impairment, an important consideration will be whether the hospital is able to provide appropriate treatment to the patient. Milieu therapy consisting of watching videos and group sessions may not be of service at all to some hearing impaired clients.

3. VISUAL IMPAIRMENT-Does the client have a visual impairment that affects his/her ability to participate in the interview/treatment? If so, what is needed to accommodate this disability? Does this impact on treatment?

4. OTHER COMMUNICATION PROBLEMS-Does the client have problems with receptive or expressive language? With uncommunicative clients, try different techniques to get them to respond to you: write them a note; ask them to nod or blink their eyes; see if they can use a keyboard. Sometimes clients' physical/medical impairments might be missed and their nonresponsiveness is otherwise mistaken for a symptom of mental illness. Do not assume that a client described as nonresponsive cannot hear or understand you. Try different methods.

5. OVERMEDICATION-Clients may be given large doses of antipsychotic drugs upon admission or if deemed necessary during treatment, with the side effect of making them groggy, unable to completely wake up, slurring their speech, or otherwise making communication with them difficult or impossible. Sometimes combinations of medications clients are prescribed for other medical conditions make them appear to exhibit symptoms of mental illness. When clients have difficulty waking up during regular work hours to participate in an interview, or if it is difficult to communicate with them, check to see if medication may be causing or contributing to the problem. If so, reschedule the interview as often as necessary until the client can participate, continuing the case if necessary. Try coming at different times of day or night.

B. MENTAL/EMOTIONAL CONSIDERATIONS

1. RESTRAINTS, SECLUSION, AND CLIENTS TOO SICK TO INTERVIEW-Upon admission or at other times during hospitalization, clients may be too sick or psychotic to participate in an attorney/client interview. Clients may be in seclusion or restraints because of their perceived dangerous behavior. Interviews with clients in these situations need to be postponed with frequent personal checks to see when they are able to participate.

2. MENTAL RETARDATION-Mentally retarded clients may be likely to try to please the attorney by giving the answers they believe the interviewer wants to hear. Be sure to discuss the commitment procedures and the legal process carefully and have the client restate his or her understanding of it to be sure that the client actually understands. In determining the client's wishes regarding venue, contesting, etc., take each issue separately.

3. ALZHEIMERS/ORGANIC BRAIN SYNDROME-If you have reason to question whether a client may be demented, be sure to ascertain whether the client is fully oriented. It is not unusual to have a lengthy interview with an Alzheimer's client with a preliminary conclusion that there is not dementia only to find out at the end of the encounter that the client believes that this is 1932.

IV. SOME INTERVIEWING TECHNIQUES

A. DETERMINE IF CLIENT IS GENERALLY ORIENTED-Early in the interview process, make sure your client knows who they are, where they are, and the current time frame (date, time, year).

B. OPEN ENDED QUESTIONS WHEN POSSIBLE-It is important to question in a manner that yields the client's wishes and direction and not to influence the answer. Do not go into the interview with assumptions as to what the client wants. Try to conduct the interview with open ended questions. If the client is unable to answer open ended questions, then gradually make the questions more specific. Remember that some clients, such as mentally retarded patients and some children are more likely to give the answer they think the interviewer wants to hear. Some clients, like adolescents and paranoid clients, may be more likely to give a negative answer to any question.

C. DEALING WITH DELUSIONS/HALLUCINATIONS-Many clients will have ideas and opinions that are a product of psychosis. There are cases in which a client is believed to be psychotic but the facts are being manipulated by the petitioner so that it appears that way or the facts are otherwise misunderstood. Some psychotic clients may be attuned to the fact that others believe they are sick and that their beliefs are delusions. These clients may ask their attorney to validate their delusions or hallucinations. Paranoid clients may want their legal advocate to agree with their delusions. This can be an issue in forming a client/attorney relationship.

Attorneys are not treatment personnel. Confronting delusions and hallucinations can be dangerous and harmful to both the patient and the attorney. On the other hand, reinforcing delusions can be unhelpful to the client. It is important not to get into a confrontation with clients regarding their delusions or symptoms of psychosis. There are many ways to handle this situation, but personal safety should always be an important consideration for the attorney.

It can be a challenge for the attorney to fulfill the ethical obligation of RPC 1.14 to "as far as reasonably possible, maintain a normal client-lawyer relationship with the [psychotic or otherwise mentally impaired] client." This is particularly true if the client wants to contest the hearing and wants the attorney to put forth a defense that is based on delusional beliefs that, in the attorney's opinion, will result in a court order of involuntary commitment. There is no single answer to how an attorney should deal with a client's delusions; the answer depends on the totality of the circumstances. However, insofar as possible, it is a good idea to walk the thin line between not confronting delusions and not reinforcing them.

Keeping in mind that it is not prudent to talk to the client about the client's delusions in any way that is likely to cause aggression by the client, it may be possible to give the client sound legal advice that his or her preferred defense is likely to fail. For instance, a client may be able to comprehend and accept a response such as "While respecting your belief that God has told you to convert people on the corner of Church and Main streets, this is so far from the experience of most people that in my opinion the court is likely to agree with your doctor that this belief is a symptom of mental illness and poses a danger to other people. That would probably lead to your commitment."

D. DEALING WITH DENIAL-It is not unusual for clients to deny mental illness, substance abuse, or evidence of danger. They may be right. Or this could be a symptom of the mental illness or substance abuse. To the extent possible, it is important for the attorney to deal candidly with the client and not to reinforce denial. For example, a client who says she does not abuse drugs, but who had a toxicology test clearly showing significant drug or alcohol use, should be told that information and informed of the evidentiary consequences of such evidence.

E. REFRAIN FROM GIVING PERSONAL OPINIONS-

    1. Opinion about what the client should do-Clients who are hospitalized on involuntary commitment are in the hospital because several people--the petitioner, magistrate, outpatient examiner, and inpatient examiner--have already substituted their judgment regarding the respondent's need for treatment for the client's own judgment. It is extremely important that the attorney maintain the role of advocate and not try to influence the patient to make a particular decision regarding whether or not to contest the commitment. Some clients genuinely look to us for advice about whether or not they should contest. If after careful interviewing a client cannot make a decision, it may be appropriate to advise a client to inform the court that they do not know what they want to do and allow the court to decide. Another course of action could be to take the position of not consenting and make the hospital prove the case.

2. Opinion about mental illness, etc.-It is advisable to avoid answering the client's questions by giving our opinions about whether or not they are mentally ill, dangerous, need treatment, or if we believe a particular delusion. There will be many times when the attorney may believe that the client is mentally ill or a substance abuser; however, that belief does not interfere with the attorney's duty and ability to zealously represent the client and advocate for the client's wishes. Often clients will accept answers such as, "I understand that you believe you are married to Elvis Presley, and that is all that is important"; or "I work for you. That means that the only thing that matters to me is what you believe and what you want. I will advocate for what you want, regardless of whatever I think"; or "I do not know if you are mentally ill or not. My job is to try to accomplish what you want irrespective of that."

V. CONTENTS OF INTERVIEW

A. BE SURE CLIENT UNDERSTANDS WHO YOU ARE AND YOUR ROLE-The client needs to know from the beginning that the attorney is appointed by the court because he or she is hospitalized under involuntary commitment.

1. NOT EMPLOYEE/AGENT OF HOSPITAL-Clients are likely to assume that anyone they see in the hospital is employed by the hospital. Affirmatively state that you do not work for the hospital.

2. RESPONSIBILITIES OF ROLE-Define your job to the client. Do not assume the client knows what your role with him or her is.

3. LIMITATIONS OF ROLE-The court appointed attorney is authorized to perform only within the limits of the appointment, that is, to represent the client in the involuntary commitment process. Many of the clients will have numerous legal issues in addition to the IVC. It is important to define the role within the scope of the appointment. That does not mean that the client cannot be referred to other appropriate resources for assistance with other legal matters. It is not the responsibility of court appointed counsel to advise regarding criminal, disability, domestic, or other legal matters.

4. PAYMENT-The client needs to know that the court will award your fee and they are not responsible for paying it.

5. HAVE THE CLIENT RESTATE ISSUES TO YOU-One of the best ways to be sure the client understands the involuntary commitment process, his or her rights in the process, etc., is to have them restate their understanding to you and then to deal with any areas of misunderstanding.

B. EXPLAIN INVOLUNTARY COMMITMENT PROCESS & ALTERNATIVES TO IVC-Be sure to explain the involuntary commitment court process to the client and the client's rights in the process. If the client has been through the involuntary commitment process before, do not assume he or she understands it. Determine if they are fully informed and re-explain it if necessary.

C. DETERMINE IF THE CLIENT IS INDIGENT-Indigent respondents are entitled to court appointed counsel. There is no provision in the statutes for a civil judgment against an indigent or nonindigent respondent who is represented by appointed counsel.

D. DETERMINE IF THE CLIENT HAS PRIVATE COUNSEL-Some respondents hire their own attorneys. Some respondents assume that their private or court appointed criminal attorneys will represent them in involuntary commitment proceedings, but as a practical matter, most private attorneys will not represent respondents (even their own clients) in civil commitment. The best practice, if appointed to represent a respondent who states that they have private counsel, is to inform the client that counsel will prepare for court and gladly stand aside if private counsel appears. If the respondent signs a release authorizing appointed counsel to contact the private attorney, it may be possible to ascertain if private counsel is actually retained. In the event that the private attorney informs appointed counsel that he or she declines or refuses to represent the respondent, it is preferable if the private attorney will communicate this decision directly to the respondent. Never assume that a client who says he or she has private counsel actually does.

E. DETERMINE WHAT CLIENT WANTS (THEY HAVE A CHOICE)-The client may or may not understand that he or she does not have to agree with treatment recommendations. It is helpful to inform the client that he or she can agree or disagree with the doctor's recommendations concerning commitment and the court will decide what will happen. There are several things the attorney needs to find out:

> **1. Client's wishes concerning venue**-If the involuntary commitment petition did not originate in the county where the 24-hour facility is located, the client has a choice of having the hearing held in the county where the facility is or in the originating county. It is necessary to determine the client's wishes regarding venue as early as possible in order to arrange for a change in venue and have the hearing scheduled in a timely manner. Different counties handle this in different ways, so an objection to venue could mean that the hearing would be held in more than 10 days from the time the respondent was taken into custody. This could influence the client's decision and could result in a continuance.

> **2. Client's wishes about inpatient treatment/outpatient treatment/medication and the basis of the client's position**-In addition to determining whether or not the client agrees or disagrees with the doctor's recommendations, it is important to know why the client feels that way. Sometimes disagreement is based on issues such as taking medication. If the disagreement is over whether or not medication is necessary at all, there is not likely to be a way to negotiate; but if the client's objections are based on a particular side effect, such as weight gain or impotence, it may be possible to negotiate a change in medication that would be acceptable to the client.

10

Sometimes clients may take a position on commitment based on issues such as placement or transportation. If a client knows he or she cannot return to their former residence and no new placement has been found, they may agree to commitment even though they object, simply because they have no where to go. This may be a situation in which the client would gladly sign a voluntary admission if permitted to do so. The court may need to be informed of the reason the client chooses not to contest.

Another reason clients may agree to commitment when they actually object is that they do not have transportation home. The involuntary commitment statutes require that involuntarily committed clients are to be transported by law enforcement upon discharge if they do not have alternative transportation. The costs of transportation can be recovered from non indigent respondents. (G.S. 122C-251).

3. If the client has an alternative position-The client may propose an alternative to the treatment recommendations, such as voluntary hospitalization at another facility, intensive outpatient commitment, or voluntary commitment. It is important to find out if there is an acceptable alternative and to see if some compromise can be negotiated. If the client admits any of the substantive allegations, it is important to establish what would be different at the time of the hearing than at the time of the petition if the court were to make an order different than the doctor's recommendations.

4. Client's wishes concerning appearing in court-In an involuntary commitment hearing based on mental illness, the client has a choice of whether or not to appear. It is important to determine if the client wants to be present or not in order to prepare the client, to arrange the appearance, or to prepare a written waiver for the judge to sign. If the respondent does not wish to appear, it is important to find out why since this decision may be based on misinformation or misapprehensions regarding the nature and possible consequences of the hearing and these issues might be alleviated by accurate information. It is also important that the client knows what impact his or her appearance or non appearance could have on obtaining the desired results. Waiver of appearance is not provided in involuntary commitment proceedings based on substance abuse.

5. The client's wishes regarding the presentation of the case-While the client generally determines the objectives of representation and the attorney determines the methods, the client may have strong wishes concerning presentation of the case. It is important to know what the client wants and any preferences he or she has about how to accomplish the intended end.

6. Witnesses-Ask the client if there any witnesses to support his or her version of the facts and/or proposed alternative to the doctor's recommendations. Be sure to get releases from the client to contact any proposed witnesses. It is not unusual for clients to believe that friends or family members will support their release when, in fact, those proposed witnesses support commitment.

F. INFORM CLIENT OF PROCEDURAL DEFECTS IN PROCEDURE & REASSESS WHAT CLIENT WANTS-If the client's constitutional or statutory due process rights have been violated by procedural deficiencies in the procedures, the client has a right to know that. There are many ways to handle this circumstance; however, determining the client's agreement or disagreement with the doctor's recommendations prior to informing the client of possible procedural defects prevents coloring the client's decision in advance.

G. DISCUSS STRATEGY

H. BE SURE CLIENT KNOWS WHAT THE HEARING WILL BE LIKE-As with any type of court proceeding, clients may be apprehensive about going to court. It is very important to give clients as much information as possible about how the hearing will be conducted. Be sure the client knows:

1. Date, time, and place of hearing.

2. How they will get there and back.

3. Who can be present-The client needs to know that the petitioner can be present, and witnesses may be in the courtroom only to testify, but the client can object to the presence of nonparties and nonwitnesses and can limit the presence of nonparty witnesses to their testimony only.

4. If allowed by the court, introduce client to court officials at hearing.

5. Appearance of the hearing room.

6. Involuntary commitments are closed hearings.

7. How judges in this district conduct court.

8. Courtroom etiquette-Particularly be sure the respondent knows when his or her case will be presented, when he or she will be able to talk, not talking at other times, not to make gestures, and what to do if the judge asks questions.

9. Medical testimony-Be sure the client knows that the doctor or other treatment personnel may testify about medical evidence and opinions.

10. Possible outcomes-Be sure the client knows what the possible outcomes are, and particularly that this is not a criminal proceeding and the court cannot order them to jail as a consequence of the involuntary commitment.

11. When they will know the outcome-Inform the client about how and when decisions are usually rendered in your district. If the client is not appearing, let him or her know when to expect you to come to see the client to report and explain the outcome of the hearing.

I. OBTAIN ANY NEEDED CONSENTS TO REVIEW RECORDS/TALK TO WITNESSES

J. PREPARE CLIENT FOR HEARING AT THIS POINT OR AFTER FURTHER INVESTIGATION AND PREPARATION-As with any case, prepare the client to

undergo examination, cross examination, what to do if there are objections, etc. Review and practice again immediately before the hearing if possible. It may be a good idea to begin examination by asking a few basic orientation questions to show the court the client's state of mind. Explain to the client why these questions are important. The client should be prepared to address the allegations in the petition, doctor's observations, his or her understanding of the diagnosis and need for medication as well as compliance with medication, and any physical conditions the client has.

K. FOLLOW UP INTERVIEW(S) WHEN NEEDED

VI. DIFFICULT SITUATIONS IN WORKING WITH CLIENTS

A. HARD QUESTIONS CLIENTS ASK

1. Client says he or she already has an attorney-See paragraph V. D., above.

2. Client "fires" appointed counsel or wants a different court appointed attorney-As in all instances of court appointed counsel, the respondent does not get to choose appointed counsel. The court should be informed if the client objects to the attorney appointed. If the client wants to represent himself or herself, the court is likely to require appointed counsel to remain to advise the client during the hearing.

2. What do you think I should do? See paragraph IV. E., above.

3. What will happen? As in all cases, it is impossible to predict the outcome of the case. However, counsel can share with the client his or her experience of the difficulty or likelihood of prevailing under the circumstances of the specific case.

4. Do you think I am crazy/an addict/dangerous/need treatment? See paragraph IV. E., above

B. WHAT IF THE CLIENT WANTS TO SAY OR HAVE THE ATTORNEY TELL THE COURT THINGS THAT THE CLIENT BELIEVES ARE TRUE, BUT THE ATTORNEY BELIEVES ARE NOT FACTUAL, BUT ARE THE PRODUCT OF THE CLIENT'S MENTAL ILLNESS?

There are times when mentally ill clients who contest commitment do not take their attorney's advice and insist on representation that is likely to provide the evidence necessary to commit them. In these cases, the attorney must provide zealous advocacy that is reasonable under the circumstances. Obviously counsel cannot knowingly perpetrate fraud, suborn perjury, or knowingly make false statements to the court. This can pose a challenge for attorneys representing clients who have belief systems that are different from most of society, even if those belief systems are the product of mental illness. If it is determined that the client is going to testify, or if the client is called by the prosecution, it is possible to ask client questions artfully to allow the client to present his or her case without violating rules of ethics or evidence. For instance, the attorney might phrase questions like:

Q: Ms. Benswanger, what was your experience of the encounter you had with the petitioner on the day of your admission?

Q: Mr. Sutter, what is your memory of the ...

Similarly, the attorney can state or argue the client's case using careful language, such as "My client wants the court to know that...," or "The respondent believes that...." In this difficult situation, such statements provide the client with an appropriate voice in court and allow their participation in the judicial proceedings that determine their commitment. Many clients who contest commitment and lose are satisfied if they feel that they have actually been heard and considered in court.

C. THREATS AGAINST ATTORNEY, STAFF, PETITIONER, COURT, OTHERS-If a client tells or suggests to counsel that he or she will or may become violent during a hearing or if the court makes a decision contrary to the client's wishes, the attorney should take action to prevent such threats from being carried out and should advise the client that he or she is doing so. Depending upon the threat, the attorney may request security or request arrangements for the hearing to be held in a space that provides additional safeguards.

VII. RESPONSIBILITIES TO CLIENT AFTER THE HEARING

A. BE SURE CLIENT UNDERSTANDS COURT RULING, HIS OR HER RESPONSIBILITIES UNDER THE ORDER, AND THE CONSEQUENCES OF NONCOMPLIANCE-Clients do not always hear or understand the court's ruling. If at all possible, ask the judge to allow you a minute outside the courtroom with each client immediately after the hearing. In the alternative, go to see the client after court or call the client if they are discharged and have left the facility. Always restate what the judge has ruled and ascertain whether or not the client understands the ruling. Be particularly sure that the client understands what he or she is supposed to do for any outpatient commitment or outpatient portion of a substance abuse commitment and what the consequences of noncompliance could be.

B. ANSWER CLIENT QUESTIONS ABOUT WHAT HAPPENED

C. DETERMINE IF CLIENT NEEDS DOCUMENTATION FOR OTHER PURPOSES-A client may need a statement from the clerk of court that his or her presence was required in court for school, work, or other purposes. The client may need a copy of the court order for personal or other legal reasons. The client should always be given a certified true copy of the order as soon as possible.

D. APPEALS-A client who loses a case should be informed of the right to appeal, the attorney's opinion of any grounds for appeal, and be informed of how long an appeal is likely to take, that appeals do not stay the order (the client is likely to be out of the hospital long before an appeal is decided), and any potential financial consequences of filing or losing an appeal.

Appendix D
Involuntary Commitment and the Federal Gun Control Act

Robert Stranahan, "Involuntary Commitment and the Federal Gun Control Act," *from* Second Annual Civil Commitment Conference (Jan. 23, 2004) (training program co-sponsored by UNC School of Government and Office of Indigent Defense Services)

INVOLUNTARY COMMITMENT AND THE FEDERAL GUN CONTROL ACT

(A) RELEVANT STATUTES

18 U.S.C. 922 (g)(4)
It shall be unlawful for any person –
  (4) who has been adjudicated as a mental defective or who has been committed to a mental institution,
to ship or transport in interstate or foreign commerce, or possess in or affecting interstate commerce, any firearm or ammunition; or to receive any firearm or ammunition which has been shipped or transported in interstate or foreign commerce.

18 U.S.C. 922(a)(6)
It shall be unlawful –
  (6) for any person in connection with the acquisition or attempted acquisition of any firearm or ammunition from a licensed importer, licensed manufacturer, licensed dealer, or licensed collector, knowingly to make any false or fictitious oral or written statement or to furnish or exhibit any false, fictitious, or misrepresented identification, intended or likely to deceive such importer, manufacturer, dealer, or collector with respect to any fact material to the lawfulness of the sale or other disposition of such firearm or ammunition under the provisions of this chapter.

18 U.S.C. 925(c) Relief from Disabilities
  A person who is prohibited from possessing, shipping, transporting, or receiving firearms or ammunition may make application to the Attorney General for relief from the disabilities imposed by Federal laws with respect to the acquisition, receipt, transfer, shipment, transportation, or possession of firearms, and the Attorney General may grant such relief if it is established to his satisfaction that the circumstances regarding the disability, and the applicant's record and reputation, are such that the applicant will not be likely to act in a manner dangerous to public safety and that the granting of the relief would not be contrary to the public interest. Any person whose application for relief from disabilities is denied by the Attorney General may file a petition with the United States district court for the district in which he resides for a judicial review of such denial. The court may in its discretion admit additional evidence where failure to do so would result in a miscarriage of justice . . . .

However, the ATF states on its website that it cannot currently entertain any individual's request for firearms restoration: "Since 1992, . . . ATF's annual appropriation has continuously prohibited the expending of any funds to investigate or act upon applications for relief from Federal firearms disabilities."
See www.atf.treas.gov/firearms/faq/faq2.htm
[ATF's current website, www.atf.gov/forms/download/atf-f-3210-1-notice.html, continues to reflect this position.]

18 U.S.C. 921 Definitions
(a)(3) The term **"firearm"** means (A) any weapon (including a starter gun) which will or is designed to or may readily be converted to expel a projectile by the action of an explosive; (B) the frame or receiver of any such weapon; (C) any firearm muffler or firearm silencer; or (D) any destructive device. Such term does not include an antique firearm.

N.C.G.S. 122C-54 Exceptions; abuse reports and court proceedings
(a) A facility shall disclose confidential information if a court of competent jurisdiction issues an order compelling disclosure.
(d) Any individual seeking confidential information contained in the court files or the court records of a proceeding made pursuant to Article 5 of this Chapter may file a written motion in the cause setting out why the information is needed. A district court judge may issue an order to disclose the confidential information sought if he finds the order is appropriate under the circumstances and if he finds that it is in the best interest of the individual admitted or committed or of the public to have the information disclosed.
[Additional pertinent subsections were added to G.S. 122C-54 by S.L. 2008-210 and S.L. 2009-299.]

N.C.G.S. 14-404 Issuance of refusal of permit; appeal from refusal; grounds for refusal; sheriff's fee.
(c) A permit may not be issued to the following persons:
>   (4) One who has been adjudicated mentally incompetent or has been committed to any mental institution.
 (This statute applies to permits for pistols and crossbows).
[Additional pertinent subsections were added to G.S. 14-404 by S.L. 2008-210.]

(B) FEDERAL REGULATIONS

27 CFR 178.11 Adjudicated a mental defective [recodifed as 27 CFR 478.11]
(a) A determination by a court, board, commission, or other lawful authority, that a person, as a result of marked subnormal intelligence, or mental illness, incompetency, condition, or disease:
(1) Is a danger to himself or others; or
(2) Lacks the mental capacity to manage his own affairs.

(b) The term shall include –
(1) A finding of insanity by a court in a criminal case; and
(2) Those persons found incompetent to stand trial or found not guilty by reason of lack of mental responsibility pursuant to articles 50a and 72b of the Uniform Code of Military Justice, 10 U.S.C. 850a, 876(b).

27 CFR 178.11 Committed to a mental institution [recodified as 27 CFR 478.11]
A formal commitment of a person to a mental institution by a court, board, commission, or other lawful authority. The term includes a commitment to a mental institution involuntarily. The term includes a commitment for mental defectiveness or mental illness. It also includes commitments for other reasons, such as for drug use. The term does not include a person in a mental institution for observation or a voluntary admission to a mental institution.

27 CFR 178.11 Mental institution [recodified as 27 CFR 478.11]
Includes mental health facilities, mental hospitals, sanitariums, psychiatric facilities, and other facilities that provide diagnoses by licensed professionals of mental retardation or mental illness, including a psychiatric ward in a general hospital.

For more information:
61 FR 47095 Notice of proposed rulemaking. September 6, 1996.
62 FR 34634 Final rule, Treasury decision. June 27, 1997.

(C) CASE LAW APPLYING 18 U.S.C. 922(g)(4)

U.S. v. Hansel, 474 F.2d 1120 (8th Cir. 1973)
Nebraska law provided a two-step procedure for determining if a patient was mentally ill and in need of hospitalization:

1) the patient may be temporarily hospitalized, up to 60 days, for <u>observation</u> if the County Mental Health Board determines he is mentally ill and in need of hospitalization, and

2) the patient may later be <u>committed</u> to the hospital if the superintendent determines he is mentally ill and should be admitted, and certifies this to the Board.

Defendant had been hospitalized under step #1. He was found not to have a serious mental disorder and was released after two weeks. Step #2 was not reached. The Court found that this **did not count** as a commitment.

U.S. v. Giardina, 861 F.2d 1334 (5th Cir. 1988)
Louisiana law provides for "admission by emergency certificate." A doctor examines the patient and certifies mental illness or substance abuse, and dangerousness. This allows for transportation and admission to the hospital. Within 72 hours of admission, examination by a second doctor is required. If the patient is to be held beyond 15 days, there must be a judicial commitment.

Giardina was admitted under this procedure, but discharged by the hospital before a hearing was required. The Court found that this **did not count** as a commitment.

U.S. v. Waters, 23 F.3d 29 (2d Cir. 1994)
New York state law allows for involuntary hospitalization based on an application for admission by a relative or other qualified person, followed by certificates from two doctors that the patient is in need of involuntary treatment. The patient can request a hearing at any time during the first 60 days of hospitalization. There is no automatic hearing. After 60 days, the hospital can request a hearing to further extend the involuntary hospitalization, or the patient can sign himself in as a voluntary patient.

Mr. Waters did not request a hearing, and signed himself in voluntarily at the 60-day mark. He was released seven months later.

The Court found that this **did count** as a commitment.

U.S. v. Whiton, 48 F.3d 356 (8th Cir. 1995)
Defendant had been involuntarily admitted to a hospital in Texas after an application for commitment, examinations by two psychologists, and a court order committing him for up to 90 days. This **did count** as a commitment.

U.S. v. Chamberlain, 159 F.3d 656 (1st Cir. 1998)
Maine law allows for involuntary emergency admission based on:
1. an application (by anyone) alleging mental illness and likelihood of serious harm,

2. examination by a doctor on the same day, certifying mental illness and likelihood of serious harm,
3. a Judge reviews the application/certification, endorses them as having been prepared in accordance with the law, and orders admission to the hospital for up to 5 days, and
4. a second doctor examines the patient within 24 hours of admission and also certifies mental illness and likelihood of serious harm.

Within those first five days of hospitalization, the hospital may seek an involuntary commitment in district court. This is a full adversarial hearing with counsel provided for the patient. The patient may also convert to voluntary status, in which case there is no hearing.

Mr. Chamberlain signed voluntary during the first five days. The Court found that this **did count** as a commitment.

U.S. v. Midgett, 198 F.3d 143 (4th Cir. 1999)

Defendant had been charged with breaking and entering in Virginia, and the court ordered an evaluation of his competence to stand trial. After reviewing the doctor's report and hearing evidence, the court concluded he was not competent to stand trial and needed inpatient care to treat his mental illness and restore him to capacity. Defendant was ordered into the hospital for treatment. After two months of treatment, doctors concluded he was not competent for trial and was not restorable for the foreseeable future, but was also not dangerous to self or others. Defendant went home after the DA declined to pursue the case.

Defendant later was arrested by the Secret Service and charged with possession of firearms in violation of 18 U.S.C. 922(g)(4). The Court concluded that defendant's confinement for restoration of competency **did count** as a commitment.

U.S. v. Vertz, 102 F.Supp. 2d 787 (2000)

Defendant was admitted to a Michigan hospital based on a nurse's petition, accompanied by a doctor's certificate stating he was mentally ill, dangerous to self and others, and in need of treatment. Defendant consented to treatment pending his court hearing. A second doctor also certified that he was mentally ill and dangerous. At the hearing, the Probate Court found mental illness and need for treatment, but discharged Vertz from the hospital after finding that less restrictive treatment was appropriate and available.

The Court found that this **did count** as a commitment.

U.S. v. Buffaloe, 449 F.2d 779 (4th Cir. 1971)

Defendant had been found not guilty by reason of insanity of a Virginia charge of maiming. After his release from the hospital, he was charged under 18 U.S.C. 922. The Court found that the NGRI hospitalization **did count** as a commitment.

See also Redford v. U.S. Dept. of Treasury, Bureau of Alcohol, Tobacco and Firearms, 691 F.2d 471 (10th Cir. 1982).

(D) **ADVISING YOUR CLIENT**

Commitment result	**Is right to firearm lost?**
Inpatient or split commitment	Yes
Substance abuse commitment	Probably
Outpatient commitment	Probably
Conversion to voluntary status before hearing	Maybe
Direct discharge before hearing	Maybe
Discharge by the court at commitment hearing	Maybe
Voluntary from start to finish	No

Your client is in the hospital on involuntary commitment papers, pending the 10-day hearing. **What can you do to minimize the damage** to his firearm rights?

1) If the client agrees to be in the hospital for treatment, convince the doctor to allow him to sign in voluntarily. For minors, get the parent or guardian to sign a request for voluntary admission (if the doctor will allow it).

2) Get the doctor to directly discharge the client before hearing. This can include continuing the case a week at a time until the client leaves.

3) If your client is a minor, advise him to expunge his commitment record when he reaches the age of 18. It is not clear that expungement will restore the right to possess a firearm, but it can't hurt.

The ethical question: If you do not advise your client about the Gun Control Act, have you violated the Rules of Professional Conduct?
In particular, consider Rule 1.4: Communication

Questions, comments, advice?
Robert Stranahan
Office of Special Counsel, Central Regional Hospital
300 Veazey Road
Butner, N.C. 27509   (919) 764-7110   Robert.P.Stranahan@nccourts.org

Appendix E
Common Abbreviations

Common Abbreviations (source unknown)

SYMBOLS

ø	none		I	independent
↓	decreased, lower, down		Δ	change
ʒ	dram		Ⓜ	mother
=	equals		Ⓕ	father
♀	female		Ⓢ	sister
↑	increase, elevate, up		Ⓑ	brother
2°	secondary to; due to			
b/c	because			
♂	male			
℥	ounce			
x	times, multiplied by			
≡	approximately			
@	at			
p̄	after			
+	and			
&	and			
x̄ , /x	except for			
ō	nothing			
c̄	with			
s̄	without			
ā	before			

List of Approved Abbreviations

A

A	attended
A.A. or AA	Alcoholics Anonymous
A_2	aortic second sound
aa	affected area
a.c.	ante cibum (before meals)
AB	abusive behavior
ACOA	Adult Children of Alcoholics
ACSW	Academy of Certified Social Workers
ACTH	adrenocorticotropic hormone (cortisone)
ad	right ear
AEB	as evidenced by
ad lib.	as desired
adm.	admission
adol.	adolescent/adolescence
ADHD	Attention Deficit Hyperactivity Disorder
ADON	Assistant Director of Nursing
aff.	affective
A/G ratio	albumin/globulin ratio
AH	Auditory hallucinations
AIDS	Acquired Immunodeficiency Syndrome
AKA	also known as
a.m.	morning
ADL	activities of daily living
amp	ampule
amt.	amount
AMA	Against Medical Advice
ANA	antinuclear antibody (test)
approx.	approximate
A&P	anterior and posterior
APAP	Acetominofen
AP & lat.	anteroposterior and lateral
appt.	appointment
aq.	aqueous (water)
AS	left ear
ART	Accredited Records Technician
A.S.A.	aspirin
ASAP	as soon as possible
ASCVD	arteriosclerotic cardiovascular disease
ASHD	arteriosclerotic heart disease
ASPD	antisocial personality disorder
AV	arteriovenous
A/V	auditory/visual
AT	Activity Therapy/Therapist
ATC	Alcohol Treatment Center
atc.	around the clock
AWOL	absent without leave

B

B	black
BAC	Breath Alcohol Content

bands	non-segmented neutrophils
baso.	basophil
BC	birth control
BCP	birth control pill
BDI	Beck Depression Inventory
beg.	beginning
bf	boyfriend
b.i.d.	bis in die (twice a day)
bili.	bilirubin
BM	bowel movement
BMR	basal metabolic rate
BO	Behavioral Observation
BP	blood pressure
BPD	borderline personality disorder
BPH	benign prostatic hypertrophy
BR	bathroom
br. sounds	breath sounds
BS	blood sugar
BUN	blood urea nitrogen
BW	body weight

C

C	Centigrade, Celsius
ca. or Ca.	carcinoma
C.A.	Cocaine Anonymous
Ca	calcium
cap(s)	capsule(s)
cath.	catheter/catheterization
CBC	complete blood count
CBS	call-back status
CCSW	Certified Clinical Social Worker
CD	chemical dependency
chem.	chemistry
cc	cubic centimeter
CHF	congestive heart failure
CHO	carbohydrate
CC	chief complaint
chol.	cholesterol
chr.	chronic
CCU	clear catch urine
cm.	centimeter
CM	case manager
CMV	cytomeglaovirus
CNS	central nervous system
c/o	complains of
CO	carbon dioxide
conc.	concentration
cont./cont'd	continue/continued
COPD	chronic obstructive pulmonary disease
conv.	convulsion
CPK	creatinine phosphokinase
CPR MB	CPK muscle band
CPR	cardiopulmonary resuscitation
CQI	Continuous Quality Improvement

C&S	culture & sensitivity
CR	cream
CSF	cerebrospinal fluid
CT/Cat Scan	computerized tomography
CPZ	Chlorpromazine
CTRS	Certified Therapeutic Recreation Specialist
CSAC	Certified Substance Abuse Counselor
cult.	culture
CVA	cerebrovascular accident
CXR	chest x-ray

D

D	divorced
d/c / dc	discontinue
D/C	discharge
DCS	Director of Clinical Services
dep.	dependent
DDH	Dorothea Dix Hospital
diff.	differential; difficulty
dig	digoxin
dil.	dilute
disp.	dispense
detox	detoxification
DMI	desipramine
DOA	date of admission
DOB	date of birth
disch	discharge
DOC	drug of choice
DLC	Developmental Learning Center
DON	Director of Nursing
DOSS	docusate sodium
DOSS + (DOSS Plus)	docusate sodium plus peri-colace
Dr.	Doctor
DR	dayroom
DSS	Department of Social Services
DSM-IV	Diagnostic and Statistical Manual of Mental Disorders, 4th Edition, Revised
DTR	deep tendon reflex
DUI	Driving Under the Influence
DVR	Division of Vocational Rehabilitation
DVT	deep vein thrombosis
DWI	Driving While Impaired
DWR	desired weight range
dx.	diagnosis

E

EA	Emotions Anonymous
EAP	Employee Assistance Program
EBV	Epstein-Barr virus
echo	echocardiogram
ECG/EKG	electrocardiogram
ECT/EST	electroconvulsive therapy
EEG	electroencephalogram
Ed/Educ	education

EENT	eyes, ears, nose, and throat
EES	Erythromycin Ethyl - Saccionate
EKG	electrocardiogram
elix.	elixir
ELOS	estimated length of stay
EMA	early morning awakening
e.m.p.	ex modo prescripto (as directed)
ENT	ears, nose, and throat
EOM	extraocular movements
eos.	eosinophils
EMG	electromyogram
EP	Escape Precautions
EPS	extrapyramidal syndrome (side effects)
ER	emergency room
et	and
etc.	et cetera (and so forth)
ETOH	ethyl alcohol
exc.	excision
Ex/e.g.	example

F

F	female
F.	Fahrenheit
FBS	fasting blood sugar
FDA	Food and Drug Administration
Fe	iron
FH	family history
FNP	family nurse practitioner
FSIQ	Full Scale Intelligent Quotient
ft.	foot/feet
FUO	fever of unknown origin
fx.	fracture
$FeSO_4$	ferrous sulfate
fld.	fluid
freq.	frequently
F/S	family session
FSH	follicle stimulating hormone
FTA	Fluorescent Treponemal Antibody (qualitative)
FTI	free thyroxine index
F/U	follow-up

G

GAF	Global Assessment of Functioning (scale)
G6PD	glucose-6-phosphate dehydrogenase
GB	gallbladder
GC	gonococcus culture (for gonorrhea)
gf	girlfriend
GGT	gamma glutamyl transferase
GI	gastrointestinal
GF	grandfather
GM	grandmother
gluc.	glucose
gm.	gram
gr.	grain
gt./gtt.	drop/drops

Gp/Grp	group
GTT	glucose tolerance test
GU	genitourinary
gyn.	gynecology

H

(H)	husband
HA	headache(s)
H&P	History & Physical
HACVD	hypertensive arteriosclerotic cardiovascular disease
H A1c	hemoglobin A1c (glycohemoglobin)
halluc.	hallucination
HbsAg	hepatitis B surface antigen
HBeAg	hepatitis B e antigen
HC	Hydrocortisone
HCG	human chorionic gonadotropin (for pregnancy test)
hct.	hematocrit
HCVD	hypertensive cardiovascular disease
HCTZ	hydrochlorathiazide
HDL	high density lipoprotein
HEENT	Head/Eyes/Ears/Nose/Throat
hgb.	hemoglobin
HI	homicidal ideation
HHH	Holly Hill Hospital
HIV	human immunodeficiency virus
H/O	history of
HOB	head of bed
H_2O	water
H_2O_2	hydrogen peroxide
hosp.	hospital
HPI	history of present illness
hr.	hour
h.s.	hour of sleep/bedtime
ht.	height
hx.	history

I

I	radioactive iodine uptake
IASD	interatrial septal defect
IBW	ideal body weight
ICF	Intermediate Care Facility
ICS	Intermediate Care Service
IgA, IgG, IgM	immunoglobulin A, G, M
IM	intramuscular
incr.	increase
ICU	Intensive Care Unit
indiv.	individual
INH	Inhalation
inj.	Injection
I&O	intake and output

inapp.	inappropriate
IOP	Intensive Outpatient Program
IPPB	intermittent positive pressure breathing
IQ	intelligence quotient
IUD	intrauterine device
IV	intravenous
IVP	intravenous pyelogram
IVSD	interventricular septal defect

J

JUH	John Umstead Hospital

K

K+	potassium
KCl	potassium chloride
kg.	kilogram
KUB	kidney/ureter/bladder (flat plate x-ray, abdomen)

L

L	liter
Ⓛ	left
lab.	laboratory
lat.	lateral
lb(s)	pound(s)
LBBB	left bundle branch block
LCSW	Licensed Clinical Social Worker
LDH	lactic dehydrogenase
LDL	low density lipoprotein
LD	learning disabled / learning disability
LFT	Liver function test
LH	luteinizing hormone
Li	Lithium
Li_2CO_3	Lithium Carbonate
liq.	liquid
LLL	left lower lobe
LLQ	left lower quadrant
LM	left message
LMFT	Licensed Marriage & Family Therapist
LMP	last menstrual period
LOA	leave of absence
LOC	Laxative of choice
LOS	length of stay
LPC	Licensed Professional Counselor
LPN	Licensed Pratical Nurse
LPT	Licensed Physical Therapist
LSD	lysergic acid diethylamide
LT	Long term
LUL	left upper lobe
lymph.	lymphocite

M

Ⓜ	Mother
ⓜ	murmur

M	male
MA	Master of Arts
maladj.	maladjustment
MAO/MAOI	monoamine oxidase inhibitor
MB	muscle band
MC	managed care
mcg.	microgram
MCL	midclavicular line
M-D	manic-depressive
M.D.	medical doctor
M.Ed.	Master of Education
m. dict.	as directed
med.	medicine/medication
mEq./l.	milliequivalent per liter
MFT	Marriage and Family Therapist
Mg	magnesium
MHC	Mental Health Center
MHT	Mental Health Technician
mi	milligram
MI	Myocardial Infarction
MJ/mj	Marijuana
ml.	milliliter
mm.	millimeter
MMPI	Minnesota Multiphasic Personality Inventory
Mn	manganese
MN	midnight
MOM	Milk of Magnesia
mono.	infectious mononucleosis
MPR	multiple purpose room
MR	mentally retarded
MS	Master of Science
M.S.	Multiple Sclerosis
ms	mental status
mo.	month
MSE	Mental Status Examination
MSL	midsternal line
MSW	Master's of Social Work
MVA	motor vehicle accident
MSN	Master of Science in Nursing
MT	music therapy
mtg.	meeting
MVI, MVI c Fe	Multivitamin with iron
MUO	May Use Own

N

Na+	sodium
NA	Narcotics Anonymous
N/A	not applicable
NaCl	sodium chloride
NAD	no acute distress
neg.	negative
neuro.	neurology/neurological
NCAC	Nationally Certified Additions Counselor
NH	nursing home
n/o	no other
NO	Nostril

noc	nocturnal
NOS	Not otherwise specified
NKA	no known allergies
NPO/npo	nothing by mouth
NR	nonreactive
NS	nothing significant
Nsg.	Nursing
NSH	no self harm
NSR	normal sinus rhythm
nml.	normal
NTG	Nitroglycerin

O

Ox4	orientation to person, place, time & condition
O_2	oxygen
OA	Overeaters Anonymous
ob.	obstetrics
OBS	organic brain syndrome
OCD	obsessive-compulsive disorder
O.D.	oculus dextra (right eye)
OD	overdose
ODD	Oppositional Defiant Disorder
oint.	ointment
O.L.	oculus laevus (left eye)
OOB	out of bed
OP	outpatient
ophth.	ophthalmology/ophthalmological
OR	operating room
orientation x 3	to person, place, time
O.S.	oculus sinister (left eye)
OT	Occupational Therapy
OTC	over the counter
O.U.	oculus uterque (each eye)
oz.	ounce
ortho.	orthopedic

P

p̄	after
P	pulse
PA	Physician's Assistant
pa.	paranoid
P&A	posterior and anterior
PAC	premature atrial contraction
PAT	paroxysmal auricular tachycardia
P&P	Policy & Procedure
Pb, Phb, øb	phenobarbital
PBI	protein bound iodine
PCPn	Pneumocystis carinii pneumonia
PC	Phone Call
p.c.	post cibum (after meals)
pCO2	partial pressure of carbon dioxide
PCN	pencillin
PCP	phencyclidine
PE	physical examination
PEG	pneumoencephalogram
per	through, by

PERRLA	pupils equal/round/reactive to light and accommodation
PhD	Doctor of Philosophy
pH	hydrogen iron concentration
PHP	Partial Hospital/Day Program
PI	Performance Improvement
PIAT	Peabody Intelligence/Individual Assessment Test
PID	pelvic inflammatory disease
PKU	phenylketonuria
p.m.	evening
PMI	point of maximum impulse
PNV	Prenatal Vitamins
p.o.	per os (by mouth)
pO2	partial pressure by oxygen
pos.	positive
postop.	postoperative
poly.	polymorphonuclear leukocyte
PPD	purified protein derivative (TB test)
p.r.	per rectum
p.r.n.	whenever necessary
prot.	protein
pro. time	prothrombin time
pt.	patient
Psych.	psychology
PT	physical therapy
PTA	prior to admission
PTSD	post-traumatic stress disorder
PTT	partial thromboplastin time
PUD	peptic ulcer disease
PVC	premature ventricular contraction

Q

QA	Quality Assurance
q.	every
q.a.m.	every morning
q.2 h.	every two hours
QI	Quality Improvement
q.i.d.	quater in die (four times a day)
QNS	quanum non satis (quantity not sufficient)
q.o.h.	every other hour
q.p.m.	every evening
q.s.	quanum satis (quantity sufficient)
QR	Quiet Room

R

R/resp.	respirations
Ⓡ	right
RA	Resident Advisor
RBBB	right bundle branch block
RBC	red blood cells
RD	Registered Dietician
RCH	Raleigh Community Hospital
retic.	reticulocyte
Rh	Rhesus blood factor

RHD	rheumatic heart disease
re:	regarding
rec	recreation/recreational
RLL	right lower lobe
RLQ	right lower quadrant
RN	Registered Nurse
RNA	Registered Nurse Applicant
reg	regular
ROS	review of systems
RPR	rapid plasma reagin (test for syphilis)
Rm	room
RMT	Registered Music Therapist
RHIA	Registered Health Information Administrator
RRR	regular rate and rhythm
RSV	respiratory syncytial virus
RUL	right upper lobe
RUQ	right upper quadrant
RT	Recreational Therapy/recreational therapist
Rx.	prescription
RNC	Registered Nurse Certified
R/T	related to
RPh	Registered Pharmacist
R/O	rule out
ROM	range of motion

S

Ⓢ	sister
S	single
SA	substance abuse
sat.	saturated
SBE	subacute bacterial endocarditis
SD	sensorium defect
sed. rate	sedimentation rate
seg.	segmented neutrophil
sep.	separated
SGOT	serum glutamic oxalacetic transaminase
SGPT	serum glutamic pyruvic transaminase
SH	social history
SI	suicidal ideation
SIB	self-injurious behavior
sig.	label (let it be printed)
signif.	significant
SL	Sublingual
sl.	slightly
Soc. Hx.	social history
SOAP	subjective/objective/assessment/plan
SOB	shortness of breath
sol.	solution
SPE	serum protein electrophoresis
spec.	specimen
SR	smoking room
SSWD	Signs and Symptoms of Withdrawl
SSE	soap suds enema
SSKI	saturated solution potassium iodide

Staph.	Staphylococcus
stat.	statim (immediately if not sooner)
STD	sexually transmitted disease
STG	short term goal(s)
Strep.	Streptococcus
Sup	Suppository
surg.	surgery/surgical
SUSP	Suspension
S&S	signs and symptoms
s/w	slept well
SW	Social Worker
sw	sterile water
sx.	symptoms
syr.	syrup

T

T/temp	temperature
TA	therapeutic assignment
T&A	tonsillectomy and adenoidectomy
tab.	tablet
TAB	therapeutic abortion
TAH-(BSO)	total abdominal hysterectomy - (bilateral salpingo-oophorectomy)
TAT	thematic apperception test
TB	tuberculosis
tbsp.	tablespoon
TC	throat culture
TCA	tricyclic antidepressant
THC	tetrahydracannabinol (active ingredient - marijuana)
TIBC	total iron binding capacity
t.i.d.	ter in die (three times a day)
TL	tough love/Tough Love
TLC	tender loving care
TM	tympanic membrane
TMJ	temporomandibular joint system
TO	telephone order
TPR	temperature/pule/respirations
TRS	Therapeutic Recreation Specialist
TSH	thyroid stimulating hormone
TSP	total serum protein
tsp.	teaspoon
tx.	treatment/therapy
TV	television

U

UDA	urine drug analysis
UDS	Urine Drug Screen
URS	urine drug screen
U/A	urinalysis
UGI	upper gastrointestinal
ung.	ointment
UR	Utilization Review
UOQ	upper outer quadrant
URI	upper respiratory infection
urol.	urology/urological

UM	Utilization Management
UTI	urinary tract infection

V

v.	very
vag.	vagina
VC	vital capacity
VD	venereal disease
VDRL	Venereal Disease Research Laboratory
VH	visual hallucinations
vit. cap.	vital capacity
VLDL	very low density lipoprotein
VO	verbal order
VQ scan	ventilation-perfusion scan
VR	Vocational Rehabilitation
VS	vital signs
Vit B6	Pyridoxine
Vit C	Ascorbic acid

W

w/c	wheelchair
w/d	withdrawal
w/e	weekend
w/o	without
WBC	white blood cells
(W)	wife
WD/WN	well-developed, well-nourished
wt.	weight
W	white
WAIS-R	Wechsler Adult Intelligence Scale - Revised
WISC-R	Wechsler Intelligence Scale for Children - Revised
WMC	Wake Medical Center
WMHC	Wake Mental Health Center
WNL	within normal limits
w/n	within
WRAT-R	Wechsler Reading Achievement Test - Revised
WTMS	Wake Teen Medical Services

X

X	time, multipled by
x̄	except

Y

y/o	years old
yr.	year

Rev. 8/85; 5/88; 3/91; 4/92; 6/93; 3/96,3/99, 7/00; 6/01, 6/02
cf, lsf

www.ingramcontent.com/pod-product-compliance
Lightning Source LLC
Chambersburg PA
CBHW080413270326
41929CB00018B/3013